The Realities of Planning

Related Titles

HUSSEY
Corporate Planning Theory and Practice, 2nd Ed.

HUSSEY
Introducing Corporate Planning, 2nd Ed.

HUSSEY & LANGHAM
Corporate Planning: The Human Factor

A Related Journal

LONG RANGE PLANNING*

The Journal of the Society for Long Range Planning and of the European Planning Federation

Editor: PROF. BERNARD TAYLOR, The Administrative Staff College, Greenlands, Henley-on-Thames, Oxon RG9 3AU, England

The leading international journal in the field of long range planning which aims to focus the attention of senior managers, administrators and academics on the concepts and techniques involved in the development and implementation of strategy and plans. It contains authoritative and useful articles describing the approaches to long-term planning as practised by modern management in industry, commerce and government.

*Free specimen copy gladly sent on request

The Realities of Planning

by

BERNARD TAYLOR

and

DAVID HUSSEY

with contributions from
A. Pettigrew, J. Robinson, R. E. Hichens, D. P. Wade,
N. Freedman, K. Van Ham, R. Young and B. James

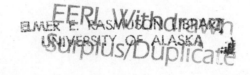
PERGAMON PRESS

OXFORD · NEW YORK · TORONTO · SYDNEY · PARIS · FRANKFURT

U.K.	Pergamon Press Ltd., Headington Hill Hall, Oxford OX3 0BW, England
U.S.A.	Pergamon Press Inc., Maxwell House, Fairview Park, Elmsford, New York 10523, U.S.A.
CANADA	Pergamon Press Canada Ltd., Suite 104, 150 Consumers Road, Willowdale, Ontario M2J 1P9, Canada
AUSTRALIA	Pergamon Press (Aust.) Pty. Ltd., P.O. Box 544, Potts Point, N.S.W. 2011, Australia
FRANCE	Pergamon Press SARL, 24 rue des Ecoles, 75240 Paris, Cedex 05, France
FEDERAL REPUBLIC OF GERMANY	Pergamon Press GmbH, 6242 Kronberg-Taunus, Hammerweg 6, Federal Republic of Germany

First edition 1982

British Library Cataloguing in Publication Data
The realities of planning.
1. Corporate planning
I. Taylor, Bernard
II. Hussey, David
658.4'01   HD30.28   80-42120
ISBN 0-08-022226-9

In order to make this volume available as economically and as rapidly as possible the typescript has been reproduced in its original form. This method unfortunately has its typographical limitations but it is hoped that they in no way distract the reader.

Printed in Great Britain by A. Wheaton & Co. Ltd., Exeter

PROFESSOR BERNARD TAYLOR

Bernard Taylor is Professor of Business Policy at Europe's oldest management college, the Administrative Staff College, Henley-on-Thames, which offers a range of long executive programmes for middle and senior management in the public and the private sector.

Before joining the College, he was founder and Director of Post Experience Programmes at the University of Bradford. At the Institute of Marketing, he established the Diploma in Marketing and a range of short courses in Marketing. Prior to this, he held responsible management positions with Procter and Gamble in marketing and with Rank Xerox in education and training.

During the past ten years he has been particularly concerned with Corporate Planning. He has organised seminars and workshops in Corporate Planning in the U.K., on the Continent, and in North and South America. He has personally trained over 600 corporate planners.

He has founded two leading international journals: the *Journal of General Management* and *Long Range Planning* - the official journal of the European Federation of Planning Societies, which he still edits. He has written or co-authored twelve books on various aspects of planning. He has been a consultant to leading companies, public enterprises and government bodies. In 1972 he was a United Nations consultant to the National Council of Applied Economic Research in New Delhi. He has also been a Visiting Professor at the University of Ottawa and the University of Cape Town.

DAVID HUSSEY

David Hussey is a leading international authority on corporate planning, and is one of the few writers with extensive practical experience as a corporate planner in industry. For twelve years he held senior appointments in companies with interests in mechanical engineering, food, pharmaceuticals, chemicals, horticulture, shipping, and road transportation. Since 1976 he has been a consultant with Harbridge House Inc., where he is a partner in the London office.

His books include *Introducing Corporate Planning* (1971), *Corporate Planning : Theory and Practice* (1974) (joint winner of the John Player Management Author of the Year Award), and *Inflation and Business Policy* (1976), and (with Mike Langham) *Corporate Planning : The Human Factor* (1979).

He was a founder member of the Society for Long Range Planning, and a former vice-chairman.

He was educated in Rhodesia, attained his B.Com. with distinction in business economics from the University of South Africa and also qualified as a Chartered Secretary (ACIS). Before his return to the United Kingdom he was employed in the field of economic planning and research, working for the Federal (formerly Rhodesian) Government until the dissolution of the Federation in 1963.

CONTENTS

viii   Contents

INTRODUCTION

The first rudimentary ideas for this book came to us in 1974. At that time we were interested in the gap between some of the textbook concepts of corporate planning and the realities of actual practice. We know that experienced planners had concerns which were frequently excluded from the books; we knew that significant elements of theory were rarely applied by practitioners. We felt that these gaps were worthy of exploration.

Lest what we thought was the inspiration of the visionary should turn out to be nothing more than the cynicism of the veteran, we arranged an afternoon meeting of experienced practitioners with whom we debated some of the issues. The meeting agreed that they were worthy of further discussions, and as a direct result we organised a series of 2½ day workshops for invited participants of known skill and standing. Three of these workshops were held, in 1975, 1976 and 1977. The first two expanded from the different approaches to objectives and strategy, the subject of chapter 2 of this book, into some of the behavioural and political aspects of planning. Both these issues appear as constant themes throughout the book.

These discussions, and other work we were undertaking in parallel, brought us to the conclusion that one of the realities of planning was that the business environment had permanently changed, and that this meant that the planning methods of the nineteen sixties would not work unless they took account of the new situation. Because of this the subject of our third discussion workshop was Government involvement in business planning, and through this we explored many facets of an extremely important new dimension.

The workshops stimulated our thinking, and the shaping of the book owes a debt to them. But in no way is this "the book of the conference". Although some of the contributions were developed from themes first introduced at the workshops, none of them are workshop papers dropped into the book without considerable further development.

The main contribution of the workshops was to help us to define what we feel are some of the important realities of modern corporate planning, around which we have structured many of our subsequent writings. It is this work which makes up the core of the book, supported by a few important contributions from others to cover areas in which we had less experience, or to provide case study examples to flesh out some of the points.

What are the realities of planning? We probably do not know them all, but the
things which seem important to us are:-

> * Corporate planning although widely practised does not make
>   the contribution it is capable of making to the development
>   and profits of enterprises in general, because a majority
>   of managers do not properly understand it, and top
>   management generally sets too low an expectation from it.
>
> * Good analysis is essential to corporate planning, but its
>   success in an organisation depends on applying an under-
>   standing of behavioural issues. Not only does corporate
>   planning affect the balance of power within an organisation,
>   and therefore is a political process, it also has to
>   stimulate creativity, motivate, be responsive to the style
>   of the organisation, and to both satisfy and make use of
>   the growing desire of managers to be involved in the
>   development of the organisations for whom they work.
>
> * Analysis remains significant, but the techniques described
>   in the textbooks of the 1960s and early seventies are
>   insufficient for the needs of complex multi-national
>   enterprises. Here the needs are for methods of strategic
>   portfolio analysis, which deal adequately with risk, and
>   which can be applied without reliance on a consultant's
>   proprietary package.
>
> * Neither corporate planning, nor the organisational change
>   it is intended to provoke, can be applied effectively as a
>   series of "cook-book" solutions. What suits one company
>   will not necessarily suit another, and may be harmful to it.
>
> * What is recommended in some of the textbooks is not always
>   right: but neither is the practice of many companies.
>   Corporate planning is not the same in all organisations,
>   and has moved along an evolutionary path with living examples
>   still remaining at each stage. Thus dialogue between planners
>   in different organisations becomes confusing because even the
>   words "corporate planning" mean different things depending on
>   the stage each has reached.
>
> * Corporate planning is no longer a matter solely for the Board
>   Room. Additional forces which are part of the reality of
>   modern planning include the requirement of wider participation,
>   intervention by and the involvement of government in the
>   strategic decisions of private business, and the growing
>   demands for Trade Union participation. But wider involvement
>   within a company may run counter to the organisational style
>   of that company, causing the planning system to become
>   divorced from the reality of decision making.

We have planned the chapters which make up this book so that they both expand on
the realities which we have observed and show practical responses to them. In
doing this we owe a debt of gratitude not only to the contributors of four of the
chapters in this book, but to participants in the workshops, and other planners
with whom we have come in contact, and whose discussions and opinions have helped
us to formulate our own thoughts.

                                          Bernard Taylor
                                          David Hussey

Part 1

NEW CONCEPTS IN PLANNING

The first chapter, by Bernard Taylor, sets the tone for the book. He compares and contrasts five different but complementary views of planning: as a central control system; as a framework for innovation; as a social learning process; as a political process; as a conflict of values. In his analysis he touches on many themes which recur constantly through this book. He concludes with the point that *there is not just one style of planning or policy making but many*, a topic taken up by David Hussey in Chapter 3 where he attempts to explain the differences between planning systems, and to suggest a classification for understanding these. (In a later chapter he raises the question about the link between planning approach and organisational style, and suggests that disappointment with planning may be because an inappropriate approach to planning is being used.)

In Chapter 2 David Hussey examines some of the approaches to planning advocated by various authorities, and explores some of the significant differences of semantics and concept which are of concern to the modern practitioner.

Chapter 1

NEW DIMENSIONS IN CORPORATE PLANNING*
Bernard Taylor

In the last twenty years corporate planning has spread throughout the free world in North America, Western Europe, Japan and into the Developing Countries. It has been adopted by large multi-national enterprises, and small businesses, service industries, agencies of central and local government and non-profit making organizations.

It has expanded to meet the challenges of competitive demand markets, shortages of resources and new pressures from society and government.

In the process the theory and practice of planning has also been extended to a point where it now provides a comprehensive range of concepts and techniques to meet a wide variety of managerial situations.

A practical challenge for planners today is *to match the planning approach to the needs of the organization*. This means abandoning the idea of the formal planning system as a cure-all or panacea and choosing a planning strategy to suit the situation. The challenge to the individual planner or senior manager is to learn to think and work in several dimensions at once - to become a kind of Renaissance Planner.

In this paper I would like to explore some of these dimensions or perspectives and their practical significance for planners.

I. PLANNING AS A CENTRAL CONTROL SYSTEM

Fundamental to Corporate Planning is the idea of the Management Planning and Control System. From Henri Fayol onwards management scholars and practitioners have thought of the management process as including 'planning, organization, command, co-ordination and control'.[1]

Melville Branch pointed out in his early account of 'The Corporate Planning Process' that in all kinds of planning 'the general sequence of operations is the same. First, there is a *sensing mechanism....* There follows a comparison of this measured performance with a *standard or desired performance....* On the basis of

---

* A presentation based on this paper was given to the Fifth International Conference on Planning in Cleveland, Ohio in July 1976.

this comparison ... *control actions* are taken....'[2]

The idea of control owes much to the engineer's concept of a control system as can be seen from comparing the pattern of control for the thermostat (Figure 1.1) with that of budgetary control (Figure 1.2).

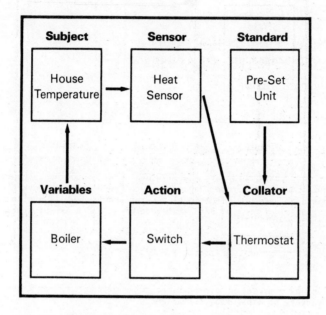

Fig. 1.1. Feedback loop control system – temperature
control.[3]

Robert Anthony in his classic study of Planning and Control Systems suggests that a distinction should be made between Strategic Planning and Management Control – though one obviously relates to the other.

Strategic Planning includes for example: choosing company objectives, planning for the organization, setting policies for personnel, finance, marketing and research, choosing new product lines, acquiring a new division, and deciding on non-routine capital expenditures.

Management Control is concerned with formulating budgets, determining staff levels, formulating personnel, marketing and research programmes, deciding on routine capital expenditures, measuring, appraising and improving management performance, etc.[4]

Clearly Corporate Planning includes aspects of both Strategic Planning and Management Control.

The notion of control of course refers not only to 'keeping operations in accordance with plans', but also 'timely revisions of plans – in minor details or major aspects.'[5]

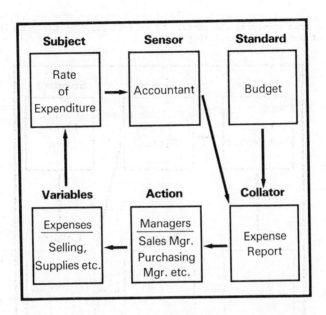

Fig. 1.2. Feedback loop for control system – budgetary control.[3]

Corporate Planning appears to have developed in the middle 1950s from the practice of the *ad hoc* 'Situation Size-up'. Company managements and management consultants conceived the idea of making this kind of Strategic Review on a regular basis, thus establishing a form of long term planning and review system for the total enterprise (see Figures 1.3 and 1.4).[6]

George Steiner's diagram (Figure 1.5) sets out a typical conceptual framework for the Corporate Planning Process[7] and it is clear from the latest Conference Board review of 83 Corporate Guides to Long Range Planning, that planning procedures still follow this broad pattern, e.g. Statement of Mission, Appraisal/Situation Analysis, Objectives, Strategies, Action Programmes, and Review.[8]

The Planning-Progamming-Budgeting System introduced into the U.S. Department of Defense and other Federal Agencies seems also to have had the characteristics of a management planning and control system. PPBS involved a move from a 1-year plan and budget based on the existing departmental organization and conventional account headings, to a 5-year plan and budget with programs and expense headings related to 'end-objectives' or missions (see Figures 1.6 and 1.7).[9]

One important reason for the widespread adoption of Corporate Planning systems has clearly been the use of diversification as a route to growth, the restructuring of companies into product divisions and corporate management's desire to maintain some control or influence over divisional management.

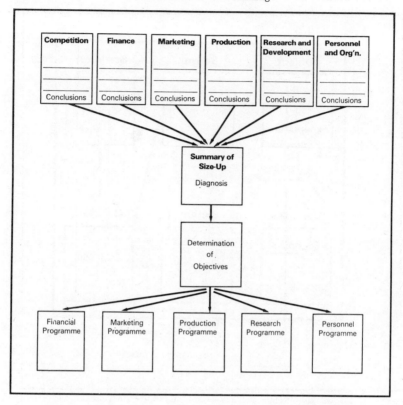

Fig. 1.3. Policy formulation - traditional approach.[6]

Research studies by Joseph Bower and others indicate that in divisionalized companies:

(1) conventional capital budgeting systems provide top management with little effective control of capital expenditure, largely because they attempt to impose an evaluation after the division management have become committed to a project. In his studies of large diversified industrial companies Bower found that 'once a project emerges from the initial stages of definition it is not only hard to change it, but in many cases hard to reject it.

Too much time has been invested, too many organizational stakes get committed, and at very high levels of management too little substantive expertise exists to justify second guessing in the proposers'.[10]

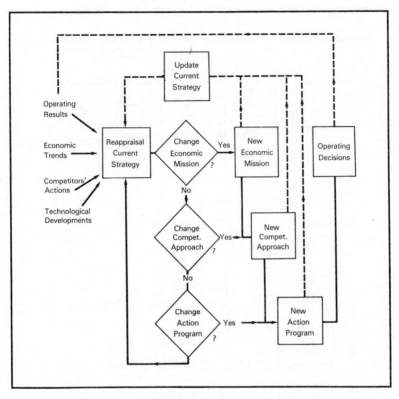

Fig. 1.4. Policy formulation - new approach.[6]

(2) the use of corporate planning procedures can provide
     better control over capital expenditure because the
     process enables management at corporate headquarters
     to influence the divisional strategy and to suggest
     that various options might be considered *before* an
     investment proposal is adopted as the 'one best way'.

Figure 1.8 shows the type of Business Screen now used in some major corporations
to foster this dialogue between corporate management and divisions about the
allocation of investment. Top management attempt to steer investments towards
products which have growth prospects, which may produce large amounts of cash in
the short term, or may build businesses in which the corporation has an important
stake.[11] Details of related approaches are given in Part 3.

THE LIMITS OF FORMAL PLANNING SYSTEMS

Formal Planning and Control Systems are now so much a part of organizational life
in large enterprises that the perspective of planning as a Central Control System
tends to dominate management thinking about Corporate Planning.

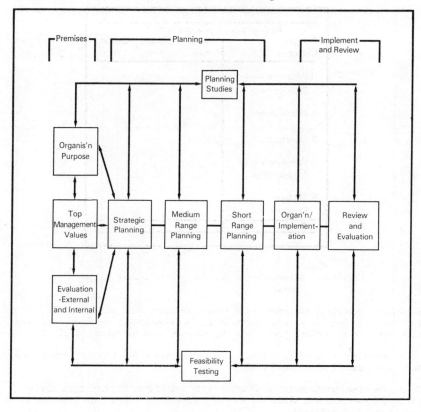

Fig. 1.5. Structure and process of business planning.[7]

However, bureaucratic procedures are inclined to become rather sterile routines and formal planning systems are no exception.

Igor Ansoff summarized the results of numerous planning surveys when he wrote:

>"Today only a handful of leading firms employ strategic
>planning to manage their forward growth thrusts. A majority
>still employ the simpler and earlier long range planning
>techniques which are based on extrapolation of the past and
>lack the systematic generation and analysis of alternatives
>characteristic of strategic planning."[12]

Of course this does not mean that strategic decisions are not being made. They may simply be made elsewhere. In their recent study of Planning and the Chief Executive the Conference Board reported 'It is clear that much planning - indeed in some companies practically all planning - is accomplished outside the context of a formal planning routine'.[13]

This phenomenon happens in government too - probably more often. One senior

Responsible Authority ($'s)			
Budget Category	Past Year	Current Year	Coming Year
1 Research and Development			
2 Procurement			
3 Construction			
4 Operations and Maintenance			
5 Military Personnel etc.			
Total			

Fig. 1.6. Department of Defense - traditional budget
          format.[9]

planner in a central government department recently remarked to me: 'I have the
feeling that there is a roller coaster of decision-making going past all the
time - and every now and then these decisions relate to our Strategic Plans'.

It is sometimes claimed that formal planning systems are ignored simply because
they are impractical or unnecessary.

Israel Unterman discovered in a survey that executives in U.S. financial
institutions found the whole process of Comprehensive Corporate Planning far too
costly and sophisticated:

> "(1) An appraisal of the many impinging environmental factors
>   demands the effort of a large planning department,
>   continuous task forces and a host of external consultants.
>   Therefore there is a considerable investment both in money
>   and time.
>
> (2) Few top executives have been trained to integrate a host
>   of many kinds of factor. The top man by experience and
>   background is usually a specialist not a generalist. It
>   takes a most exceptional skill to use what Peter Drucker
>   calls a 'holistic' approach. Relatively few executives
>   have this ability.
>
> (3) Even where the process is operational there are some on-
>   going problems.... When profit centers become highly
>   successful there is a tendency to overlook the total plan
>   and the holistic process is not enforced."[14]

Eric Rhenman, a Swedish sociologist concluded after a 5 year study of long range
planning in Scandinavia that:

Program Element	Projected Force	Projected Program Cost (Total Authority Expenditures)			
	(No. of Units) 1966-1972	R and D 1966-1972	Investment 1966-1972	Operating Cost 1966-1972	Total 1966-1972
General War Forces B-52 Bomber Syst. Minuteman Syst. Polaris Syst. etc.					
Limited War Forces Armored Divs. Infantry Divs. Carrier Task Forces etc.					
Mobility Forces C-141 Trans Syst. C-5A Trans Syst. Logistics Ships etc.					
Grand Total.					

Fig. 1.7. Department of Defense – program budget format.[9]

"(1) Strategic Planning is seldom necessary. Most organiza-
       tions survive successfully by regarding environmental
       changes as independent of each other.

 (2) The procedures of strategic planning make it more
       difficult to observe and deal with strategic problems.

 (3) The major problems are caused not by changes in technology
       but by changing values and norms in the environment.

 (4) To change an organization requires power to handle the
       political system (an inextricable part of the organiza-
       tion)."[15]

THE NEED FOR A BROADER MORE FLEXIBLE APPROACH

There is a growing consensus that new styles of planning are needed. After
studying strategy-making in a wide range of institutions in Canada, Henry
Mintzberg of McGill University wrote:

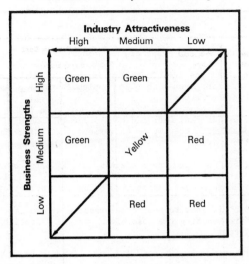

Fig. 1.8 Portfolio management - General Electric 'Business
Screen' used in allocating resources to different
businesses.[11]

"Planning is not a panacea for the problems of strategy-
making. As obvious as this seems, there is little
recognition of it in planning books or by planners. Instead
one finds a focus on abstract simple models of the planning
process that take no cognisance of other modes of strategy-
making. Little wonder then that one finds so much frustration
among formal planners. Rather than seeking panaceas we should
recognize that *the mode used must fit the situation*."[16]

Yehezkel Dror, a former consultant with RAND Corporation, writing on the basis
of experience of policy-making for U.S. government agencies makes a similar point:

"Many of the proponents of Comprehensive Planning seem to
assume explicitly or implicitly that comprehensive planning
is an ideal mode of direction for all types of systems, and
should therefore be encouraged as much as possible. This
opinion stems from a lack of familiarity with other types of
system direction which often are not only more efficient but
are also more effective."[17]

John Friend and a group of colleagues in the Tavistock Institute of Operational
Research, after studying planning in the construction industry and in local
authorities in Britain concluded that in these situations:

"The goal of imposing a comprehensive solution to the organization of planning activities is bound to be illusory.... The
innovator should recognize the limitations of what he can
achieve through the medium of central control systems of a kind
that rest on explicit ground rules for dealing with clearly

defined classes of situations."[18]

POLICY ANALYSIS AND STRATEGIC MANAGEMENT

In general, however, the researchers feel that the action required is not to
stop using formal planning systems but to supplement these procedures where
necessary with other approaches.

For the public sector Yehezkel Dror and others are recommending a multi-
disciplinary approach which they refer to variously as Policy Sciences, Policy
Analysis or Policy Studies.

Dror finds that 'there is a growing awareness that efforts to improve decision-
making in organizations through methods such as analysis and Planning-Programming
Budgeting cannot succeed unless accompanied by broader organizational changes'.[19]

The problem says Dror is 'how to introduce urgently needed improvements in
decision-making while avoiding the possible boomerang effects of comprehensive
formal planning systems'.

Table 1.1 illustrates the distinction which Dror makes between Formal Planning,
referred to as 'Systems Analysis' and Policy Analysis. He suggests that the new
features to be included in Policy Analysis are that increased attention would be
given to:

> (1) encouraging innovative and creating thinking
>
> (2) attempts to change the overall organizational climate
>
> (3) the political aspects of policy-making, i.e. power
>   inside and outside the organization
> (4) speculative thinking on the future as an essential
>   background for current policy-making
> (5) qualitative considerations (instead of viewing all
>   decision-making as resource allocation).[19]

TABLE 1.1 A Comparison of Systems Analysis and Policy Analysis.

	Systems Analysis	Policy Analysis
Criteria	Economic – Efficient Allocation of Resources	Economic + Social and Political Effectiveness
Emphasis	Quantitative	Qualitative and Innovative + Quantitative where possible
Methods	Economic Analysis Quantitative Models	Economic Analysis + Qualitative Models, Future Thinking and Intuition
Expected Results	Better Decisions on Limited Issues. Boomerang Effect on Complex Issues	Slightly Better Decisions on Issues Better Information for and Education of Decision Makers
Location	Financial Groups	Near Decision Makers

With regard to business organizations, Igor Ansoff and his colleagues at
Vanderbilt University have reached the same conclusion. They suggest that

"a particular style of planning should be seen as *part* of a
complex vector of managerial capabilities which are required
to support entrepreneurial activity within the firm.... Unless
the other components are aligned to accept its results
strategic planning can be a distortion akin to a rubber band
being stretched whilst its two ends are held fixed. Like the
bank, the capability tends to snap back once the distorting
force is removed.

"In this perspective, the wonder is not that competitively
competent organizations will resist strategic planning, the
wonder is that top management coersion can sometimes force
planning to take root in the organization. More likely is the
outcome exemplified by the McNamara Story."[20]

Igor Ansoff calls the wider, more comprehensive approach to strategy-making
'Strategic Management'. He shows the differences between Strategic Planning and
Strategic Management in Figure 1.9.[21]

(1) Strategic Planning is concerned with the 'external linkages' of the firm,
    e.g. Product-Market Strategy. Strategic Management is also concerned with
    internal arrangements, e.g. organizational systems and organizational change.

(2) Strategic Planning focuses primarily on the formulation of strategy as a
    problem-solving process. Strategic Management also includes the problems of
    implementation and control.

(3) Strategic Planning concentrates on technological, economic and informational
    aspects of strategy-making. Strategic Management pays more attention to
    social and political factors inside and outside the organization.

What then are these 'other approaches' and perspectives which need to be added to
Formal Planning Systems?

In the remainder of this chapter I will describe four other approaches to planning
which I believe will be useful to planners and which are already in the process
of development. In embryo we may have here our new concept and methodology of
planning - the basis for Policy Analysis or Strategic Management.

II. PLANNING AS A FRAMEWORK FOR INNOVATION

A second viewpoint as fundamental to Corporate Planning as the Planning and
Control System is idea of 'organized entrepreneurship' or institutionalized
innovation.

At certain times in history, e.g. in nineteenth century England and in modern
Japan the notion of change and growth seems to be accepted as an ideology by
Society, to work and to generate material wealth become accepted as a system of
beliefs.

Peter Drucker argues as follows:

"In a world buffeted by change, faced daily with new threats
to its safety, the only way to conserve is by innovating.
The only stability possible is stability in motion."[22]

The implications of this philosophy were spelled out for the individual, for
organizations and for society at large by John Gardner, the former U.S. Secretary

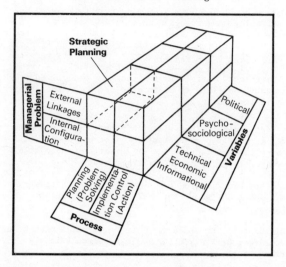

Fig. 1.9. Strategic management.[21]

of Health, Education and Welfare. In his book 'Self-Renewal' he wrote:

> "A society whose maturing consists simply of acquiring more
> firmly established ways of doing things is headed for the
> graveyard - even if it learns to do these things with greater
> and greater skill. In the ever-renewing society what matures
> is *a system or framework within which continuous innovation,
> renewal and rebirth can occur*."[23]

One of the concerns of politicians in relation to society and of top management
in large organizations is how to foster this innovation.

In *Small is Beautiful*, E.F. Schumacher points to a conflict of values between
'order and freedom' which is inherent in politics, in management and in personal
life.

> "Without order, planning, predictability, central control,
> accountancy, instructions to the underlings, obedience,
> discipline - without these, nothing fruitful can happen,
> because everything disintegrates. And yet - without the
> magnanimity of disorder, the happy abandon, the *entrepreneur-
> ship* venturing into the unknown and incalculable, without
> the risk and the gamble, the creative imagination rushing in
> where bureaucratic angels fear to tread - without this, life
> is a mockery and a disgrace.
>
> The centre can easily look after order; it is not so easy to
> look after freedom and creativity. The centre has the power
> to establish order, but no amount of power evokes the creative
> contribution. How then can top management at the centre work
> for progress and innovation?"[24]

```
┌──────────────────────────────────────────────┐
│  ┌──────────────────────────────────────────┐ │
│  │        Sequence For "Breakthrough"        │ │
│  ├──────────────────────────────────────────┤ │
│  │                                           │ │
│  │  1. Breakthrough In Attitudes             │ │
│  │     • Belief That a Breakthrough          │ │
│  │       is Desirable and Feasible           │ │
│  │                                           │ │
│  │  2. Feasibility Study                     │ │
│  │     • Analysis of the Key Issues          │ │
│  │                                           │ │
│  │  3. Breakthrough In Knowledge             │ │
│  │     • Organisation of Groups or           │ │
│  │       Departments                         │ │
│  │       (A) To Gather and Analyse the       │ │
│  │           Facts                           │ │
│  │       (B) To Direct and Mobilise          │ │
│  │           Support for the Changes         │ │
│  │                                           │ │
│  │  4. Breakthrough In Cultural Pattern.     │ │
│  │     • Discover Social Effects of          │ │
│  │       Proposed Changes and Deal With      │ │
│  │       Resistances Created                 │ │
│  │                                           │ │
│  │  5. Breakthrough In Performance           │ │
│  │     • Implementing the Plan of Action     │ │
│  │                                           │ │
│  │  6. Control                               │ │
│  │     • Achieving Control At The New        │ │
│  │       Level of Performance.               │ │
│  │                                           │ │
│  └──────────────────────────────────────────┘ │
└──────────────────────────────────────────────┘
```

Fig. 1.10.   Sequence   for 'Breakthrough'.[25]

Joseph Juran contrasts these two essential processes of management as Control and Breakthrough:

> "Control means staying on course, adherence to a standard,
> prevention of change. Under complete control, nothing would
> change – we would be in a static, quiescent world....
> Breakthrough means change, a dynamic, decisive movement to
> higher levels of performance.... As with living organisms,
> the products, processes, methods etc. of industry, are only
> mortal. They are doomed from birth. If the company is to
> outlive them, it must provide for a birthrate in excess of
> the death rate."[25]

Juran suggests that it is possible to establish a sequence for Breakthrough which may be applied as generally as the well known Planning and Control Cycle. His sequence for Breakthrough is shown in Figure 1.10. This sequence bears a striking resemblance to the process used by Stanford Research Institute and others who try to plan for innovations.

Juran also remarks that the processes of Breakthrough and Control as well as being complementary are often sequential. For a period innovation and growth is paramount, but in due course these new projects have to be integrated into the usual operation. (See Figure 1.11.)[25]

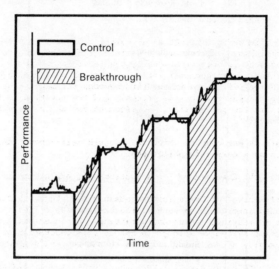

Fig. 1.11. The sequence of Breakthrough and Control

ORGANIZED ENTREPRENEURSHIP

In business, if top management wants to provide for succession in terms of products, processes and people, entrepreneurship has to be systematized. In particular the original founder has to find a way of communicating the 'theory of the business' so that it can be interpreted at different levels and in various parts of the organization and so that it can be reviewed and up-dated.

To quote Peter Drucker again:

> "Every one of the great business builders we know of - from the Medici to the founders of the Bank of England down to Thomas Watson in our days - had a definite idea, a clear 'theory of the business' which informed his actions and decisions. Indeed a clear simple and penetrating 'theory of the business' rather than 'intuition' characterizes the truly successful entrepreneur, the man who not only amasses a large fortune but builds an organization that can endure and grow long after he is gone.
>
> But, the individual entrepreneur does not need to analyse his concepts and to explain his 'theory of the business' to others, let alone spell out the details. He is in one person thinker, analyst and executor. Business enterprise, however, requires that entrepreneurship be systematized, spelled out as a discipline and organized at work."[26]

In certain firms, at certain times top management are able through Corporate Planning to foster innovation in an enterprise, to stimulate creativity in various parts of the organization, and to use these ideas to build the business and in the process open up new opportunities for the individuals or groups concerned and for company employees generally.

In the words of Donald Schon:

> "The firm defines itself as a vehicle for carrying out a special kind of process. It defines itself through its engagement in entrepreneurship, the launching of new ventures, or in commercializing what comes out of development. The principal figure in the firm becomes the manager of the corporate entrepreneurial process; and the question is this: what are the potentials in development for new commercial ventures?"[27]

Texas Instruments is one company which has adopted Self-Renewal and Organized Entrepreneurship as a corporate philosophy.

Patrick Haggerty, the Chairman of Texas Instruments, explains:

> "Self Renewal at Texas Instruments begins with deliberate, planned innovation in each of the basic areas of industrial life - creating, making and marketing. With our long range planning system we attempt to manage this innovation so as to provide a continuing stimulus to the company's growth."

Approaches to Corporate Development vary enormously from highly structured procedures which attempt to hold line management accountable for the development of new projects as well as the on-going operations, to informal processes designed to launch a new initiative such as a Diversification Task Force.

One of the best known approaches follows the pattern developed by Stanford Research Institute.[28]

This involves a programme of meetings with the top management team to:

(1) assemble relevant information

(2) determine the growth potential

(3) analyse the total situation

(4) establish development projects with project teams and resources

(5) receive reports and review progress.

Simultaneously planning teams are set up in various parts of the organization:

(1) to receive suggestions in the form of Provisional Planning Issues from individuals,

(2) to group and sift the ideas, and to submit them to senior management.

This approach has the advantage of involving line management and members of staff at all levels. An approach similar to this has recently been employed with success in the large British retailer W.H. Smith & Son.[29]

LIMITS TO GROWTH

The Limits to Growth argument has added a new dimension to the philosophy of
self-renewal. Reporting in 1969, the Committee on Resources and Man, of the
National Academy of Sciences Research Council projected the likely impact of
national and corporate growth policies on the quality of life and concluded:

> "The quality of life, which we equate with freedom of action,
> is threatened by the demands of an expanding economy and
> population. This happens in three principal ways:
>
> (1) through the restrictive and harmful effects of pollution;
> (2) through the increasing frequency and complexity of
> unconstructive but unavoidable human contacts; and (3) through
> the necessary increase in regulatory measures – all in
> consequence of increasing use of and competition for resources,
> space, recreation, transportation, housing and even education
> facilities."[30]

Since 1969, the Limits to Growth issue has been transformed from a long term
concern into an immediate reality. With the Arab oil embargo and the threat of
other raw materials cartels, the prospect of easy supply markets has receded.
The decline in the demand for automobiles, steel and other goods has heralded
increased world competition for demand markets. Higher rates of unemployment
particularly among young people and minorities have emphasized the human and
social costs of recession, and most governments are struggling to cope with the
problems produced by high rates of inflation. Clearly, the expansive days of
the 1960s are to be followed by what the U.S. Chamber of Commerce has called 'a
new economic era for business enterprise'.

Some writers on 'self-renewal' have responded by emphasizing that growth may be
qualitative as well as quantitative and self-renewal may be thought of in terms
of people as well as in terms of technology and markets. For example:

Willard Wirtz of the National Manpower Institute puts the following argument for
educational renewal:

> "The depletion of natural resources leaves us only two
> choices. One plainly is to shrink which is against our
> nature and probably contrary to the laws of institutional
> or system survival. The other, no less plain is *to rebuild
> our ideas and plans around the fuller development of those
> other resources which are called 'human' and which are in
> limitless supply.*"[31]

Educational Renewal is described by the National Manpower Institute in their
Prospectus for an Education-Work policy:

> "Some kind of provision for interspersing the earning and
> learning of a living, for interweaving employment and self
> renewal, is going to have to be recognized as the essential
> condition for an effective career as a worker, citizen or
> human being."

This will require a variety of new initiatives by government agencies, by
business organizations and by colleges and universities to provide a programme
of 'life-long learning' in which (1) education for young people is better matched
to the jobs available; (2) adults, particularly women, can be readily re-trained

for a second or third career; and (3) people will be educated not just for work but for increased leisure, and for retirement.

III. PLANNING AS A SOCIAL LEARNING PROCESS

A new and increasingly popular concept is that planning should be viewed as a social and organizational learning process.

Donald Schon suggests that a fundamental problem in modern society is the loss of 'the stable state' - the fact that technological change at an unprecedented rate is continually calling for changes in our personal and social arrangements.[32]

He writes of the belief he once held that his life would at some time reach a stable situation - when he grew up, found a job, or got married and how it somehow refuses to 'settle down'.

No doubt many of us are familiar with the feeling of uncertainty produced by the pressures of change.

It is this rate of change which makes it necessary for us to develop planning as a social learning process.

> "The loss of the stable state means that our society and all of its institutions are in *continuing* processes of trans-formation ... we must learn to understand, guide, influence and manage these transformations....
>
> We must invent and develop institutions which are 'learning systems' - systems capable of bringing about their own trans-formation."

This 'sociologist's' view of planning as a social learning process tends to confront the 'classical' concept of planning as a rational analytical system. Its exponents challenge the notion that Corporate Planning can be a tidy sequential process carried out logically and leading to the possibility of clear and final solutions. They point to difficulties in practice - elements of uncertainty, disturbance from the external environment and the actions of employees, which make the application of a coherent and rational strategy and plan difficult and rare.

They suggest that top management and planning specialists often seek the security of the familiar, the quantifiable, and the controllable; they therefore focus on financial and efficiency goals and neglect the human aspects of change. These sociologists claim that 'rational planners' see the company as a technical system designed to achieve technical and economic objectives and they regard human beings as necessary but unpredictable elements in the system. They argue that managers and technologists who have a Control concept of the firm derived from engineering see it in terms of information and product input and output. Human beings are seen as weak links in this potentially efficient system and it would be preferable if they could be replaced by machine links. The sociologists on the other hand see the firm as a fluid system in which human beings play a major role in determining attitudes and behaviour.[33] The 'Social Learning' school are also worried about the bureaucratic nature of formal planning systems and the fact that procedures can so easily become meaningless rituals. As Hasan Ozbekhan reminds us:

> "Planning is adaptive to evolution in the environment only

in so far as continuous exchanges between it and the
environment permit it to operate in an adaptive mode. More
often, however, because of growing rigidity and institution-
alization, plans become non-adaptive and tend to lose touch
with surrounding evolutionary trends."[34]

The Corporate Planner who uses a Social Learning mode aims to develop a planning
system not so much for predicting and controlling but for coping with change and
uncertainty. He aims to help senior executives to adapt and to be adjustable
so that no matter what happens they can re-think their situation in strategic
terms. He also sees himself in the role of influencing a total cultural system
and of developing a 'systemic' competence up and down the hierarchy in coping
with change.

The approach of the Sociologist is very tentative. Donald Michael has pointed
out in his book *On Learning to Plan and Planning to Learn* why public planning
must be a learning process:

>   (1) The social technologies for understanding and defining
>   complex social systems are underdeveloped.
>
>   (2) Our theory and methods for Organization Development need
>   much research and development.
>
>   (3) A particularly difficult research and development activity
>   will have to do with learning how to incorporate members
>   of the environment into the long range planning process.
>
>   (4) There are no ready-made tested 'solutions' or even humane
>   coping procedures for dealing with major societal tasks.[35]

Planning is therefore seen as a process of trial and error. It is:

>   (1) *Incremental*. "If knowledge is revealed to us only in
>   fragments and sequentially, a flow concept must come to
>   replace the now outdated notion of learning as a fixed
>   stock of knowledge."
>
>   (2) *Experimental*. "A willingness to explore alternative
>   futures in the search for new possibilities of action is
>   an important part of the learning orientation."
>
>   (3) *Managed*. "The planner or policy analyst accordingly is
>   not seen as a man having a superior knowledge in some
>   field, but a superior ability to learn ... with tools
>   for exploring complex situations ... and models useful
>   for strategic intervention."
>
>   (4) *Shared*. "Unless potential client groups can be taken
>   along on this learning trip, the expert's models will ...
>   simply remain models. Expert and client must share in
>   the learning experience so that a joint reconceptualiza-
>   tion of problems can occur, and the possibilities for
>   concerted action be discovered. The policy analyst must
>   be able also to structure the learning experience of
>   others, to be a teacher and a learner at the same time."
>
>   (5) *Based on Recent Information*. "In a situation of acceler-
>   ated change and only limited autonomy, this will require
>   a tightening of feedback loops of information about change
>   in both internal and external environmental states, a

general attitude of openness towards the future, and a
quickening of the response times to new learning."[36]

These remarks were made in relation to public sector organizations and the
'Social Learning' school seems to be making an important contribution to planning
in local government, in hospitals, in education authorities and universities. It
is often apparent in these situations that it would be premature to employ
rational comprehensive planning systems such as PPBS except on a very restricted
basis. The first natural step is to enable the various groups involved in
management - and it is usually a team or several teams - to explore the possibilities of improving planning and co-ordination with interested parties inside and
outside the organization.

In business organizations similar approaches are being used. They usually involve
collaboration between Planners and Management Development or Organization
Development specialists. In one rapidly growing Unilever company for example
400 managers were involved in planning discussions within their own departments
and they in turn reported to a top management group called 'The 1977 Committee'
because this was their 5-year planning horizon.   The process in this case
evolved out of an Organization Development training programme based on a version
of the Managerial Grid.

The Management of another large European company recently employed a similar
approach to try to develop a new strategy. Again a series of workshops were
held taking a 'diagonal slice' of managers starting with the Board and some
senior staff and moving down through middle management. Sometimes the managers
met in departmental teams, on other occasions they met in cross-functional groups.
At various phases the groups were asked to:

     (1) define the present strategy
     (2) carry out an external appraisal
     (3) make an internal appraisal
     (4) generalize and evaluate alternative strategies
     (5) identify key strategic issues
     (6) suggest courses of action

(A case history of this project appears in chapter 11.)

Among the advantages of 'learning to plan and planning to learn' are:

(1) The process involves the decision-makers. It moves at their pace and deals
     with the key issues which they choose.

(2) The approach is usually based on an analysis of data, e.g. - to quote two
     actual cases - a scenario for the U.S. Health System or a prior assessment
     of key issues for an education authority (e.g. pre-school education).

(3) The discussions which take place strengthen informal contacts inside the
     organization and help to evolve a consensus about what needs to be done.

(4) Recommendations for action tend to be integrated with established management
     processes and procedures. In the jargon of consultants the planner is
     trying to manage a process; he is not selling a package.

(5) As the approach is incremental and proceeds in steps and with the various
     groups participating at each stage, this raises much less anxiety than the
     installation of a comprehensive planning system.

It will be clear that Organizational Learning focuses on informal processes
rather than the establishing of formal procedures. Recent research into policy-

making in British Boards of Directors emphasizes the importance of these informal
processes both in developing a consensus about objectives and in generating
product policy. Interviews were held with 91 directors in 21 companies. Most of
the firms claimed to be using some type of formal planning system. However, the
researchers found that there was virtually no consensus in any of the Boards on
corporate objectives except about a vague notion of 'profitability' (Figure 1.12).
And when directors were asked what sources of information they used for strategic
decisions, written communications were less important than informal meetings with
colleagues (Figure 1.13).[37]

The research emphasizes the need to foster informal planning processes as well
as developing formal planning procedures where they may prove useful.

	Stated By Individual Directors	Agreed By 2/3 of Board
Profitability	21	19
Market Penetration	15	3
Product Development	14	3
Market Development	13	2
Company Image	9	1
Corporate Productivity	7	0
Customer Service	7	0
Industrial Relations	7	1
Liquidity	6	1
Others	33	5

Fig. 1.12. Setting company objectives - 91 Directors in
21 Companies.[37]

IV. PLANNING AS A POLITICAL PROCESS

The political view of planning, though familiar to practitioners, has only
recently received attention from researchers concerned with long range planning.
The broad argument is that in contemporary society what happens to an organization
is determined by external and internal organized interests. And these external
interest groups (owners, suppliers, governments etc.) and internal interest groups
(departments, divisions etc.) form coalitions in which the balance of power is
crucial.

For example, on the basis of his investigations into long range planning in
Scandinavia, Eric Rhenman suggests that organizations may be classified according
to whether or not they have goals. These goals may be external - imposed from
outside by government, a parent company, a group of members or shareholders. Or
internal, e.g. objectives negotiated between managers at the centre and those in
departments or divisions. Rhenman suggests that organizations may be divided
into four main categories according to whether they have or do not have internal

	No. of Companies	Ranked Importance
Informal Meetings With Colleagues	20	1
Written Communications Within the Company	19	2
Informal Meetings With Subordinates	18	3
Informal Meetings With Customers	15	4
Formal Meetings Within the Company	15	4
Press and Other Media	14	6
Informal Meetings with Competitors	8	7
Market Research etc. From External Agencies	6	8

Fig. 1.13. Sources of information for strategic decisions.[37]

and external goals (see Figure 1.14):

(1) *Marginal Organizations*. These are organizations which have little power over their environment, e.g. small entrepreneurs. Internally, power is in the hands of a single entrepreneur and he does not typically set internal goals; nor does he accept goals from an external organization. Marginal businesses do not have the power to dominate their environment and their key strategic skill lies in anticipating changing circumstances, and in adapting to the moves of other more powerful enterprises.

(2) *Appendix Organizations*. These are organizations like sales companies or government agencies which have goals imposed on them by an outside body. Power is with the management of this external unit and they make the strategic decisions. The managers of the appendix enterprise are not in a position to choose their own internal goals although they may assume they have an autonomy which they do not in fact possess. In a showdown the parent organization is bound to win. A key strategic skill for the management of this organization therefore is to learn how to match their results to the requirements of the parent body.

(3) *Corporations*. In large private companies power is usually located in the top management, but their authority is limited by the presence of power bases on other parts of

Internal Goals / External Goals	Without Internal Goals	With Internal Goals
Without External Goals	**Marginal Organisations** e.g. Small Entrepreneur	**Corporations** e.g. Large Companies
With External Goals	**Appendix Organization** e.g. Sales Company Government Agency	**Institutions** e.g. Public Corporations Co-Operative Societies

Fig. 1.14 Types of organizations

the organization. The corporation does not have goals imposed upon it by outside bodies and it can achieve dominance over its environment principally through the development of new products, processes and systems.

(4) *Institutions.* These are enterprises such as public corporations and co-operative societies which have both social objectives set by outside agencies, and commercial goals decided by management.

Power in these systems is divided between management and other supporting groups. Management therefore have a dual task; they must be able to deal with strong social and political pressures and also they need to have the technical and marketing talent to generate new business systems. Because power lies largely outside the Institutions, management has to work through joint consultation with other interest groups.[38]

Other writers on strategy[19] categorize power systems within organizations into three main types:

(1) *Individual.* In these organizations power is in the hands of a single person, e.g. the President of a country or the owner of a firm. He makes the key decisions and the planner who wishes to influence policy must work with him. Typically, however, he does not use a formal planning system. He usually has a strategy but it is largely implicit and to retain the initiative in negotiations with subordinates he may prefer not to reveal his hand.

As Ed Wrapp once wrote 'Good Executives Don't Make Policy Decisions' - they often keep their colleagues in the dark about future policy and act in an opportunistic fashion.

(2) *Hierarchy*. This is the typical situation in a large company where power is formally in top management, but they normally find it sensible to consult with other groups, e.g. general managers of product divisions, heads of corporate staff groups and chief executives of national subsidiaries. In this situation, planning procedures provide a useful basis for the dialogue which has to occur between these various parties.

(3) *Coalition*. In certain situations power is not located in one top manager nor in a senior management team but in several interest groups located inside and outside the organization. As one strategic planner recently remarked of a hospital, 'The problem is to find the decision maker'. In the hospital, power is shared among three main groups - the doctors, the nurses and the administrators. Increasingly, also, the blue-collar workers are also claiming a say in hospital policy.

A university Vice-Chancellor also finds himself faced with several power groups: e.g. the faculty, the administration and the students.

In local and national government power is always divided between the politicians and the officials, and the problem varies depending on whether the politicians are grouped as

        (a) one dominant party
        (b) two or more evenly balanced parties
        (c) individuals with no party alignment and owing their first
            loyalty to their constituents.

In the Coalition it is not normally possible to gain agreement to long term commitments. The nominal leader often has to proceed by incremental steps, taking one issue at a time. The idea of developing a comprehensive, rational, long range plan is an unrealistic pipe dream. *Ad hoc* decision-making is the usual pattern.

The idea of 'setting corporate objectives' is politically naive. As American Presidential candidates know well, a wide coalition of interests is best kept together by the use of well-phrased platitudes. Yehezkel Dror refers to the value of 'goal-opaqueness' in coalition situations. It certainly seems that the development of explicit objectives and policies will frequently explode a coalition by making conflicts of values and aspirations overt rather than implicit. The leader can only unite his coalition on specific issues and by careful negotiation.

PLANNING AS AN INTER-ORGANIZATIONAL PROCESS

Research, and practical experience suggests that Corporate Planning also involves decision-makers in interactions with powerful groups outside the enterprise. A 5-year research programme by the Tavistock Institute in British local authorities, led the researchers to conclude that:

        "Corporate Planning is not enough - the making of strategic
        decisions must be considered not merely as a corporate but
        also as an inter-organizational process. The more

comprehensively those in large organizations seek to plan
the more they find themselves dependent on the outcome of
other agencies, both public and private; also, the more
aware they become of the many subtle relationships –
economic, social, political and ecological – that extend
into other parts of their environment – which may be less
clearly structured in formal organizational terms."[39]

The Tavistock researchers, and others working on the political dimensions of
planning, stress the importance of building informal contacts and 'networks' both
inside and outside the enterprise as a means of *influencing decisions*.

The argument for 'network building' is that:

(1) An organization's scope and influence tend to be defined in
    practice through bargaining with government and other
    organizations.

(2) As inter-organizational contacts are important, the policy-
    making activity needs to include Foreign Policy, i.e. the
    policies to be adopted and the relationships to be developed
    with other organizations and interest groups. These policies
    should be in the shape of broad guide-lines allowing discretion
    for local interpretation.

(3) An organization may expand its scope and influence by
    building and maintaining information and support networks
    with other groups and enterprises. It is necessary therefore
    to allocate time and resources and to select and train
    management who have the marketing and political skills to
    sustain and develop inter-organizational collaboration.

Figures 1.15 and 1.16 show two formats – which have proved useful in analysing
support and influence networks in Local Government and in business.

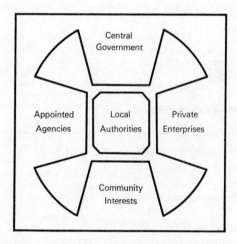

Fig. 1.15. Planning in Local Government.[39]

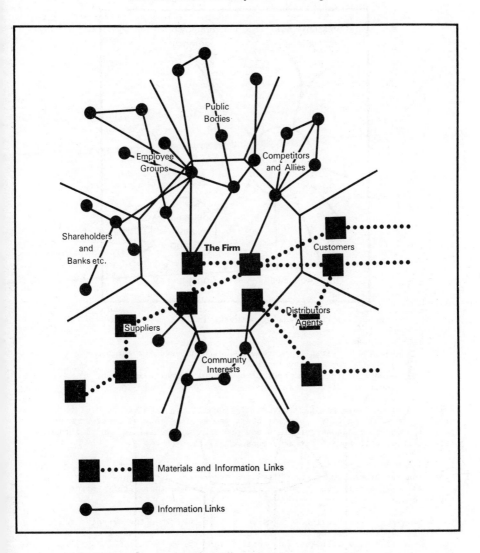

Fig. 1.16. Planning networks in business.

Figure 1.17 illustrates the types of networks which are developed by policy-makers in local government:

    (1) within the organization which employs them,
    (2) in their own professions and associations (including trade
         unions),
    (3) in other adjacent agencies - Water Boards, Health Authorities,

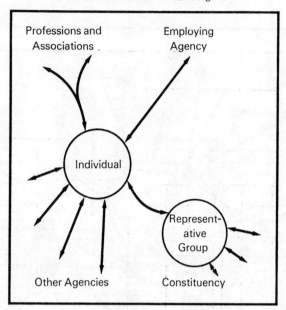

Fig. 1.17.   Policy-making networks in local government.[39]

Gas and Electricity Boards, and with private enterprises –
such as property developers.
(4) with the elected members of the local council, and with
their constituencies.[39]

This kind of analysis provides few revelations to top managers much of whose life
is spent cultivating these informal contacts, working on government commissions,
participating in trade associations and professional activities and maintaining
relationships with social action groups of all kinds.

This is why doors are open to some people and not to others, why some organizations can influence government policy and others cannot. These influence
networks are essential to Corporate Planning although they rarely appear in the
formal plans.

The management's political resources become apparent when the organization is
challenged by some outside body. To handle a monopoly investigation or a lawsuit
on product liability will test the enterprise's strength at law. A public
confrontation with protest groups may require access and the ability to use
television and other news media. The threat of a strike will test the credibility
of management and their negotiating skills with Trade Unions. A takeover bid
requires the mobilization of shareholder support. A negotiation with distributors
and dealers may require the backing of other manufacturers. To stop or modify
parliamentary legislation which may damage the business may need access to civil
servants and politicians.

Clearly, organizations vary in their dependence on external political networks.
In certain fields – e.g. defence, construction, health, transportation, communica-

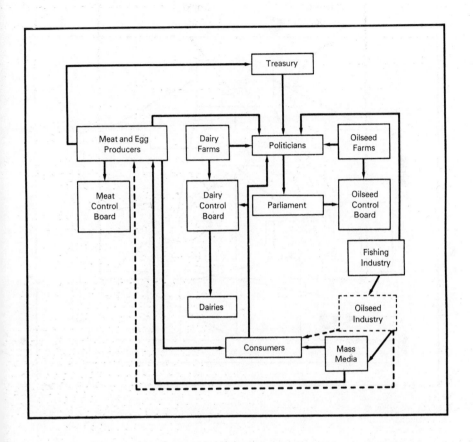

Fig. 1.18. Political systems in the food industry –
introducing margarine into South Africa (1966).[40]

tions, energy, and agriculture – the managers of an individual enterprise are
inevitably going to be deeply involved with governments and various external
interest groups. In other fields – e.g. retailing and distribution, most
consumer goods and capital goods which are not vital to the national infrastructure – external political activities seem to be less central to policy-
making. Figures 1.18 and 1.19 show the importance of political networks in the
Food Industry and in the Building Industry.

CORPORATE PLANNING WITH GOVERNMENT AND UNIONS

Traditionally, business executives in the 'western world' have assumed that in
general they were free to make the major strategic decisions for their enterprises –

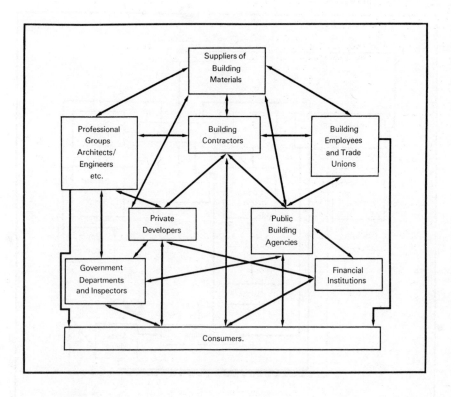

Fig. 1.19.   Interactions between groups in the building
             industry.

without referring to government officials, trade union leaders and self-appointed
representatives of the public. There is now a strong movement in many countries
towards the greater involvement of employees and unions on the one hand and local
and national government officials on the other in the informal and formal
processes of Corporate Planning.

In the Developing Countries government has always been heavily involved in
business - both as owners of public corporations and through the regulation of
private enterprise.

Figure 1.20 - by Robert Kerwin of Bosphorus University in Istanbul - shows the
typical pattern of decision-making between government and industry for a private
enterprise in a Developing Country, based on an organizational setting in Turkey.

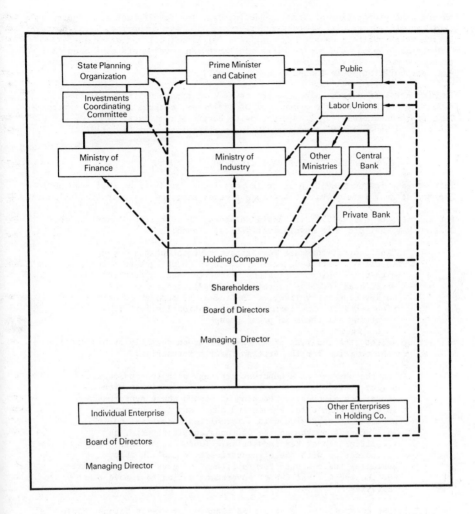

Fig. 1.20. The decision-making process in a typical
            private enterprise in a mixed economy.

In Western Europe, increasingly, employees and trade union officials are
consulted in advance about key decisions such as major capital investments, plant
closures, mergers, and working arrangements likely to affect the employees. Many
West European countries have established processes by law for this consultation
through: (a) the appointment of Worker Directors - usually on a second tier
'Supervisory Board', and (b) the use of Works Councils with powers to veto and
rights of consultation. Government involvement in business is extensive. In
France and Sweden the central government attempts to influence business policy

through the preparation of broad guidelines for the development of industry as a
whole and for particular sectors and regions. In most countries, large parts of
business are publicly owned, e.g. railways, airlines, oil and other energy
industries. During the recent recession, European governments have been obliged
to become more deeply involved in financing and planning for depressed industries,
e.g. shipbuilding, pulp and paper and automobiles.

In many parts of Europe, also, there has been an expansion in legislation
affecting business for the protection of employees, consumers and the environment.
In certain countries, e.g. the U.K., price controls and restrictions on wages,
rents and dividends have been imposed in an attempt to control inflation.

FROM CONSULTATION TO PARTICIPATION

This advance in government intervention has led to predictions that some nations
are moving away from private enterprise towards a system of centralized planning.

For example, in March 1975 Sir Ronald McIntosh, the Director-General of the
British National Economic Development Office, stated:

> "The central forecast for Britain over the next few years
> is one of continued decline.... If we do not get to grips
> with our industrial problems before the next upturn in
> world trade occurs ... this could spell the end of the
> market economy by 1980.... To find a way through the situa-
> tion requires some form of planned national effort ...
> involving all the main power groups."

Sir Arthur Knight, the Chairman of Courtaulds, wrote recently of his experience
with government policies for the British textile industries:

> "In the absence of a coherent strategy with the consequent
> policy conflicts, one is bound to make comparisons with
> situations elsewhere. Looking at others whose performance
> is better than ours, France and Japan are two obvious
> examples of countries with a formulated industrial policy.
> This depends on the choice of fundamental criteria, and
> identification of key industries. There is not only
> communication with these industries to establish what
> obstacles there are to the fulfilment of government objectives,
> but the unequivocal use of government action to remove these
> obstacles."[41]

The call is not generally for centralized planning by Trades Unions, Employers'
Federations and Government Departments - even if this were feasible - but there is
a general recognition of a need for better understanding and closer co-operation.

John Davies, a former Minister and ex-Director-General of the Confederation of
British Industry summarized the position as follows:

> "Here we stand today, gazing with disillusion at one another:
> Government perplexed that its benevolent enthusiasm should be
> so lukewarmly reflected, and management vexed to find that
> all that is expected of it is maximum disclosure, but not
> participation in decision.... What is needed is the replace-
> ment of the concept of consultation - which has become

practically and rightly a dirty word by one of partnership."

TRADES UNIONS AND EMPLOYEES

There is also a recognition that Trades Unions and employees need to be involved *before* the event, in major decisions which affect their lives. The damaging strikes that have occurred in various parts of Europe – and in North America – have frequently been the natural response of employees to being presented as a 'fait accompli' with strategic decisions in which they have had no say and which might have serious consequences for them and for their families.

The process of collective bargaining clearly has to expand outside the traditional area of wages and working conditions to cover the structuring of work and the design of the working environment. In a recent survey when asked: *What advances are most important to achieve?* British workers answered:

		(per cent)
(1)	More information from the top on what is happening and why	26
(2)	Better incentives to improve productivity and efficiency	23
(3)	Better pay	21
(4)	Bigger say in day-to-day running of the company	19
(5)	Bigger say in how work is planned and organized	15

When asked to name *Advances least important to achieve* they said:

(1)	Bigger say in management decisions on finance and investment	31
(2)	Workers having seats on Board[42]	26

The need for better communication of company policies to employees was confirmed by a Confederation of British Industry Survey of Employee Attitudes.[43] Asked *How much profit does an average company make before tax out of every £100 sales?* against an *actual* average of £10, shop floor workers estimated £31, and managers estimated £20.

The survey showed that 60 per cent of employees had no idea what profits their *own* companies made.

The survey also suggested that greater worker participation might lead to better motivation and higher production. A high proportion of employees of large organizations clearly feel alienated and demotivated. In the CBI study an extraordinarily high proportion of workers agreed with the statement: 'I could do more work in my present job without much effort'

		(per cent)
(1)	Workers in nationalized industry	57
(2)	Workers in private industry	42
(3)	Managers	29

Trade Union officials, too, clearly need to be involved in evolving corporate strategy – otherwise they will use their power to stop the new policies being implemented. This has occurred in Britain with the Ten Year Strategy for the

British Steel industry even though it had been previously agreed between the management and the government.

New processes of joint consultation have now been evolved in many of the British nationalized industries and in British Leyland and Chrysler (UK), which ensure that Trades Unions are consulted in the planning process - both as regards broad Corporate Strategy and concerning the detailed implementation of the Strategy. Some organizations have also established an early-warning system to enable representatives of government, unions and management to get together several years before a possible plant closure to discuss alternative strategies and if necessary to arrange for the retraining and redeployment of employees. Government legislation in Europe frequently assumes that this consultation will take place. In Sweden the Ministry of Industry's regular survey of companies asks for details of future plans for:

> *New Factories* - home and overseas
>
> *Investment Trends* (year by year)
>   - in total,
>   - for product development,
>   - for marketing, etc.

Finally the form asks management *Have you consulted the central trade union for the company?*

>   - if *Yes* how did you consult them?
>   - if *No* why did you *not* consult them?

In Britain the recent Labour government launched its New Industrial Strategy (which some said was not new, not industrial, and not a strategy) on the basis of 'Tripartite Planning' involving co-operation between government, management and unions:

> (a) at national level through contact with Ministers and
>   senior officials
> (b) at sector level - through on-going discussions in the
>   National Economic Development Committees
> (c) in large private companies where the top management are
>   invited to discuss their broad strategies and plans
>   with government and unions through the process of
>   Planning Agreements.

Olle Hammarstrom, a Swedish labour ministry official summarizes the political realities of Corporate Planning in Europe. 'If you want more industrial peace,' he says, 'give the unions more power'.

The evidence is overwhelming. The facts may not be fully reflected in the literature on Corporate Planning, but in practice, planning is becoming a highly political process. Moreover, the balance of power is changing and in most cases it is no longer sensible for managers to assume that they can make their strategic decisions without full consultation with their employees, with the Trades Unions and with government agencies.

V. PLANNING AS A CONFLICT OF VALUES

This perspective emphasizes that planning is not merely a rational, cognitive process; it is also about commitment to goals, and values.

The supporters of this view of planning criticize planners for being too much concerned with making strategies and plans for the perpetuation of existing institutions and present systems and for spending too little time considering what these institutions and systems are for, and what social purposes they serve.

The significance of this view of planning for current and future planning practice arises from two main trends:

1. 'Futures Creative Planning'

The development in government and business of Futures Forecasting and Planning for large socio-technical systems.

2. Planning for Cultural Change

The appreciation that planning must be concerned with identifying, appraising and modifying the values or belief systems in an institution and ensuring a better 'fit' between the 'dominant ideas' or values within an enterprise and the expectations of the society in which it must exist.

FUTURES CREATIVE PLANNING

In 1968 a group of leading academics meeting at an OECD symposium in Bellagio published the following Declaration on Planning:

> "The pursuance of orthodox planning is quite insufficient, in that it seldom does more than touch a system through changes of the variables. Planning must be concerned with the structural design of the system itself and involved in the formation of policy.
>
> Mere modification of policies already proved to be inadequate will not result in what is right. *Science in planning today is too often used to make situations which are inherently bad, more efficiently bad.*
>
> The scope of planning must be expanded to encompass the formulation of alternative policies and the examination, analysis, and explicit stipulation of the underlying values and norms."[44]

This suggests the need for a new approach to planning which will not take present institutions and arrangements as given but will explore the possibilities of creating new social and technological systems. Erich Jantsch, an exponent of the 'new' planning argues that:

> "Three essential features of the 'new' 'futures creative' planning make it radically different from the 'old' (non-creative) planning:
>
> (1) The general introduction of *normative thinking* and *valuation* into planning ... placing emphasis on invention through forecasting;
>
> (2) The recognition of *systems design* as the central subject of planning (i.e. acting upon structures rather than variables of systems);

(3) The conception of *three* levels
  . normative or policy planning (the 'ought')
  . strategic planning (the 'can')
  . and tactical or operational planning (the 'will')."[45]

The exploration of social and technological futures may seem to be a task for
public planners, but it is clear that business and research organizations will
have to be involved in the design, marketing and managing of these large systems
and the systems will frequently require collaboration between government and
industrial groups on an international basis.

As Donald Schon points out:

> "The movement towards business systems further erodes the
> boundaries between private and public enterprise. Firms ...
> have come to identify themselves with broad social functions.
> In part, this reflects the growing market for public systems
> such as housing, transportation, waste management and the
> like. In part, it reflects recognition that if a new
> technology is to be introduced into a public system, the
> whole system must be restructured."[46]

Erich Jantsch predicts that:

> "Industry will have to develop the capability to plan, design,
> build, manage and perhaps even operate the big systems of the
> future - systems for transportation, communication, education,
> health, urban living, etc. - and this challenge can only be
> met by a flexible inter-institutional response from industry
> as well as other planning, research and operating institu-
> tions."[47]

There is, here, a role, for the use of Futures Research techniques - scenarios,
delphi studies etc., to explore and examine alternative possibilities for
systems serving major social functions and to provide a common background for
policies which will have to be developed on an inter-institutional and possibly
on an international basis. There is also a function for 'Think Tanks' and
'Look Out' Institutions whose function is 'to conceive possible futures; to
create standards of comparison between possible futures; to define ways of
getting at such possible futures by means of the physical, human, intellectual
and political resources that the current situation permits to estimate'.[48]

For example Visual Communications is a field which is at present being thoroughly
explored by futures research in an attempt to determine the future implications
of present decisions.

Figure 1.21 lists some of the new technological developments, Figure 1.22
suggests a number of the social implications and Figure 1.23 sets out some of the
key policy decisions which need to be made. Raymond Williams, the author of this
study,[49] examines three alternative scenarios:

Scenario I - Global TV Corporations

Unprecedented control by a few multinational corporations, based on U.S. or
U.S.S.R. monopoly rights to satellite TV, financed by multi-national advertising
and networked programmes, with national networks operating mainly as sub-
contractors.

New Receivers	• Portables and Micro-Receivers • Large-Screen (6 ft × 4 ft) • Flat Wall Screen
Cable Systems	• Retransmission • Independent Broadcasting • Services on Demand: News, Education, Information, Programmes, Public Discussions, Medical Consultancy, Printed Material
Visual Information Systems	• Domestic Visual Devices: Telephone, 'Readers', Printers, Closed Circuit TV
Satellite TV	• Via Ground Stations • Direct to Augmented or Normal Receivers
Video-Cassettes	• Video Recordings • Special Programmes • Cassette Library
Videotape Equipment	• Cheap Production • Community TV
Interactive TV	• Push Button Purchasing or Voting • Interaction Equipment

Fig. 1.21.   Television 1990: the new technology[49]

Scenario II - Dominant National Networks

Increased power for remote centralized broadcasting corporations with state control or commercial monopoly, centralized production with cable transmission of national network programmes, national licensing of satellite TV, cable TV and video cassettes.

Scenario III - Community TV Services

Increased democratic control by local communities, and control of cable and satellite TV by representative international agencies. Cable TV would provide a comprehensive service to the local community and there would be many independent production companies.

This scenario identifies the decisions to be made, sets out the technological alternatives, and explores the social and political implications.

PLANNING FOR CULTURAL CHANGE

Those who stress the importance of goals and values in planning tend to view a social system as a total culture.

The notion of 'culture' is borrowed from the anthropologists who define it as:

New Receivers	• Heavy Capital Investment
	• Centralized Control
	• Pay TV for Large Screen?
Cable Systems	• New Pay TV in Urban Areas?
	• Local Community TV?
Visual Information Systems	• New Information Utilities?
Satellite TV	• New Multinational Corporations?
	• Democratic or Dominated by Super-Powers?
Video Cassettes	• Multinational Corporations?
	• Public Library Service?
	• Independent Producers?
Videotape Equipment	• Independent Producers?
	• Community TV?
Interactive Equipment	• Commercial Uses (Advertising)
	• Community Information Services
	• Politics (Voting)

Fig. 1.22. Television 1990: social effects of new
           technology.[49]

> "a body of learned behaviour, a collection of beliefs,
> habits and traditions shared by a group of people and
> successively learned by new members who enter the Society."[50]

Donald Schon refers to the 'theory' of a social system:

> "When a person enters a social system, he encounters a
> body of theory which more or less explicitly sets out not
> only the 'way the world is' but 'who we are', 'what we are
> doing' and 'what we should be doing'. The theory of an
> industrial firm, for example, includes what the business
> is, how it works, what the market and competition are like
> and what kinds of performance are valued. The theory of
> an agency for the blind includes notions about what a blind
> person can learn to do, what is an appropriate service, what
> professional behaviour consists in, the difference between
> good and bad clients, what the objectives of providing the
> service are.... Value systems correspond to, and are
> inseparable from theory.... It is in a way misleading to
> distinguish at all between the social system and its theory,
> for the social system is the embodiment of its theory and
> the theory is the conceptual dimension of the social
> system."[51]

Sir Geoffrey Vickers focuses on the 'ecology of ideas' - the way the ideology of
a social system must evolve and adapt in response to a changing world: His
theme is 'the process by which men and societies change the values by which they
live'.

> "Human life" he writes, "is sustained culturally, no less
> than biologically, by what seems to be a highly precarious

A. **Cable and Visual Information Systems**
   1. Channel Size and Range of Services?
   2. Contracts—Commercial vs Public Service?
      Existing vs New Contractors?
      Extent of Access and Coverage?

B. **Satellite TV**
   Open Skies World Wide TV Service
   • U.S./Russian Monopolies?
   • National Sovereignty Over Air Space?

C. **Video-Cassettes and Video-Tape Recording**
   1. Increased Access to Independent Producers?
   2. Commercial or Public Service?

D. **Interactive TV**
   Range of Uses
   • Commercial only vs Public Information and Politics?

Fig. 1.23. Television 1990: communications policy: key
decisions.[49]

social process. Each generation takes over, makes over,
and passes on a heritage which consists basically in
specific ways of appreciating and acting in its situation.
It is essential to any society that its 'appreciative
system' shall change sufficiently to interpret a changing
world yet should remain sufficiently shared and sufficiently
stable to enable mutual understanding and common action, and
to make sense of personal experience."[52]

"All dreams" he suggests, "even the American Dream, must
constantly be dreamed anew".[53]

NEW ASSUMPTIONS

The view of the organization as a culture makes very different assumptions from
the 'classical-rational' view of planning.

1. Setting of goals in an enterprise is part of a complex social process

J.C. March for example writes:

"It seems to me perfectly obvious that a description that
assumes goals come first and action comes later is frequently
radically wrong.

Human choice behaviour is at least as much a process for
discovering goals as for acting on them."[54]

Eric Rhenman discovered in his research into long range planning in Scandinavia
that the real planning process is far more confused than the Planning and Control
theory assumes:

> "One of the basic notions of the normative theory of
> planning and decision-making is that the decision process
> starts with the formulation of goals. The decision-maker
> then seeks alternatives which can fulfil these goals. This
> 'goal first, plan second' hypothesis was found not to be
> suitable.... It turned out that the real planning process
> can best be described as a learning process in which the
> goals and the methods of achieving them are changing all
> the time and where the goals depend very much on successive
> insights into the alternatives available."[55]

2. <u>Organizations contain many sub-cultures and value systems competing for
   dominance</u>

One of the tasks of top management is to maintain a balance between these various
sub-cultures so that the organization will remain stable but innovative. Igor
Ansoff contrasts the goals, values and attitudes of the Operating Manager (con-
formist, conservative, short-term, own-industry) with the wider orientation of
the Entrepreneurial Manager (less conventional, more innovative, concerned with
the longer term and the social implications of policies)[56] (see Figure 1.24).
Richard Normann, of the Scandinavian Institute for Administrative Research puts
forward a theory of a 'dual culture': one part of this culture is preoccupied
with the techniques, management, stabilization and exploitation of *established*
businesses. Another part is concerned with the ability to create new businesses.[57]

	Narrow Perspective	Wider Perspective
Environment	— Immediate Environment of Firm, Industry, Nation, Technology	— Multi-Industry, Multi-National, Social and Political as Well as Economic and Technological
Social Values	— Optimizing Immediate Profits	More Aware of Social Values
Personal Values	— Money Power Stability/Conformity	More Concern with Self-Actualization, Change, Deviance
Skills	Narrow Experience — Intuitive, Extrapolative Planner, Conservative	Border Experience, Professional, Analytical Entrepreneurial

Fig. 1.24. Operational manager vs strategic manager.

3. <u>Strategy tends to emerge in an irregular way over time through a complex
   interaction between the various factions and in response to changes in the
   environment</u>

Henry Mintzberg of McGill University has analyzed the evolution of strategy over
a long period in Volkswagenwerk, the U.S. Government (Vietnam Policy) and
Saturday Night Magazine. He concludes that:

> a) A strategy is not normally a deliberate plan conceived
>   in advance of the making of decisions. It is best thought
>   of as 'a pattern in a stream of decisions'.

b) 'Strategy formation is not a regular, nicely sequenced
    process running on a standard five year schedule or
    whatever ... patterns of strategic changes are never
    steady but rather bumpy and *ad hoc* with a complex inter-
    mingling of periods of continuity and change, etc.'.[58]

c) The active policy-maker - the hero of virtually all the
    planning literature - can be dangerous, e.g. offering
    explicit strategies to a strong bureaucracy in a
    turbulent environment may result in the forceful applica-
    tion of policies which are no longer appropriate. Often -
    to avoid resistance or because he is uncertain - he must
    implement his strategy slowly and by stages.

4. Control in human affairs is often not achieved so much through formal
procedures and budgets, as through the operation of group norms and self-
control

This emphasizes the need in an enterprise for a strong sense of purpose and a
value system to which the staff can become committed. Each individual is a
member of many other reference groups (e.g. scientists, professionals, trade
unionists) which have competing and conflicting value systems. In essence when
a person enters an organization, the employee and the management enter into a
'psychological contract'. He commits himself to the organization and its goals
and the management aims to provide him with job satisfaction and recognition,
the ability to grow in his job etc. When this contract is broken employee
motivation becomes a problem.

5. A major strategic problem for management appears to lie in up-dating the
'dominant ideas' in the enterprise

Eric Rhenman, after a comprehensive research study into Long Range Planning in
20 public and private organizations in Scandinavia decided that the major strategic
problem facing them was not changing technology or competition for markets, but
the difficulty of matching the values and attitudes within the organization to
the values and attitudes in the organization's environment. Moreover, the main
obstacle to innovation lay not in resistance to change in the organization but in
top management's insensitivity to the expectations of the environment.

Rhenman concluded that management in private enterprise should become more
responsive to social changes:

> "If private enterprise is to survive in a free economy
> without serious disturbances, it must be prepared to take
> part in active regional planning, to promote industrial
> democracy, to work for a better environment and to pursue
> various other political goals."[59]

One of the conclusions from this writing and research on values is that the
planner should be continually aware of the repercussions and the value implications associated with various courses of action. Various organizations have
developed methods for mapping goals and values for an organization. These
approaches include: the Social Audit, the Stakeholder Analysis, the use of
attitude surveys inside and outside the organization and surveys of opinion
leaders in relation to specific issues.

The Cultural Impact of Technical Change

Planning of course is about change and it is bound to have an impact on 'culture'. The capacity of institutions to resist change is legendary. Generals and admirals remain deaf to new ideas or persist in outdated concepts of warfare despite all the evidence presented to them. Work forces and trades unions frequently refuse to accept new technologies which demand new approaches or threaten to make their present skills obsolete. Professional and managerial staff strive to preserve established routines and relationships long after they have outlived their usefulness. Donald Schon argues that all social systems exhibit not merely 'inertia' - a tendency to move steadily along their present courses unless a contrary force is exerted upon them - but 'dynamic conservatism' that is they *fight* to remain the same.[60]

He also suggests that a community, a whole industry, or a single institution must be regarded as a total system - which incorporates an existing technology and traditional values and norms of behaviour:

> "It is always futile to seek a single 'cause' for a system's
> being the way it is. There is always a complex of inter-
> acting components. The social system contains structure,
> technology and theory.
>
> The structure is set of roles and relations among individual
> members. The theory consists of the views held within the
> social system about its purposes, its operations, its environ-
> ment and its future. Both reflect, and in turn influence the
> prevailing technology of the system. These dimensions all
> hang together so that any change in one produces changes in
> all the others." [60]

In 1951, the anthropologist Margaret Mead was asked by UNESCO to produce a report on the problem of introducing new technologies into Developing Countries. In her report she suggested that innovators should take certain precautions - to anticipate the social impact of technical change, and to facilitate its absorption by the culture. Some of the points made in Margaret Mead's report are summarized in Figure 1.25. They seem equally relevant to the changing of technology, organizational structures and procedures at the level of the enterprise.[61]

Research by Mumford and Pettigrew into the choice and installation of major computer systems in Britain suggests that in most cases important social and political problems occurred because top management and the management services specialists involved, typically insisted on regarding the problem as a technical and financial choice and seemed unaware of the need to consult and involve the staff of the operating departments at every turn.[62]

                    CONCLUSION

The Realities of Planning

As many practitioners and writers have pointed out, there is a gap between our theory which sees planning as a deliberate, rational, sequential process and our practice, where we find that many of the processes are *ad hoc*, informal, non-rational and concerned with values or power.

1. **Social Effects**—Be aware that your are dealing with a pattern of human habits, beliefs, and traditions. Discover just what will be the *social effects* of your proposed technical changes.

2. **Established Order**—Do not attack the established order. It is an attack on long standing beliefs and thus on the believer and (sometimes even worse) on those who taught him those beliefs.

3. **Social Learning**—Provide opportunities for the group to learn by experience. 'Living through a long series of situations in which the new behaviour is made highly satisfying and the old not satisfying'.

4. **Social Climate**—Establish a social climate favourable to the changes by 'consistent, prompt attachment of some form of satisfaction'—praise, approval, increased status, sense of participation and material reward.

5. **Participation**—Secure the active participation of those who will be affected both in the planning and in the execution of the change.
   —Work with the recognized leadership of the culture. Only members of the culture understand the habits of the culture.

6. **Timing**—Choose the right time and provide sufficient time for the mental changes to take place. Start small, keep it fluid. Avoid surprises. One of the main reasons why culture develops is that it makes life predictable.

7. **Integration**—Reduce the impact of changes by weaving them into an existing broader pattern of behaviour.

Fig. 1.25.   Cultural patterns and technical change.[61]

Every planner has to live with this incompatibility between his theory and his practice and it sometimes results in a kind of schizophrenia - a form of 'Planners' Neurosis'.

We have an elegant theory of planning which argues very persuasively that planning should be:

(1) comprehensive
(2) rational
(3) sequential
(4) formalized.

In practice the planner finds that the process is not comprehensive but *partial*. Total integrated planning systems like total integrated information systems exist only in textbooks and in the dreams of management scientists. He finds that his planning process, to be kind, exhibits only 'limited rationality'. His ambitions for producing a sensible allocation of resources based on a global strategy, are frequently defeated through the machinations and the deviousness of operating managers who do not accept the logic that labels their division a 'Cash Cow' to be 'milked' for the benefit of other people's calves.

Often they find their financial and economic calculations, and their logical arguments are inexplicably discounted or altered because of some senior person's 'intuition'.

We do, of course, have a planning procedure - but that is not to say that this is where the decisions are made. The chief executive often seems quite happy that everyone else should use the system but one has the feeling that he is not always frank about his own strategies and future intentions. There are many planners who have first learned about company acquisitions and other important

moves in the financial press. Added to all this is the problem known in the
literature as 'implementation'. Planning theory is eloquent about formulating
long range plans but somewhat less forthcoming on the subject of how plans should
be carried out. In practice it is sometimes difficult to know whether plans are
being 'formulated' or 'implemented'. Even when you think you have a plan agreed
it turns out simply to be a basis for further negotiation. It may be overturned
by resistance from sections of management and groups of employees, the opposition
of Trades Unions, protests from the community, legislation, moves by competitors
or Acts of God. As one executive remarked it seems that 'No plan survives
contact with reality'.

What is Policy Analysis?

We are now in the process of rewriting our theories about planning and remaking
our planning processes in an attempt to reflect 'the realities of planning' for
different activities under differing conditions in various parts of the world.
The past decade has seen the growing acceptance of expertise in decision-making
and it has been recognized that management specialists of various kinds are able
to contribute to the policy-making process. To the established groups of
technologists, accountants, economists and management scientists, have been added
experts in organizational behaviour, corporate and public affairs, and futures
research.

We are in the first phase of building a science and practice of policy-making
which will be 'truly multi-disciplinary and multi-function' - 'a new "supra-
discipline" devoted to the study and improvement of policy-making in all kinds
of systems.'[63]

Some writers have suggested that the result will be a new approach to strategic
planning to be called Strategic Management or Policy Analysis.

But what is Policy Analysis or Strategic Management? As yet it hardly exists
except as a way of thinking - as reflected in a number of publications and
university programmes. However, we have in our current thinking and practice the
elements for a new more realistic approach to planning.

A fundamental characteristic of this approach is that it is multi-dimensional.
The planner or policy-maker usually comes to his task with a way of thinking
about the organization which has been acquired through study of a single
discipline and experience in a particular function. It is clear that not one of
these traditional viewpoints - not even the conventional view of planning,
provides a sufficiently rounded view. To plan *realistically* the planner needs
to use a number of different perspectives or 'conceptual lenses'.[64]

The old story of the Blind Hindus and the Elephant provides a useful illustration
of this point. It seems that there were four blind men walking along a road,
they came across an elephant and each tried to touch it to find out what it was.

The first Hindu took hold of the elephant's trunk and he said, 'It is a snake'.
The second Hindu grasped the tail and he said, 'It is a rope'. The third Hindu
put his arms around one of the legs and he said, 'It is a tree'. The fourth man
put his palms on the elephant's side and he said 'It is a wall'.

The moral of the parable is that each of the Blind Hindus had found a part of
the truth but none of them had the whole. The problem with planning is similar.
All too often progress in planning is limited because the planning team think of
planning in one particular context or dimension. I have suggested five perspec-

tives on planning each of which contribute part of the total picture:

1. *Planning as a Central Control System*

This view emphasizes the need for

> (a) explicit objectives, strategies and plans
> (b) a rational, analytical approach
> (c) a regular review procedure.

2. *Planning as a Framework for Innovation*

This views planning as a framework for self-renewal of products, processes and people, a process of organized entrepreneurship through which the enterprise can be regenerated.

3. *Planning as a Social Learning Process*

This perspective suggests that planning must be conceived as a learning process through which individuals and groups develop a sense of direction, feelings of mutual trust, confidence, and methods for coping with unfamiliar problems in an uncertain environment.

4. *Planning as a Political Process*

As strategic decisions affect the balance of resources, and the status of individuals and groups in an enterprise, planning is naturally not only about consensus but also about conflict and bargaining among interest groups inside and outside the organization.

5. *Planning as a Conflict of Values*

Planning at the highest level is not just about improving efficiency or choosing strategies, it concerns the development within the individual enterprise and in society, of cultures which can claim the allegiance of employees and which are accepted as socially useful by the community at large.

It is also concerned with an attempt to influence the shape of the world in which we will live tomorrow.

When we put all these perspectives together we may still not have a 'total' picture of planning - the whole elephant.

The analysis is intended to be illustrative not exhaustive.

I wish to suggest that to succeed in planning we must take a broad view using many disciplines and forms of analysis. *We need a 'total systems' view which sees planning and policy-making as a central human activity: rational, but also creative and intuitive; bureaucratic, yet dynamic and evolving; political, and at the same time concerned with important choices between human values.*

The Role of the Planner

Finally, we should ask 'What does this analysis imply for the planner and the policy-maker?'

First and foremost it emphasizes that *the job of the planner is not merely to*

*design, install and maintain a formal planning system. His task is to help the
decision-makers to identify what are the key decisions to be taken - and to
assist them in taking these decisions with the best available information and in
the most effective fashion.*

Also, he should realize that the task is not simply to find a rational technical
solution but to discover an approach which is culturally acceptable and politically
feasible.

He may of course also be involved with the political negotiations and the educational processes which in all probability will be needed to implement the
decisions

Secondly, it suggests that *there is not just one style of planning or policy-
making but many.*

The job of the planner or the senior manager responsible for planning is:

> to try to understand planning in its many dimensions;
>
> to diagnose the situation he is in from several points of
> view; and
>
> to match his planning approach to the condition of the
> organization he is concerned with.

Fitting the planning 'mode' to the situation will require a good deal of skill
and experience:

> (a) In a large bureaucratic organization, this will probably
> require the introduction of a formal planning system.
>
> (b) In circumstances where growth or innovation are required
> it will be important to organize for new projects.
>
> (c) In an uncertain situation with many interest groups
> involved, it may be advisable to use an incremental or
> organizational 'learning' process - to improve mutual
> understanding, to explore the problem, and possibly to
> evolve a consensus.
>
> (d) If it is necessary to influence decisions in other
> organizations there may be a need for special arrange-
> ments to improve formal and informal contacts, e.g.
> through joint committees, liaison officers, etc.
>
> (e) Where there is a 'crisis of identity' in the organiza-
> tion (e.g. if it is not thought to be socially valuable,
> or if the future of the enterprise is tied up with the
> creation of a new technology with important social
> implications) it may be particularly important to re-
> examine the future role of the enterprise in society.

I do not wish to be misunderstood. I am not advocating a rejection of rationality,
a neglect of systems and procedures - a return to 'muddling through'. To quote
one of Britain's business leaders, Sir James Goldsmith, Chairman of Cavenham
Limited:

> "Muddling through is a euphemism for failing to plan forward.

It means acting tactically and without a strategy; it means
confusing the means with the end.... If we continue to avoid
facing the facts ... the epitaph on the grave of our
democracy will be:

> 'They sacrificed the long term for the short term, and
> the long term finally arrived'."

REFERENCES

1. Henri Fayol, *General and Industrial Management* (trans. Storrs), Pitman,
    London (1961).

2. Melville C. Branch, *The Corporate Planning Process,* p.132, American
    Management Association, New York (1962).

3. Joseph M. Juran, *Managerial Breakthrough,* McGraw Hill, New York (1964).

4. Robert N. Antony, *Planning & Control Systems - A Framework for Analysis*,
    p.67, Harvard University, Boston (1965).

5. Robert Y. Durand, *Business: Its Organization, Management & Responsibilities*,
    p.389, Prentice-Hall, Englewood Cliffs, N.J. (1958).

6. F.F. Gilmore, *Formulation & Advocacy of Business Policy*, Cornell University,
    New York, (1968), pages 8-10 & p.20.

7. Adapted from G.A. Steiner, *Top Management Planning*, MacMillan, New York
    (1969), p.33.

8. See Rochelle O'Connor, *Corporate Guides to Long-Range Planning*, pp.24-95,
    The Conference Board, New York (1976).

9. G.H. Fisher, *The World of Program Budgeting*, RAND Corporation Paper (1969).

10. Joseph Bower, *Managing the Resource Allocation Process*, p.54, Harvard (1970).

11. David C.D. Rogers, *Essentials of Business Policy*, Harper & Row, New York
    (1975), p.52.

12 Igor Ansoff *et al., From Strategic Planning to Strategic Management*, p.39,
    Wiley, London (1976).

13. *Planning and the Chief Executive*, p.5, Conference Board, New York (1972).

14. Israel Unterman, American Finance: Three Views of Strategy, *Journal of
    General Management*, 1 (3), (1974).

15. Eric Rhenman, *Organisation Theory for Long Range Planning*, p.4, Wiley, New
    York (1972).

16. Henry Mintzberg, Strategy-Making in Three Modes, *California Management
    Review*, pp.44-53 (1973).

17. Yehezkel Dror, *Ventures in Policy Sciences*, p.118, Elsevier, New York (1971).

18. John K. Friend *et al.*, *Public Planning: The Inter-Corporate Dimension*, p.375, Tavistock, London (1974).

19. Yehezkel Dror, op. cit., p.38.

20. Igor H. Ansoff *et al.*, op. cit., pp.1-14 and 39-78.

21. Igor H. Ansoff *et al.*, op.cit., p.2.

22. Peter Drucker, *Landmarks of Tomorrow* (1959).

23. John W. Gardner, *Self-Renewal - The Individual and the Innovative Society*, p.5, Harper & Row, New York (1963).

24. E.F. Schumacher, *Small is Beautiful - A Study of Economics as if People Mattered*, p.209, ABACUS, London (1975).

25. Joseph M. Juran, *Managerial Breakthrough*, p.2, McGraw-Hill, New York (1964). (See also pp.6 & 16).

26. Peter F. Drucker, Entrepreneurship in Business Enterprise, *Journal of Business Policy*, 1 (1), Autumn (1970).

27. Donald A. Schon, *Beyond the Stable State*, p.67, Temple Smith, London (1971).

28. See E.G. Malmlow, Corporate Strategic Planning in Practice, pp.2-9, *Long Range Planning*, September (1972).

29. Bennett.

30. Quoted in Economic Growth: *New Views and Issues*, p.11, U.S. Chamber of Commerce, Washington (1975).

31. Willard Wirtz, *The Boundless Resource*, p.3, National Manpower Institute, New Republic Books, Washington (1975).

32. Donald A. Schon, op.cit., p.30.

33. For a detailed discussion of these concepts see Enid Mumford and Andrew Pettigrew, *Implementing Strategic Decisions*, p.16, Longman, London (1975).

34. H. Ozbekhan, Towards a General Theory of Planning, in: E. Jantsch, ed., *Perspectives of Planning*, OECD, Paris (1969).

35. Donald N. Michael, *On Learning to Plan and Planning to Learn*, p.19, Jossey-Bass (1973).

36. J. Friedmann, The Future of Comprehensive Urban Planning: A Critique, *Public Administration Review*, 31 (3), 325 (1971).

37. Peter H. Grinyer and David Norburn, Strategic Planning in 21 U.K. Companies, *Long Range Planning*, August (1974).

38. Eric Rhenman, *Organisation Theory for Long Range Planning*, John Wiley, London (1973), p.55.

39. John Friend *et al.*, op.cit., p.xxiii.

40. I.C. MacMillan, Business Strategies for Political Action, *Journal of General Management*, Autumn (1974), p.59.

41. Arthur Knight, *Private Enterprise and Public Intervention*, Allan & Unwin, London (1974).

42. Opinion Research Centre November 1974 Survey of 2000 private sector employees.

43. *Study in Employee Attitudes and Understanding*, Confederation of British Industry, London, May (1976).

44. E. Jantsch (ed.), *Perspectives of Planning*, OECD, Paris (1969).

45. Erich Jantsch, *Technological Planning and Social Futures*, p.14, Associated Business Programmes, London (1972).

46. Donald A. Schon, op.cit., p.75.

47. Erich Jantsch, *Technological Planning and Social Futures*, p.145, Associated Business Programmes, London (1972).

48. Hasan Ozbekhan, *The Idea of the 'Look-Out' Institution*, Systems Development Corp., Santa Monica (1965).

49. Raymond Williams, *Television Technology & Cultural Form*, Fontana (1974).

50. Margaret Mead (ed.), *Cultural Patterns and Technical Change*, UNESCO, Paris (1951).

51. Donald A. Schon, op. cit., p.35.

52. Geoffrey Vickers, *Value Systems and Social Process*, Penguin (1970).

53. Geoffrey Vickers, op. cit., p.67.

54. J.C. March, The Technology of Foolishness, *Civilokonomen*, May (1971).

55. Eric Rhenman, *The Problems of Large Organisations in a Structurally Changing Environment*, p.25, SIAR, Stockholm (1973).

56. H. Igor Ansoff *et al.*, op. cit., p.47.

57. Richard Normann, *Creative Management*, SIAR, Stockholm (1976).

58. Henry Mintzberg, *Patterns in Strategy Formation*, p.15, University of Aix-Marseille, March (1976).

59. Eric Rhenman, *Organization Theory for Long-Range Planning*, p.49, Wiley, London (1973).

60. Donald A. Schon, op.cit., pp. 32 & 33.

61. Margaret Mead (ed.), Cultural Patterns & Technical Change, UNESCO, Paris (1951), discussed in Joseph M. Juran, op. cit., pp.142-157.

62. Enid Mumford and Andrew Pettigrew, *Implementing Strategic Decisions*, Longman, London (1975).

63. See Yehezkel Dror, From Management Sciences to Policy Sciences, in Michael
     J. White *et al., Management and Policy Science in American Government,*
     pp.267-295, Lexington, Mass. (1975).

64. This term is borrowed from Malcolm Allison *Essence of Decision* (Little,
     Brown & Company, Boston 1971), a fascinating analysis of the Cuban Missile
     Crisis using three different frames of reference - viewing government as a
     'rational actor', as a bureaucracy, and as a political machine.

Chapter 2

CHANGING PRACTICE IN CORPORATE PLANNING
David Hussey

It is difficult to say exactly when corporate planning began, but certainly by the mid-1960s there was a very evident trend to planning by major companies on both sides of the Atlantic. Until about 1965 the companies which were attempting a planning process were like a small stream. By 1970 they had become a fast flowing torrent, and virtually every company that considered itself advanced in its management thinking had flirted in some way with the concept of corporate planning.

Over this period, too, the first significant books on corporate planning were published: H.I. Ansoff's *Corporate Strategy* (McGraw Hill, 1965), E.K. Warren's *Long Range Planning: The Executive Viewpoint* (Prentice Hall, 1966) and B. Scott's *Long Range Planning in American Industry* (American Management Association, 1962) and G. Steiner's *Managerial Long Range Planning* (McGraw Hill, 1963).

The academic world also reached take-off point at this time. Corporate planning began to be taught at business schools, in all types of seminars, and appeared as an appropriate subject for research and doctorial theses.

Professional planning societies were formed. In the U.K. The Society for Long Range Planning came into being in January 1967. By September Pergamon were publishing the Society's official journal *Long Range Planning*, which soon became international in content and circulation.

Many of the promises of these early years of corporate planning were never kept. The reality of what could be planned was at variance with the heavenly delights offered by many of the early practitioners. Those early planning systems tended to be characterised by a naive feeling that whatever was planned became almost an inevitability, and accompanied by an unhealthy rigidity of system and over-formality of paper work. Some of the changing patterns of thought from the inevitable disillusionment of disappointed expectations have already been traced in the first chapter.

One of the by-products has been a healthy scepticism about corporate planning, and a growing tendency to question those planning theories which do not appear to be routed in reality. At the same time there has come to be a greater understanding of what planning can do, and a realisation that although planning may be about strategy and control, it is also very much about people. The human dimension, in many forms, has been illustrated in chapter 1.

Our purpose now is to explore some of the significant variations between actual approaches to planning and the theories described in the literature. Leading authorities themselves often offer widely differing advice about what is good practice, and some of these differences will also be probed. By exploring these issues we hope to open up the subject of the changing practice of planning to reinforce the arguments of chapter 1, and to prepare the ground for a considera- tion of some of the other realities faced by modern business. The fundamental reality is that business can no longer be regarded solely as an issue for cold, analytical logic: society is changing rapidly, and modern management, and therefore modern planning, has to respond to a new environment of employee participation, union involvement in strategic decisions and government inter- vention.

The Reality of Objectives

There can be few books published on planning or management decision-making which do not devote some space to "objectives" and related concepts such as "goals", "aims", "purpose" and "constraints".

One substantial problem is that of semantics. There is no common management meaning given to words such as "objectives" and "goals". Although many authors use them in the same general sense, there are often nuances of meaning which become apparent only after detailed study of the literature. Sometimes the differences are very wide. The most extreme differences are when the meaning of some of the words are reversed. For example, many writers use the term "objectives" in the sense of the fundamental purpose of the organisation in relation to the interpreted desires of its shareholders (or stakeholders where the author considers that others with an interest in the firm, such as employees have a fundamental right to influence the purpose of the company: those authors who do not accept the stakeholder concept consider the restraining influences of these parties to be a "constraint" on the objectives). Objectives in this sense might include growth, profit and return intentions, and a statement of the business the organisation considers itself to be in. Some authors use the terms "mission" or "charter" to distinguish "what business we are in" from the other objectives. Those authorities using objectives in this fundamental sense will probably interpret the term "goals" in the sense of mile-stones which show the point which should be reached by a defined period of time if the organisation is implementing the strategy devised to fulfil its objectives: examples are divisional profit targets, market shares, new product launch dates, and the like.

But other authorities consider that the term "goals" better describes the long term aims of the business, while the milestones are called "objectives".

This is not the end of the story. "Objectives" may emerge once again in the "management by objectives" (m.b.o.) sense – related to the "milestone" concept, but dealing with the individual standards and results that each manager may have to achieve if he is doing his job properly. In this sense "objectives" may, for many jobs, have only the most tenuous of links with the purpose of the firm or the major strategies being followed.

Within these broad different patterns of usage there are also nuances of meaning which further complicate the position and many readers have their own company or private meanings which they attach to the words as they read them: meanings which are often different from the intention of the author.

If every person clearly defined his or her own usage of the words, was consistent, and checked out the meaning of the authorities he was using, problems would not arise. But human nature is not always as logical as this. What is of real significance is not just words, but the real differences in underlying concept which occurs between authors. The two extremes of view are well illustrated by Ansoff (1965)[1] and Lindblom (1959),[2] and it is of value to explore these differences before giving thought to the reality of objectives in modern organisations.

Ansoff uses these definitions:

> "Objectives are decision rules which enable management to guide and measure the firm's performance towards its purpose".[3]

> "Constraints are decision rules which exclude certain options from the firm's freedom actions".[4]

> "The adjective 'business' has traditionally meant that the firm is an 'economically' or money-motivated *purposive* social organisation. This implies that a set of objectives can be identified in most firms, either in explicit form as a part of the firm's business plan or implicitly through past history and individual motivation of the key personnel".[5]

In contrast, Lindblom argues that the literature usually preaches what few actually practise. "The hallmarks of these procedures ... are clarity of objective, explicitness of evaluation, a high degree of comprehensiveness of overview and wherever possible, quantification of values for mathematical analysis".[6]

He compares this method which he calls the root approach with what he argues is more general practice, which he calls the branch approach "... continually building out from the current situation, step-by-step and by small degrees" differs dramatically from the root method, "... starting from fundamentals anew each time, building on the part only as experience is embodied in a theory and always prepared to start completely from the ground up".[7]

Under the root method good policies are those which meet the test of being demonstrably the most suitable means to the desired end. Under the branch method, various analysts might find themselves agreeing on a policy without a consensus that it is the best way to achieve their own particular objectives.

Another contrast is that under the root method the clarification of values and objectives is a prerequisite of the analysis of various policies, whereas under the branch method objectives do not precede analysis but are closely intertwined with it.

Whatever the conceptual arguments in favour of each of the approaches, the practical situation is that the majority of companies come closer to the branch method than the root method advised in the literature. In these cases objectives become a control tool, derived from the strategies, rather than the first step in analysis demanded by the literature. This suggests that the branch approach has empirical respectability, even if it does not fit the theories.

There are other differences of interpretation over what are valid objectives. A large body of opinion argues that at least in the business enterprise, the main objective of the business is to earn profits for the shareholders. This leads to the contention that the basic objectives of the business should be expressed in some form of profit terms, such as growth in earnings per share, discounted cash flow rate of return, or simply growth in total profits plus a return on capital employed target. Figures such as these can provide the basis for the use of the gap analysis technique described in much of the literature. (Gap analysis is no more than an exploration of forecast expectations compared with objectives, and is used as a tool to help the organisation find ways of closing the gap between aspirations and expectations.)

This interpretation is challenged by Galbraith (1967).[8] He argues that control has passed from business owners to professional managers and white collar workers in the majority of firms of any size and that this "technocracy" is not motivated to maximise profits but to retain control. Thus the company prefers to avoid the risk of failure rather than to seek means of enhancing profits and, so long as profits can be maintained or enhanced with a moderate growth, the technocracy is more secure if it avoids risks. The objective becomes the survival of the technocracy and this is only threatened when profits fall. At the same time an increase in power is sought - but measured in terms of increases of turnover and employees (which allow the technocracy to expand) and not in terms of maximum profits.

This fits in with the concept of "satisficing" planning distinguished by Ackoff (1970)[9] where management takes actions which allow the companies to do well enough but do not try to do as well as is possible.

If this is the reality, it follows that the calculation of profit objectives is much more than a matter of combining logical analysis with business judgment. The total approach to strategic decision making will be different, seeking different ends, and heavily influenced by internal power politics. And this is without the additional complications of views that "social responsibility" should play a dominant part when objectives are set.

Whether the Galbraith view is valid for all business is an open question. But it does raise the issue of whether profit objectives can be defined in a meaningful way so that they do influence corporate strategy. The fact that they are not so defined in many organisations may be one of the realities of planning, where theory and practice do not coincide.

Social responsibility, or rather the belief by many that business should demonstrate socially responsible behaviour, has an impact on objective setting to the degree that it is considered to be a relevant issue. Two views have already been mentioned: that these matters are fundamental to the purpose of business: that they are "constraints" or influences which have to be considered to the extent that they affect the organisation's ability to devote all of its attention to the profit motive. Either path presents a great dilemma to management: a dilemma of choice and a dilemma of conflict. Satisfying the needs of one "stakeholder" can mean failure to satisfy the needs of another. And some of the social responsibility issues may involve business in conflicts of behaviour and law between two sovereign states, or may lead to the view that instead of doing its duty business is using the role of government. Some of the influences which are changing the traditional view of business as nothing more than a profit making vehicle will be examined in later chapters.

There are those that see considerable changes in the acceptance by business that its purpose includes social responsibility. Hayek (1960)[10] argues that any role other than that of serving the shareholders will eventually put companies under

the control of government or other interests. He quotes Friedman[11] "If anything
is certain to destroy our free society, to undermine its very foundations, it
would be a wide-spread acceptance by management of social responsibilities in
some sense other than to make as much money as possible."

Most text books assume that we live in a well ordered society, and that when
there is an intention to change approach or systems the intention rapidly becomes
fact. In practice we work in varying degrees of chaos, although the best
companies are much less chaotic than the worst! The reality of planning today
is that it is no longer a clever, strictly analytical activity. People are one
of the greatest considerations in modern planning, and the work of the
behavioural scientists is of increasing relevance to the corporate planner. The
people issue, which in part involves a bringing together of personal and corporate
objectives, is discussed in the case studies in chapters 11 and 12.

The Realities of Strategy

Views on how a company should approach strategic choice and decision making bear
some relation to views on corporate strategy. Those who press for formal
objectives are likely to argue for a similar formality in strategic choice. Those
who dispute the relevance of profit objectives will have a different view of the
criteria and methods of selection of strategies to that held by those who hold
that profit is the only valid objective.

Once again Lindblom (1959)[12] and his comparison of the root and branch methods
provides an illustration of the two extremes of viewpoint.

The difference is illustrated in these further quotations:

Root	Branch
"Policy - formulation is therefore approached through means - end analysis. First the ends are isolated, then the means to achieve them are sought."	"Since means and ends are not distinct, means - end analysis is often inappropriate or limited."
"Analysis is comprehensive every relevant factor is account."	"Analysis is drastically limited: (i) Important possible outcomes are neglected. (ii) Important alternative potential strategies are neglected. (iii) Important affected values are neglected.
"Theory is often heavily relied upon."	"A succession of comparisons greatly reduces or eliminates reliance on theory."

It is often difficult to distinguish the branch approach from haphazard management, and we wonder to what degree it is an apology for what is frequently
practised, rather than a recommendation of what should be done. One of the
realities of planning is that many organisations can improve their strategic
decision making process, but that they often do not because of a refusal by
senior management to acknowledge that an improvement is possible.

In many organisations what really happens is that strategies come about in an almost random manner without very much thought about their role in taking the company to its objectives. This haphazard selection of beads is then strung on a thread in the hopes that the resultant necklace will have value: in other words the reality of the corporate plan in many companies is that it gives little attention to evaluation and choice.

Not only is this in complete contrast to the analytical processes recommended by writers such as Ansoff (1965),[13] but it tends to be a self-defeating exercise since plans produced in this way are abandoned every time a new idea comes into the boardroom. Decisions tend to be made on a mixture of whim and internal power.

While the modern approach should certainly give considerable attention to the human dimension in planning, including internal power structures, the complex companies are finding new tools of strategic analysis - the portfolio techniques. These provide the means of making rational decisions in companies with activities which have a great diversity of product and/or geographical area of operation. A later chapter will examine some of these methods, which offer a way of making the "root" approach work in complex situations. There is also a link with objectives, one aspect of which has already been mentioned, in the work of Ackoff (1970).[14] He classifies decision making into three distinct patterns - the optimisers, satisficers and adaptivisers - although in practice mixtures also occur.

"Satisficing" plans aim to do well, but not as well as is possible; to do enough to satisfy, but not to do more than this. Objectives set by satisficing planners are always feasible - there is no question of their being used in a behavioural sense to "stretch" individuals and the organisations. Strategies always try to avoid conflict, and rarely involve organisational change or major variations from the part. Satisficing planners tend to produce "one point" plans; that is, their plans contain only one set of strategies, envisage only one possible outcome and make no provisions for things that might go wrong or not turn out as forecast. An artificial certainty is given to all planned actions. As the organisation is considered to be flexible enough to cope with the unexpected, and because of this artificial certainty, there are seldom formal systems for monitoring and controlling the plans.

Ackoff (1970)[15] sums up satisficing. "Not surprisingly, satisficing planning seldom produces a radical departure from the past. It usually yields conserva- tive plans that comfortably continue most current policies, correcting only obvious deficiencies. Such planning there appeals to organisations that are more concerned with survival than with development and growth."

Satisficing planning adds little to the company's knowledge of itself or its markets. Its value to the company must be seriously questioned: although it may be the reality of planning for many organisations, it can hardly justify the management effort put into it.

The "optimising" planner takes a completely different view of his job. He aims always to choose the best possible course of action, and relies very heavily on operational research techniques and mathematical models. He formulates his objectives and goals in quantified terms, and tends to ignore all those he cannot so quantify.

Ackoff (1970)[16] considers "This can distort the value of his work and produce justifiable discomfort in the consuming managers who must moderate quantitative

results with their own qualitative judgements on important problems that have
not been taken into account".

The optimiser is only as good as his models. Perhaps his biggest fault is that
he tends to underrate the human issues, because few of these can be quantified
in the terms required by his model. Control systems can be built into his
models but tend to measure only the things foreseen when the models were built.
The unforeseen is in danger of being ignored until it is too late.

"Adaptivisers" have the belief that the main value of planning lies in the
process and not in the plans themselves. What is sought is quality of thought
rather than accurate plans: accuracy may in fact prove that plans are easily
achievable and unambitious.

Perhaps more significant is the adaptiviser's belief that the main purpose of
his plans is to prevent crisis from arising: to use the plans as a basis for
continually adapting the organisation and systems so that difficulties are
avoided and so that management does not have to spend most of its time resolving
the problems caused by past inadequacies snd inefficiencies.

The adaptiviser differentiates three types of risk in all future events. Some
aspects are virtual certainties, for which the best solution is to ensure that
adequate plans are made and actions committed so that the company may exploit
these events.

Many more events are a matter of varying degrees of probability: here the plans
would be backed up with contingency plans for various foreseeable probabilities.
Finally there are those events which simply cannot be foreseen at all, for which
the only planning solution is flexibility and speed in response.

Early books on planning stressed the relationship between the company and its
markets, and the company and its environment. The tendency now is for planners
to see the business environment in a much more integrated way and to recognise
that it impacts on the firm itself, its market and on the expectations of the
firm's stakeholders. There is a complexity of inter-relationships which
requires study and attention. Unfortunately, despite periods of reaction caused
by traumatic events such as the 1973 inflation explosion, few companies give
adequate consideration to the environment in which they operate. This is a pity,
because the reality is that the environment is critical to corporate strategy,
and surprises are inevitable for those who ignore it.

The other reality of strategy to which more companies are giving attention is
of concern mainly to complex companies. It faces up to the problem of comparing
and choosing between options which do not arise from the same marketing opportunity. It is not difficult to design priorities or allocate resources between
three or four products which are each intended for different segments of the
same market. It may even be possible to deal easily with two or three different
markets and the ranges of products that go with them.

Where the problems commence are when the company has a number of divisions or
subsidiaries, numerous products, and operates internationally. The question top
management faces is no longer how to exploit a particular opportunity, but which
of many opportunities to exploit. The difficulty is in seeing the total corporate
plan as a whole, rather than as a consolidation of the intentions of the various
divisions. It is in choosing a portfolio of activities that balance growth and
decline, cash flow contributions and cash hungry products, risk, and the long
term objectives of the company that the difficulties occur.

Conventional discounted cash flow techniques, ideal for distinguishing between options in a single project, lose their value because high returns can often be achieved from working in an area which on the aggregate is unsatisfactory. An example is an investment in cost reduction which by itself may yield significant returns, but which should not be made because the product as a whole would still have poor prospects and little profit.

To some degree it is possible to rely on the chief executives of each division to reject most of their own bad eggs. But this still leaves the problem of allocating resources of capital, talent and facilities. There are now strategic portfolio analysis techniques which offer a solution and are being increasingly used.

What happens in many planning processes is that almost all attention is devoted to only one aspect of strategy: the reaction of the company to market and environmental conditions. The plan might select strategic business areas for growth, holding or decline; plan market expansion; commit research and development to new products; or do any number of things related to the market.

But the reality is that what we commonly think of as strategy should not be a free-standing thing. It should be related to structure, people and systems. If strategy changes, there is a strong likelihood that the organisational structure should also be altered, and that existing systems will be wrong for the new situation, and that different types of people with new skills will be needed.

The relationship is dynamic, in that a change in organisation structure or personnel systems can sometimes cause a *de facto* alteration of strategy. Without consideration of the mutual interaction of these elements there may be no change in the *planned* strategy. What actually occurs may, of course, be vastly different from the plan.

It is probably not difficult for any reader to think of examples from his own experience where the management system – and the term is used in its widest sense to embrace every form of system – hindered a new strategy instead of helped it, or when the strategy could not be achieved with the existing organisation.

Despite this, most plans consider only strategy. Research among corporate planners (Knowlson (1974)[17]) showed that only 45% of companies attempted organisation planning in any formal way (out of a sample base of 385).

The Realities of Management

Much of the thought about corporate planning follows the analysis of the management task first set out by Fayol (1949)[18] and built on by numerous writers right up to the present day. This breaks down the management task or functions into a series of elements. Words such as "organise", "plan", "motivate", "control" and "set objectives" occur in most of the analyses: a comparison of the views of selected writers is given in Table 2.1.

Some of the early thinking about corporate planning latched on to the idea that it was the way in which managers should fulfil the planning element of the management task, and initially this seemed a valid rationale for formal planning. If the job had to be done, why not utilise a way of doing it more effectively? Later writers, for example Hussey (1974),[19] drew attention to the fact that corporate planning was in reality concerned with *all* the elements of management.

TABLE 2.1 Elements of Management Task Functions or Process Distinguished by
Certain Writers

Name	Reference	Elements identified
P. Drucker	*Practice of Management*, Pan, 1969, pp.409-12.	Set objectives, organise, motivate and communicate, measure, develop people.
H. Fayol	*General and Industrial Management*, trans. C. Storrs, Pitman, 1969, pp.3, 5-6.	Planning, organisation, command, co-ordination, control.
E.L.F. Brech	*Organisation*, Longman, 1966, p.14.	Plan, motivate and co-ordinate, control.
W.H. Newman	*Administrative Action: The Techniques of Organisation and Management*, Prentice Hall, 1963.	Planning, organising, assembling resources, supervising, controlling.
L.F. Urwick	*The Pattern of Management*, University of Minneapolis Press, 1956, p.52	Forecast, plan, organise, direct, co-ordinate, control, communicate.
G.F. Milward	*An Approach to Management*, Macdonald and Evans, 1946, pp.35-6.	Forecasting, planning and programming, organisation, command, co-ordinate, control.
H. Koonz	*Towards a Unified Theory of Management*, McGraw-Hill, 1964, pp.248-9.	Planning, organising, staffing, direction, control.

(Note: The reader is referred to R.N. Antony, *Planning and Control Systems: a
framework for analysis*, Harvard University Press, 1965, for a more detailed
treatment of this subject.)

Source: *Inflation and Business Policy*, D.E. Hussey, Longmans, 1976.

This argument was that corporate planning could not succeed unless, for example,
it included organising, motivating, controlling, setting objectives, etc.

Perhaps this widening of thought to match the reality of management was just as
well. Mintzburg (1975)[20] analysed numerous diary studies of how managers
actually spent their time, and found that what they actually *did* bore little
relationship to what had hitherto been described as the essential elements of
their task. The four "myths" disproved by the evidence are:

* The manager is a reflective systematic planner.

* The effective manager has no regular duties to perform.

* The senior manager needs aggregated information which a
  formal management information best provides.

* Management is, or at least is quickly becoming, a science
  and a profession.

Hussey and Langham (1979)[21] state "The gaps between what managers do, and what we popularly believe they do, and what they ought to do, give us a good clue as to why corporate planning is more difficult to implement in practice than the logic of its theories would suggest".

REFERENCES

1. H.I. Ansoff, *Corporate Strategy*, McGraw Hill, 1965.

2. C.E. Lindblom, The Science of Muddling Through, *Public Administration Review*, vol.19, Spring, 1959, published in H.I. Ansoff (ed) *Business Strategy*.

3. H.I. Ansoff, 1965, op. cit. p.38.

4. H.I. Ansoff, 1965, op. cit. p.38.

5. H.I. Ansoff, 1965, op. cit. p.3.

6. C.E. Lindblom, 1959, op. cit. p.43.

7. C.E. Lindblom, 1959, op. cit. p.44.

8. J. Galbraith, *The New Industrial State*, Houghton Miffin Co., 1967, Chapter 15, pp.166-78.

9. R.L. Ackoff, *A Concept of Corporate Strategy*, Wiley Interscience, 1970.

10. R.A. Hayek, The Corporation in a Democratic Society: in whose interest ought it and will it be run? in M. Anshen and G.L. Bach, *Management and Corporations*, McGraw Hill, 1965 - reproduced in H.I. Ansoff (ed), *Business Strategy*, Penguin, 1969.

11. M. Friedman, quoted in Hayek, op.cit.

12. C.E. Lindblom, 1959, op.cit. p.45.

13. H.I. Ansoff, 1965, op. cit.

14. R.L. Ackoff, 1970, op. cit.

15. R.L. Ackoff, 1970, op. cit.

16. R.L. Ackoff, 1970, op. cit.

17. P. Knowlson, *Organisation and Membership Survey*, Society for Long Range Planning, March 1974.

18. H. Fayol, *General and Industrial Management*, Pitman, 1949.

19. D.E. Hussey, *Corporate Planning: Theory and Practice*, Pergamon, 1974, Chapter 1.

20. H. Mintzburg, The Manager's Job: Folklore and Fact, *Harvard Business Review*, July-August 1975.

21. D.E. Hussey and M.J. Langham, *Corporate Planning: The Human Factor*, Pergamon, 1979, p.32.

Chapter 3

THE EVOLUTION OF PLANNING APPROACHES*

David Hussey

Few thinking people would claim to be satisfied with the progress of the British economy since the war. There are many reasons why our performance lags behind that of countries like Germany and France, and why many forecasts position us as the poor men of Europe of the not so far distant future. This chapter will concentrate on only one aspect, the quality of corporate planning which in itself is a reflection of the quality of management.

The modern business environment is complex and in a state of change. Management has to operate in a society whose values have changed dramatically over the last decade, in a political climate which encourages an increasing amount of government involvement in business affairs, and under economic conditions which increase the risk of business decisions. How can we cope?

The only way is by developing management skills and in particular improving corporate planning skills. At first sight this emphasis on corporate planning might seem odd. Many management thinkers stress planning as one of the important elements in the total management task. Other elements are organising, motivating, co-ordinating, communicating and controlling – the list varies slightly with the author.

DON'T WE DO IT ALREADY?

In addition, doesn't every organisation that matters already have a corporate planner? Isn't planning on the syllabus of many professional examinations, taught at business schools and universities, and written about regularly in management journals? Didn't Government once get interested through planning agreements? Isn't it something that we all know and do well?

Let us examine these points. Firstly, a process of corporate planning is an approach to the total management task. It is a future-oriented, integrated way of running an organisation. Its job is to plan, organise, motivate, co-ordinate, communicate and control. There is research evidence that corporate planning does improve an organisation's performance. One reason why corporate planning often falls short is that many organisations see it only in the light of the narrow

---

*Originally published in *Professional Administration*, April 1979.

planning task of management, and not as the total management process that it
really should be.

A DEFINITION OF CORPORATE PLANNING

> Corporate planning is a comprehensive, future oriented,
> continuous process of management which is implemented
> within a formal framework. It is responsive to relevant
> change in the external environment. It is concerned with
> both strategic and operational planning, and through the
> participation of relevant members of the organisation,
> develops plans and actions at the appropriate levels in
> the organisation. It incorporates monitoring and control
> mechanisms and is concerned with both the short and the
> long term.

Secondly, while most organisations purport to practise corporate planning and it
is possible to find planners in most large companies, there is considerable
research evidence, supported by the opinions of informed observers, that very few
companies obtain optimum benefit from their planning efforts. Many plan very
badly. The pitfalls in planning are well documented, but despite this many
companies approach planning from somewhere deep down in the elephant trap.

TEN MAJOR PITFALLS IN CORPORATE PLANNING

1. Top management's assumption that it can delegate the
    planning function to a planner.

2. Top management becomes so engrossed in current problems
    that it spends insufficient time on long range planning,
    and the process becomes discredited among other managers
    and staff.

3. Failure to develop company goals suitable as a basis for
    formulating long range plans.

4. Failure to obtain the necessary involvement in the
    planning process of major line personnel.

5. Failure to use the plan as standards for measuring
    managerial performance.

6. Failure to create a climate in the company which is
    congenial and not resistant to planning.

7. Assuming that corporate comprehensive planning is
    something separate from the entire management process.

8. Injecting so much formality into the system that it
    lacks flexibility, looseness, and simplicity and
    restrains creativity.

9. Failure of top management to review with departmental
    and divisional heads the long range plans which they
    have developed.

10. Top management's consistently rejecting the formal

planning mechanism by making intuitive decisions which
conflict with formal plans.

(Adapted from a study of 215 companies by George Steiner:
published as *Pitfalls in Comprehensive Long Range Planning*.
Planning Executives Institute, 1972.)

Why has the academic world through its teaching, had more influence on the way
corporate planning is carried out? Many who lecture on business policy and
corporate planning are unknown outside of their own academic environment: too
few have added to the knowledge from practical experience, significant research,
or writing. No British academics have written extensively on planning, and most
of the significant authors on this subject are practitioners or consultants.

SOME FACTS AND FIGURES

Selected findings from the SLRP Organisations and Membership
survey.

(a) 54 per cent of corporate planners have less than five
    years involvement in corporate planning.
(b) 73 per cent of corporate planners are 36 years of age
    or older.
(c) 53 per cent of corporate planners have been concerned
    with corporate planning in no more than one organisa-
    tion.
(d) 64 per cent of planners were appointed to their position
    from within the company.

Lack of experience of planners can be compensated for by the
use of consultants. In the U.S.A. J.L. Brown and R. O'Connor
(Planning and the Corporate Director, *The Conference Report
No.627, 1974*) found that some 27 per cent of U.S. companies
used consultants in planning either at start up or on a
continuing basis, and a further 51 per cent employed consultants for *ad hoc* studies connected with planning. I know of
no parallel research in the U.K., but would be surprised if
the British figures exceeded 10 per cent and 25 per cent
respectively.

Those who have studied corporate planning at business schools or for professional
examinations are rarely in a position to influence the way in which their
organisation approaches corporate planning, although the skills learnt may well
help them do their own jobs in a better way.

TOO EASILY SATISFIED

One of the problems is that management frequently understands little about
corporate planning, and is too easily satisfied. If its standards are too low,
it will often accept an approach which is considerably below the
achievable. Many senior managers rightly accept that strategy is part of their
job but lack the required depth of knowledge, and do not know that they do not
have it.

The development of corporate planning is made difficult by the nature of the job.
Planning is not a profession, such as accountancy or chartered secretaryship.
Although it has an able association in the Society for Long Range Planning, it
does not have examinations or professional qualifications. It does not generally

offer a career in itself, but positions in a total general management career. It attracts good people, most of whom get promoted very quickly to other jobs. The result is breadth rather than depth of experience: several people in an organisation with some planning knowledge, but too few with very much.

Two-thirds of planning jobs are filled from within the organisation, which reduces the opportunity of learning for those with experience of other companies. About half of the people in planning jobs have had planning experience in only one company.

HOW IT HAS GROWN

Figure 3.1 tracks the evolution of planning concepts, and at once illustrates some of the problems of improving planning in the U.K. Each of the forms of planning illustrated is still practised by some organisations, even though the process of development has moved on. Many of the organisations which claim to practise corporate planning are in fact using what are outdated concepts, some of which no longer fit the social environment in which we operate. They may still benefit the organisation, but at a sub-optimal level.

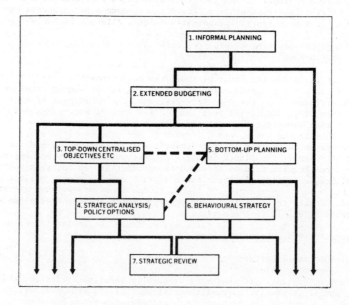

Fig. 3.1 Evolution of planning approaches

The figure of course simplifies. There are variations within each of the labelled boxes, and some overlapping of concepts. Also the evolution is of planning thinking, not a process through which every organisation must pass. Most join at a particular point on the evolutionary tree. It must also be stressed that

success may result from any of the stages: the argument of this chapter is that
the aim should be to do even better, rather than being satisfied with current
levels of success. The right approach to corporate planning can bring the
additional degree of success.

Let me explain the stages in Figure 3.1:

1. Informal Planning

This is the state known to everybody, where top management keeps its plan in its
heads, and does not attempt to make a formal plan for the organisation. It
works, often very well, for the autocratic, opportunistic entrepreneur with
flair. Unfortunately many who approach their planning by this method also lack
flair. It is an approach which becomes increasingly untenable under modern
pressures for more participation.

2. Extended Budgeting

Hesitating steps were taken on the road to corporate planning when organisations
began to extrapolate the annual budget into the future. Usually an accounting
exercise, it represented an attempt to see the logical future consequences of the
chosen course of action. It fails because it is unresponsive to environmental
changes, carried an implicit and incorrect assumption that present policies will
continue into the future, and has a tendency to become a mere figures exercise.
Few organisations practise it in its extreme form, although it has not become
extinct.

3. Top-down Planning

Here we begin to follow the first of two forks, which might loosely be termed
'analytical' and 'behavioural'. Top down planning involves only a few at the
top of the organisation, sets objectives without the involvement of those who
have to attain them, and is frequently dominated by O.R. approaches and corporate
models (not that these are bad in themselves).

Three forms might be typified: 'ivory tower', where a planner remote from the
organisation prepares the plans, 'tablets from the mountain', where objectives
and guide lines are produced on the assumption that all wisdom is concentrated
in head office, and 'boffin', where the corporate model produces all the answers,
but only the expert can operate the model. These types of planning are still
widespread, despite the fact that lack of involvement ensures that plans are
rarely implemented.

4. Strategic Analysis/Policy Options

The analytical branch evolves into a more rational approach to strategic thinking,
moving to a planning role of presenting management with policy options, rather
than one solution plans. It uses very worthwhile techniques like portfolio
analysis, and is responsive to environmental changes. Many organisations would
benefit by getting this far along the evolutionary tree: comparatively few have.
Its main danger is under-rating the significance of human behaviour.

5. Bottom-up Planning

The rationale for this style of planning is to involve those who are concerned
with implementing the plans. A very common sub-form is the 'church collection
method'. It works like this. Everyone in the organisation is asked to write a
plan for his own area. His contribution is dropped into the corporate hat.

Someone adds it all up, rejecting a few obvious faked coins, but usually accepting
with gratitude what is donated. This becomes the plan.

It fails because the board room ignores it and carries on with strategies which
are outside of the plan, and because the involvement is a sham: it is too narrow
to be real. Another version attempts to combine top-down with bottom-up by
issuing objectives as edicts and inviting managers to say in detail how they will
attain them. Variations of bottom-up planning are very common.

6. Behavioural Strategy

This attempts to broaden the degree of involvement of managers in planning.
There are various approaches. One is a form of planning conference where all
managers identify and work through the issues facing the company, aiming to
produce an outline plan as its end product. Another is a carefully structured
organisational development approach to strategy, which encourages individual
creativity and wide involvement.

Philips of Eindhoven have been leading exponents of an O.D. approach. The
weaknesses of the behavioural approach are the difficulties of reconciling the
actions from the initiative with the top management strategy, the problem of
quick response to changing circumstances, and the fact that measures such as this
tend to become less effective as they are repeated in successive years.

7. Strategic Review

Finally we have the latest stage in the evolution, a deliberate attempt to take
what is best from each branch and blend analysis with behavioural in a structured
way. Typically the approach defines objectives and strategic guide lines in a
participative way, but ensures that the decisions taken are founded on sound
analysis. Those who are interested can find a case study of the approach in
Corporate Planning at Rolls Royce Motors Ltd by R. Young and D.E. Hussey, *Long
Range Planning*, April, 1977.

Government could take a lead in improving the quality of corporate planning in
the U.K. So far its approach has been largely through the planning agreements
initiative. One of the biggest difficulties this faces is the practical one.
Many organisations either do not have corporate plans and therefore have nothing
which they can agree with government, or they produce plans in which top management has little confidence. To have a planning agreement one presumably needs
a plan.

My feeling is that government has gone down the wrong road. What it should be
doing is getting the process of planning more widely discussed and practised.
One way of doing this is by an enquiry into corporate planning, to do for planning
what the Sandilands Committee did for inflation accounting.

The purpose of such a study might be to examine the research evidence of good and
bad planning, to study alternative approaches, to examine how corporate planning
can be made more participative, to see what the business schools and professional
bodies are teaching in this area, and to establish the things that should be done
to help the entire country improve its corporate planning efforts.

Something needs to be done.

Part 2

THE POLITICS OF PLANNING

There are two major aspects of corporate planning as a political process: the relation of the enterprise to the political events in the business environment in which it operates; the internal political issues of power and influence within the firm itself.

The first aspect is taken up by Bernard Taylor in Chapter 4. He describes the pressures which make it essential for the modern company to take account of the political environment in its plans, and to include strategies for influencing the political process.

David Hussey supplements this analysis in Chapter 5 by tracing the trends which are leading to more claims by Government and Public Bodies in the Western World for more involvement in the process of corporate strategic decision making.

In Chapter 6 we include a contribution by Andrew Pettigrew, a leading researcher into the political issues of decision making within organisations. His assumption is that strategy formulation can be understood as a process of political decision making.

Chapter 4

THE POLITICAL DIMENSION*
Bernard Taylor

INTRODUCTION

I believe that to avoid serious planning failures in the 1980s requires:

(1) a thorough re-orientation in the thinking and practice
    of Corporate Planning;
(2) the development of new relationships and new under-
    standings between businessmen, government officials and
    trade union leaders and possibly the establishment of
    some new institutions and new procedures;
(3) the appointment of new kinds of top managers, admini-
    strators and trade unionists and an ambitious programme
    of training and development to give them the necessary
    skills to cope with the new planning environment;
(4) finally, it will require the use of new approaches and
    new techniques for forecasting analysis and planning -
    what we might call legislative planning or political
    planning both for the short term and the long term.

THE NEW POLITICAL ENVIRONMENT

During the last decade, the social, political and legal framework of business has
been transformed. The businessman's traditional "right to manage" his own
enterprise has been repeatedly and successfully challenged by one pressure group
after another, in the cause of equal rights for women, racial equality, consumer
protection, pollution control and "the quality of working life". Social responsibility which was once an option has become a legal requirement.

The new-found power of blue-collar workers has resulted in an extension of the
legal rights of employees and their unions. And in Western Europe, the limited
liability company and the Board of Directors are now in the process of being
reformed to provide for the representation of employees and community interests.

---

*An earlier version of this paper was presented at the 7th World Planning
Congress, London, 24-27 September, 1978.

A natural response of businessmen to this avalanche of legislation is to look
for a moratorium on new laws, a breathing space in which to allow their organisations to absorb the changes which have occurred. But there seems to be little
chance of this. Instead, the 1980s offer the prospect that government involvement
in business will continue and will probably increase.

In retrospect, the Energy Crisis of 1973/74 appears as a watershed in the history
of the Western World - the end of an era of affluence, continuous growth and
relative stability. Since then, the business environment has changed fundamentally
and, I would argue, it is essential for us to arrange some kind of collaboration
between government and industry in order to deal with the problems which have
emerged. I believe that these problems are outside the scope of an individual
company's management. They require action on the level of a whole region or on
a national or international basis. It could be that they will prove to be
temporary difficulties which will disappear over the next few years. I think
that they will probably remain with us throughout the 1980s and businessmen will
have to get involved with government bodies, trade unions and other social groups
in the search for solutions.

Among the most important challenges facing Western governments and businesses
are the following:

(1) Lower Growth in World Markets and Intensive International Competition

Much of the competition - from Japan, Russia and the Third World countries - is
seen by our competitiors as part of a national economic strategy which includes
the availability of cheap finance and protected domestic markets.

This trade war has resulted in demands from western industrialists for similar
support and protection from government.

(2) The Stagnation or Decline of Major Industries

Major industries have been traditionally regarded as the main supports of our
economy, for example, railways, docks, steel, shipbuilding, aircraft, textiles,
shoes, motor cars, power plant, machine tools, etc. This has led some companies
like British Leyland and Alfred Herbert to become dependent on government support
and has resulted in the nationalisation of industries like aircraft manufacture
and shipbuilding.

(3) High Unemployment and the Shortage of Key Skills

The present high levels of unemployment will probably persist throughout the
1980s owing to the combined effect of the reduced demand for labour from manufacturing industry and an increase in the working population, and the large
numbers of unemployed in development areas and among particular groups, e.g.
teenagers and especially black youths, will present our societies with major
social problems. At the same time business growth is held back by shortages of
skilled workers. Despite high unemployment, instrument maintenance personnel,
computer staff, electronics engineers and tool-makers are all in short supply.

The planning of manpower is complicated because of the long lead times involved,
in educating and training new staff, in re-training existing employees for new
jobs, in laying off people in declining industries and creating jobs for them

elsewhere, and in persuading employees to accept new technologies.

(4) Producer Cartels and Shortages in Supply Markets

Since 1973 managers in the industrialised world should have learned not to take
the supply of energy, food and essential raw materials for granted. To achieve
secure sources of supply for important commodities in the future will probably
require international agreements by national governments and free trade areas
like the EEC. The price of oil is negotiated annually with OPEC countries. And
there is now a continuing North-South dialogue aimed at stabilising commodity
markets. I believe that long term contracts for raw materials will probably form
an essential element of planning in the 1980s.

Already we have international supply agreements on energy, food crops and fishing.
The Japanese also have long term contracts for the supply of metals, rubber and
other key commodities. And access to the major commodity suppliers in Africa and
the Middle East has become a key political issue between the West and the
Communist bloc.

(5) Hyper-Inflation and Fluctuating Exchange Rates

The years since 1973 have seen the highest rates of inflation since the Second
World War and popular demands for governments to control wages, prices and
dividends. Also, exchange rates have fluctuated violently and governments have
tried to defend their currencies by increasing interest rates and by imposing
stringent controls on the export of capital.

This turbulence in financial markets has added a new dimension of uncertainty to
business management and the government has made regulations affecting the most
important decisions in management - the levels of prices, wages and dividends,
the cost of money and the prices of raw materials.

I believe that these problems are with us to stay and represent a changed
political environment for corporate planning.

PLANNING AS A POLITICAL PROCESS

Corporate planning was originally conceived in the 1960s as a mechanism for
internal co-ordination and control within a company hierarchy with a single
decision-making system focused on the chief executive and the Board.

To work effectively today, corporate planning needs to be developed as an inter-
organisational process so as to include relationships with other organisations
and interest groups (inside and outside the business) whose decisions and actions
are likely to have an important impact on the firm.

We can all think of important projects - new factories, mines, reservoirs,
airports and new products - motor cars, aeroplanes, drugs, pesticides - whose
progress was delayed or stopped because of opposition from some social or
political group.

And we know of industries where production targets and delivery dates are never
met, where restrictive practices continue to hamper production and factories
are grossly over-manned but workers are not made redundant because the production

system is in fact controlled not by the management but by the trade unions and the work force.

We are also aware of the growing involvement of government in business over the last decade - controls on prices and incomes; legislation for the protection of employees, consumers and the environment, and to provide equal opportunity to women and ethnic minorities; direct intervention in specific industries through the use of incentives, sanctions, outright expropriation and nationalisation.

In the 1970s there has been a dramatic decline in managerial power and authority, and many planning failures have been caused because management are over-estimating their power to carry through their decisions. A manager can only plan with confidence *managerially* to take decisions which are under his own control. For decisions which are made by other groups or individuals outside his control he must plan *politically* to influence their decisions.

To avoid "strategic surprise" in the 1980s it is important that the senior managers should take a realistic view of their power position. In most cases they should abandon any illusion that they are "the captain on the bridge", guiding the corporate destiny and recognise that they must often operate like a politician, maintaining formal and informal contacts with other organisations, negotiating and bargaining with them, forming alliances with friendly groups and trying to influence potential opponents.

Some industries, e.g. armaments, energy and transportation, are traditionally close to government, and political activity there has always been an important part of management. Others, e.g. the consumer industries, have been less subject to government intervention and for their management, politics is a new world.

Regardless of the management's political experience, I would argue that "Corporate Affairs" or "External Relations" is an important area of business which requires top management attention and should be the subject of plans, forecasts and analyses like other corporate functions such as finance, marketing or manufacturing. And in many cases companies will need to employ specialists who know the relevant political systems. In many cases, the Corporate Affairs activity fits conveniently in the Chairman's Office alongside Corporate Planning.

PLANNING IN A MIXED ECONOMY

Political debates about economic planning usually propose two alternatives - Centralised Planning, or communism, on the one hand, and Free Enterprise, with a minimum of government interference, on the other.

Industrial planning in Britain has been bedevilled by this ideological battle ever since the Second World War. The example of the British Steel industry is a classic case - first nationalised, then de-nationalised, then nationalised again. As a consequence vital investments in the industry were put back for a decade and we are now trying to re-structure the industry in the middle of an international economic recession.

It is generally assumed that businessmen are in favour of free enterprise. In my experience businessmen are not so much concerned with the colour of the government as with achieving some kind of stability in government policy. However ridiculous the government policy, businessmen will adapt to it in time. What management find difficult to cope with is a policy towards industry which changes every four or five years - not on the basis of rational analysis but because the new politicians have a different dogma from the ones they replace.

In any case, I believe that the politicians are offering a false choice. Central
Planning and public ownership of the means of production would be unacceptable
to the majority of the population in Western European countries. And it would
take strong action on the part of West European governments to break the
monopoly power of large companies and large unions if we wished to develop a free
market economy. In Britain the Trade Union Closed Shop has the support of law
and in 20 out of 22 major industrial sectors, three firms control over 50% of
the market. The only feasible alternative for us is a form of industrial planning
on the pattern which is already well developed in France, Japan and Sweden and
exists in most other European countries. This is _not_ centralised government
planning of all areas of economic activity on the East European model. Nor is
it Corporatism such as was common under the National Socialist governments of
the thirties - where the government often achieved a consensus by force and free
and open debate was prohibited.

In broad terms, Capitalist Planning means a process similar to that described
below:

> (1) Government puts forward certain broad economic policies
>   and strategies or priorities for industrial and
>   regional development;
>
> (2) These guidelines then become the basis for widespread
>   debate among industrialists who are represented on a
>   number of councils or committees. In these meetings
>   businessmen discuss with government officials and trade
>   unionists the prospects for their particular sector of
>   business activity. And the government representatives
>   offer incentives in the form of cheap credit loans and
>   grants or sanctions such as restrictions on building
>   and limits on the import of technology.
>
> (3) In addition to these private negotiations there is
>   often - as in Sweden - a public debate in the course
>   of which businessmen, government officials, political
>   parties and other interest groups put forward their
>   own "long term forecasts" for particular industries
>   or regions.
>
> (4) This has been described as "convergent planning". In
>   most cases, by a process of negotiation, government
>   officials and the leaders of business reach an under-
>   standing and the open debate where this occurs serves
>   to test public reactions to the proposed economic and
>   industrial policy. Occasionally, as with the proposed
>   rationalisation of the Japanese automobile industry,
>   businessmen and government officials agree to differ.

If this is the likely future, how should be prepare for it? In countries like
Britain which have very little experience of this kind of dialogue between
government and industry, we have a great deal to do:

> (1) We need to develop the relationships and the mutual
>   confidence which is necessary before government
>   officials and industrialists can work effectively
>   together. Often it seems that they live in separate
>   worlds and speak a different language.

(2) New procedures and possibly new institutions are
     required to enable civil servants and businessmen to
     discuss industrial planning - both formally and
     informally, on a continuing basis.

(3) A great deal of research and data collection will be
     required before industrial policies and sector plans
     can be developed on the basis of reliable information
     regarding market trends, trends in technology,
     availability of skilled manpower, etc.

This is broadly the approach which is being adopted in the British National
Economic Development Office through the activities of the Sector Working Parties.
Perhaps we could regard the activities of NEDO as sector planning in the embryo
stage.

What then are the implications for business?

(1) to make effective contact within the various government
     departments which they deal with;

(2) to work directly and within the Trade Associations and
     in other forums like NEDO and the Industrial Training
     Boards: to recommend *positive policies* which will
     encourage the development of the industry and to
     minimise the impact of regulations which may be damaging;

(3) to work with government where possible in planning
     jointly for the future development of the industry -
     helping government officials to understand the industry's
     problems and opportunities for the future.

The task for government officials is similar:

(1) to develop continuing contacts with businessmen and a
     real understanding of industry's problems;

(2) to advocate to politicians a stable industrial policy
     which can be maintained over a period of time;

(3) to try to co-ordinate the policies of different
     departments so that industrialists do not continually
     receive conflicting messages, e.g. from an industrial
     policy which encourages the rationalisation of
     industry and a competition policy which tends to
     discourage the concentration of market power;

(4) to attempt to develop jointly with industry broad
     strategies to guide the future development of key
     sectors.

PLANNING WITH EMPLOYEES AND UNIONS

In my opinion the question for management in Europe is not *whether* we should try
to involve employee representatives in Corporate Planning but *how* we involve
them. The last decade has seen an increase in the power of employees and unions
to the point where in general they can, and in many cases do, prevent the achieve-

ment of corporate objectives and the implementation of company plans. In part,
their power arises from the vulnerability of large technological systems to
industrial action by a few workers, e.g. computer staff, power workers and air
traffic controllers. The power of the trade unions also arises from their
effectiveness as political organisations, in particular the alliances which they
have forged with left-wing political parties. One might contrast the comparative
weakness of businessmen in putting their case in the media, in parliament and on
public platforms.

In most European countries employees have now been granted certain legal rights
to participation in management - on the shop-floor, in works councils, and
through direct representation at Board level. Also, the employer's rights have
been tightly circumscribed in relation to health and safety at work, sickness
benefits and pensions and the treatment of workers in cases of redundancy. If
management continue to present their plans to their work forces as a *fait accompli*
they must not be surprised to find their employees delivering a veto to the plans
in the only way available to them - by taking industrial action.

Recent experiments in employee participation, organisation development and
autonomous work groups, have led some trade unionists to conclude that any form
of participation which includes no say in formulating objectives and plans but
concentrates on discussing *how* the plans might be achieved is likely to be
something of a charade.

Two alternative approaches are being advocated:

> (1) The consensus approach: This suggests that employee
>   representatives at different levels in the business
>   should be consulted and involved at various stages in
>   the preparation of the Corporate Plan. The work force
>   should be made aware of the broad objectives and plans
>   for their part of the organisation and performance
>   should be reviewed against these plans on a regular
>   basis. This is the form of Corporate Planning which
>   was adopted by the British nationalised industries
>   under pressure from the previous government. A similar
>   tripartite pattern of corporate planning is envisaged
>   in that government's proposals for Planning Agreements
>   which have so far appeared in private industry only in
>   Chrysler UK, and in a modified form in British Leyland.

> (2) The adversary approach: Another view adopted by many
>   trade unionists suggests that the interests of the
>   work force and management will always be different.
>   Agreement can therefore only be achieved on a temporary
>   basis through negotiation. Any attempt by management
>   at achieving a consensus through employee participation
>   is therefore doomed to failure and, moreover, entails
>   the risk that trade union representatives will be
>   implicated in decisions for which management should take
>   the responsibility.

> The supporters of the adversary approach, therefore,
> forecast that trade unions may seek to become involved
> in Corporate Planning through an extension of the
> collective bargaining process. The unions may simply
> ask for the disclosure of more information about the
> company's future plans in order to be able to consider

the implications for their members before management takes
any action.

Or, in critical situations, trade union representatives may
come together, e.g. in shop stewards' committees at various
levels in the enterprise to develop their own *Alternative
Corporate Plans*. This has already happened in the U.K. in
Lucas Aerospace and in parts of the British Steel Corporation.
And in Norway in the Union of Computer Staff.

TECHNIQUES FOR POLITICAL PLANNING

The management tradition, in the U.K. at least, is one of political neutrality.
Politicians are elected by the democratic process and it is expected that the
government will act in the best interest of the nation as a whole. On the other
hand, it is widely assumed that business is best left in the hands of businessmen
with a minimum of government involvement.

Clearly, for a variety of reasons, the energy crisis, unprecedented levels of
inflation, persistent unemployment, the need to rejuvenate declining industries,
etc., *the rules have changed*.

In recent years there has been

    (1) a rapid growth in government spending and purchasing
        power;
    (2) an expansion of public ownership of industry;
    (3) the use of new government agencies to regulate and
        restructure industry;
    (4) an attempt to intervene in specific industries and in
        individual companies to influence management decisions
        on investment and employment;
    (5) a flood of legislation expanding the range of government
        controls over prices and incomes, industrial democracy,
        "the quality of working life", environmental protection,
        race relations, equal opportunity for women and consumer
        protection.

In the face of a continuous pressure from government agencies, left-wing
politicians, trade union officials and members of various social pressure groups,
management have belatedly begun to realise that whether they like it or not their
businesses are involved in a political process. There is a debate going on
continuously about the future of industry and its place in society. Proposals
are being made by various pressure groups which are likely to have a critical
impact on business and to contribute effectively to the discussion and management's interventions must be planned well in advance.

It is not at all clear what form political planning or legislative planning will
take. It will clearly vary with the size of the business, the degree of
government influence and the issues at stake. However, the broad outlines of
political planning are clear:

(1) Political Mapping

The first stage is to gather information about the nature of the political
environment. This means producing a "political map" of the main organisations
and pressure groups which are active in each industry and region and in relation

to important issues, e.g. legislation, planning permission, purchasing policy, government grants, import duties, etc. A number of political studies of this kind have been done by consultants and academics.

(2)   Analysis of Political Networks

Another approach is to trace the formal and informal networks which exist to determine who is in a position to take the relevant decisions affecting the business and which individuals or groups can influence these decisions, together with an analysis of their relationships with the decision-makers and the pressures which they can bring to bear. This technique has been well demonstrated by the Tavistock Institute and other sociological research groups.

(3)   The Political Agenda

Also, it is important to have an agenda of the social and political issues which are being debated in various political parties and action groups and which may become the subject of legislation or regulation in the next five to ten years. Typically, these issues are signalled well in advance. They are the subject of campaigns by pressure groups. They are the basis of proposals at trade union conferences. They appear in party manifestos, are the subject of Royal Commissions and White Papers before they ever reach the statute book.

General Electric (U.S.A.) have done well-publicised studies of this kind, analysing the demands of social pressure groups and attempting forecasts of sociological trends.

(4)   Assessing Political Response

In relation to specific projects or products, it is important to evaluate the likely response of social and political groups. This can be done conveniently by the use of some form of cross impact analysis, e.g. by listing organisations or groups involved and estimating their likely reaction to a particular project, or alternatively, by looking at a political change, e.g. an item of legislation and evaluating its likely impact on various parts of the business.

Shell use a format for this purpose called a Societal Response Assessment Matrix.

(5)   Organised Lobbying

Effective political action requires an organised pressure group. This means:

        (i)   a permanent organisation with sufficient funds to appoint skilled professionals, not merely an *ad hoc* group hastily assembled to fight nationalisation or some other immediate threat;

        (ii)   an alliance of diverse and competitive interests representing an industry or a locality, e.g. a chamber of commerce or an industry association rather than an individual firm;

        (iii) the development of constructive and politically feasible proposals, in a form which politicians and officials can use, instead of the more usual complaints and protests.

(6) Communications Programmes

Management has the continuing task of marketing the company to the "stakeholders" -
shareholders, financial institutions, dealers and distributors, suppliers and
employees as well as the local community and various agencies of government.

Recent experience in Britain provides ample illustrations of this trend:

- the anti-nationalisation programmes of Tate and Lyle,
  the banks and the building industry;

- the employee communications campaigns of Chrysler UK,
  British Airways and IBM;

- the regular use of opinion surveys and corporate image
  studies among employees, shareholders and various opinion-
  forming groups.

In most cases top management and the corporate planning team are closely involved
in mounting these communications efforts and in certain cases, e.g. Chrysler UK,
the Corporate Plan has become the basis of a regular review of performance with
employees.

(7) Economic Impact Studies

The political process makes it possible for taxes to be raised and laws to be
passed without any attempt being made to assess their effect on business. Often
the effect is disastrous. In recent years changes in Value Added Tax in the U.K.
have crippled the boatbuilding and television tube industries and the taxation
of stock appreciation did great damage to manufacturing companies before the
taxation rules were amended. In the U.S.A., the Environment Protection Act has
had a punitive effect, virtually outlawing a number of industries and handicapping
others in international competition. And the field tests now required by the
Food and Drug Administration have meant that only the largest firms can now
afford to launch new drugs.

A most effective response to such legislation appears to be a well-publicised
evaluation of the damage it is doing. Merrett and Sykes produced a most
effective assessment of the British stock appreciation tax which led to its
amendment. The British Food Manufacturers' Federation regularly surveys the
effect of government price controls on the industry's cash flow and investment.
Dow Chemicals have published widely their estimates of the inordinate cost of
environmental protection.

(8) Futures Forecasts

A novel aspect of politics in recent years has been the growth of futures
research as a background to the analysis of public policy. Nowadays, the public
debate about major policy issues frequently entails the consideration of
"alternative futures" for society. In Britain, future government policies on
Energy, Industry, Telecommunications and Education have become the subject of
widespread public debate.

Certain States of the U.S.A., e.g. Hawaii and Iowa, have launched elaborate media
campaigns to try to engage the public in debates about the future of their
regions. And in the U.S.A. and in Western Europe, it is now common for governments to employ the services of Think Tanks and Futures Research Groups.

Private institutes, such as Hudson, Battelle and Stanford, are widely used.
Industry groups such as the Inter-Bank Research Organisation and the Chemical
Industries Association are also engaged on Futures Studies.

It is essential that the point of view of business should be represented in
these futures debates, by industries putting forward their vision of the future.

Indeed Theodore Levitt's injunction applies as much to industries as to
individual companies: "If you don't know where you're going, any road will lead
you there".

(9)   Regular Meetings with Government

In some nationalised industries it is common practice - typically in June or
July - for the top management team to review a limited number of key strategic
issues with the relevant minister and his staff. This gives them an opportunity
to influence government policy and to inform the politicians in advance what
impact their policies may have on the industry. It also allows time for an
interchange of views about the broad strategy for the business, before the
preparation of detailed investment plans in the autumn.

I believe that regular contacts with government could also prove helpful to the
management of large private firms and in Britain it may become more common for
businessmen to have regular discussions with government officials and politicians
about industrial strategy, energy strategy, transportation policy etc.

        CONCLUSION

If we are to avoid major problems in government-industry relations, we need to
revise our ideas about Corporate Planning.

(1)   The Changed Political Environment

We must recognise that in recent years there has been a *shift of power in society*.
At one time the autonomy of management was unquestioned. Now management decisions
are regularly and successfully challenged by groups of employees, community
interests and by numerous agencies of government.

Management is now faced with:

    (a)   Trade unions which have unprecedented political
          strength based on monopoly power, a close alliance
          with left-wing political parties and the proven
          ability of small groups of workers to bring modern
          society to a halt by industrial action.

    (b)   Pressure groups which are organised as never before
          to promote the cause of Consumer Protection, Conserva-
          tion, Equal Opportunity for Women, and Racial Equality.

    (c)   Political parties and government officials which are
          committed to involvement in the management of industry
          in a way previously not contemplated *except in times
          of war*: through outright nationalisation, direct
          investment via government holding companies, the
          regulation of prices, wages and dividends and a whole
          spate of legislation affecting conditions of employment,

industrial relations, industrial democracy, and
programmes directed at the promotion and protection
of specific industries and regions where jobs (and
votes) are at stake.*

(2) Planning as a Political Process

In these changed circumstances it is unrealistic for management to regard
Corporate Planning as a process which concerns management alone. They must find
ways of involving and influencing the decision-processes of other interests and
organisations who have the power to prevent their plans from being realised. It
is natural, too, that representatives of public authorities, groups of employees
and community interests should wish to influence the decisions of businessmen
regarding numbers of workers to be employed, conditions of work, levels of
investment, location of factories, arrangements for pollution control, etc.

Corporate Planning must be regarded not merely as a process internal to the
company but also as a political and inter-organisational process. Firms, in fact,
need to have a "foreign policy" towards other groups and organisations.

(3) Sector and Regional Planning

If we are to solve the problems which face societies in Western Europe: re-
generating manufacturing industry, meeting international competition, creating
new jobs, finding secure sources of supply for food and raw materials, and
controlling inflation, I believe we must have more effective industrial planning
by sector and by region.

There is no alternative in many industries to a partnership between government
and industry. Competition in certain industries - shipbuilding, steel, aerospace,
even motor cars, takes the form of competition between alliances of major
companies and national governments and there is no way in which an individual
European company is going to compete successfully with a foreign company - in
Russia, the U.S.A., Japan or the Third World - which has government backing.

However, to have effective industrial planning involves the creation of new
institutions, new procedures and new relationships between government and
industry. In Britain the idea of industrial policy is debated in terms of
political ideologies - as if the choice is between *either* a Free Market Economy
or a state on the East European model. Instead of discussing political dogma we
should follow the example of the Japanese, the Swedes and the French and get
down to the practical task of developing the institutions we need to plan a new
industrial structure. This will require the efforts of our best businessmen,
civil servants and trade union leaders.

(4) Employee Participation in Planning

One of the most remarkable developments in recent years is the demand of
ordinary people - workers and citizens - for the right to participate in the
decisions which affect them. And one of the greatest challenges to managers and
administrators is to find a way to widen the planning process so as to engage
the interest and mobilise the ideas and energies of large groups of employees
and citizens.

From their point of view, on the shop floor and in the neighbourhood, much of

---

*Since the time of writing in 1979, the Thatcher government has come to power but
we have yet to see a fundamental move towards de-regulation.

present-day planning is a charade, a confidence trick, a way of short-circuiting
the democratic process. When managers and public officials talk about strategic
plans, the man in the street is likely to ask "Whose plans?", "Whose objectives?".
They are the ones who suffer the plans or receive the plans but they have little
or no say in determining their own future.

Present approaches to participation do not go far enough - organisation
development programmes, works councils, autonomous work groups, all have the
common feature that they concentrate on ways and means of achieving objectives
and implementing plans which have been developed elsewhere.

Now, groups of workers are appearing who are producing their own Corporate Plans,
and groups of citizens are coming forward with their own plans for new airports
and new roads. If management do not find a way of including workers in the
debate about the future of the enterprise, they may find their employees working
with their unions and government agencies to achieve their own Alternative
Corporate Plans.

(5) Political Planning

To plan effectively in the 1980s requires new skills, new approaches, and new
techniques which we might label collectively Political Planning or Legislative
Planning. Some businesses - in the defence industries, in transportation and
in energy - have traditionally had close contacts with government, and their
managers have had to develop the necessary political contacts, an understanding
of the world of government and the industry-wide organisations which are required
to lobby government effectively. In other industries the need for political
activity is novel. The information system, the relationships and the political
organisation have yet to be developed.

In small and medium-size companies it is likely that the Chairman and the Board
of Directors will be able to handle government and industry relations through
professional and trade associations. In large companies, however, it will be
necessary to appoint specialist staff to deal with "Public Affairs" or "Corporate
Affairs".
And we may see a wider use of formal techniques for analysing and forecasting
the political environment and for planning and organising business activity in
this area in a more constructive and systematic way.

Chapter 5

INVOLVEMENT OF GOVERNMENT AND PUBLIC BODIES

David Hussey

There was once a time when it was reasonable to argue that business should mind its own business, and that any involvement with the public sector should be at the broadest possible level. Certainly it made sense to fight hard to change government policies so that they were closer to the interests of the firm. One of the best, and successful, examples of this is the long battle that Courtaulds had to change government policies towards the textile industry. Early corporate planners in the U.K. would have argued for co-operation at the broad strategy level, where business could influence the national policies, but few would have suggested that Government should get involved in the strategies of individual firms.

Obviously it often has, either through the application of its general policies or from time to time by direct intervention. The Ferranti episode of the mid-sixties is a good example, where an adjustment was forced on the company because it was held to be making excess profits on government contracts.

The reality of planning in the U.K. today is that Government and public bodies are much more closely involved in the planning of individual firms, that this process is steadily intensifying, and that it is likely to continue regardless of the political colour of the government of the day. Although there is a strong body of thought that government should create the right conditions and leave industry alone to get on with the job, there are many others who feel that some involvement is desirable and helpful to all parties. The social environment has changed considerably in the last decade, and what was once an acceptable attitude by managers also has to change.

Few managers support the ultimate in government involvement, public ownership. This too, has increased in intensity in recent years, and this form of inter-vention is one reason why business distrusts the less extreme forms of involvement which they otherwise might favour. Certainly the threat of nationalisation is a real one for many businesses. It may abate when governments change, but will not disappear if the normal situation of regular changes of political fortune overtake successive governments. There are those whose political aims are dedicated to the destruction of private enterprise, and they too are part of the reality of the world in which we must plan.

The U.K. does not stand alone on its inevitable trend to more government involve-ment. In many ways it is not as far along the path as many other European countries, although the mechanisms for intervention often vary. Even the U.S.A., which is the staunchest defender of private enterprise, is moving along the same path.

Before looking in detail at the way trends have been developing in the U.K., it is of interest to study the global trends.

Two Forms of Intervention*

To a realistic corporate manager, anything that he must do or cannot do - either now or in the future - as a result of governmental action represents "intervention", no matter what the source of the motive. Nevertheless, there are two distinct mainstreams of governmental intervention which differently affect business enterprises:

> . Nationalistic Intervention: These are the governmental actions directed wholly toward foreign investment, exclusively because it is foreign.

> . General Intervention: These actions flow from a government's overall view of its role in the economy of its country. In implementing policy in support of this view, a government deals no differently with foreign-owned firms than with nationally owned ones; instead, it confronts the private sector as a whole.

The distinction between these two mainstreams of intervention becomes more obvious through focusing on individual countries that may be strongly committed to one of them, but only marginally to the other. In Sweden, for example, governmental intervention in the private sector is unusually pervasive, yet there is little exhibition of highly nationalistic intervention.

The Shaping of Interventionist Policy

In many countries, governmental intervention in the private sector is an all-of-one-piece weaving together of economic, social, political, and cultural threads into a comprehensive, internally consistent and relatively stable framework. Although the form it may take in such a country may be deeply rooted in national tradition, the interventionist system is often imposed virtually in its entirety at a particular historic juncture. Three different examples are those of India, Sweden and Yugoslavia.

India: At the time of independence, the new government established a structure characterized by the following features:

> - Centralized five-year planning.
> - The Gandhian concept of highly decentralized small production units in many industries, especially labour-intensive ones, so as to raise the standard of living and level of employment in rural areas.
> - The Socialist doctrine of reserving ownership of all heavy industry (for example, iron and steel, heavey electrical equipment, mining) for the state and of dictating joint public - private ventures in other

---

* This section, including Figure 5.1, was almost entirely provided by J. Schnapp, Harbridge House Inc. Boston, to whom an acknowledgement and thanks are due.

   industrial sectors, such as non-ferrous metals, chemicals
   and pharmaceuticals.
- The nationalization of all credit mechanisms to provide
  control over investment flows.
- The licensing of every new industrial production facility
  under terms awarding the government the right to
  investigate operations; direct changes in them; assume
  management control if warranted; and control supply,
  distribution and price.

Sweden: The Social Democratic governments that began to dominate the Swedish
political scene in the early 1930s instituted a system whose features have
remained essentially unchanged for more than 40 years:

- Extensive redistribution of income, financed by high
  progressive income taxes and effected through an
  elaborate array of governmental human services.
- A stress upon private ownership and management of the
  means of production but involving worker participation
  in decision-making through workers' councils and worker
  representation on boards of directors.
- Considerable governmental influence on the timing and
  form of industrial growth through an incentive system
  which encourages corporations to deposit nearly 20 per
  cent of their pre-tax profits in a reserve account which
  can be tapped only with governmental approval.
- A series of policies which emphasise full employment -
  but balancing this with high technological efficiency
  and the encouragement of overseas investment.

Yugoslavia: At the rupture with Stalinist Russia in 1948, the Yugoslavian
government began devising a system which, by the early 1950s, was characterised
by:

- State ownership of all productive assets except those in
  businesses employing five or fewer workers or in farms
  smaller than 10 hectares.
- Worker self-management of all enterprises through the
  mechanism of worker councils and a management board of
  each council which hires a director as chief executive
  officer.
- A competitive market economy with the use of price
  controls only to combat inflation.
- Funds for worker compensation and funds for reinvestment
  both vary depending on surplus of revenues over external
  cost (that is, raw materials, power, interest expense)
  and both allocated by the worker councils according to
  its view of short and long term interests of workers.
- Opportunity for any enterprise to merge with other
  enterprises; to spin off new enterprises; and to borrow
  growth capital from community, regional, or national
  financing entities.
- Requirements of all worker councils to co-ordinate the
  plans of their enterprise with the social plans of the
  community and the five-year national economic plan.

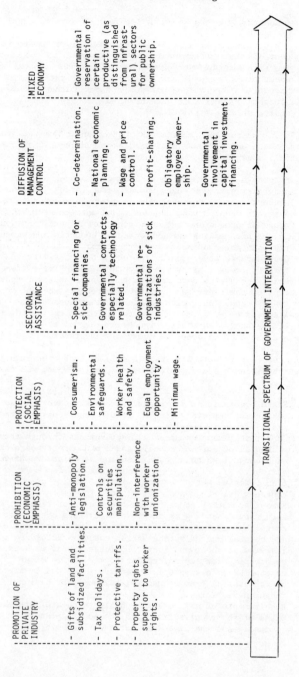

GOVERNMENT INTERVENTION SPECTRUM

PROMOTION OF PRIVATE INDUSTRY	PROHIBITION (ECONOMIC EMPHASIS)	PROTECTION (SOCIAL EMPHASIS)	SECTORAL ASSISTANCE	DIFFUSION OF MANAGEMENT CONTROL	MIXED ECONOMY
- Gifts of land and subsidized facilities.	- Anti-monopoly legislation.	- Consumerism.	- Special financing for sick companies.	- Co-determination.	- Governmental reservation of certain productive (as distinguished from infrastructural) sectors for public ownership.
- Tax holidays.	- Controls on securities manipulation.	- Environmental safeguards.	- Governmental contracts, especially technology related.	- National economic planning.	
- Protective tariffs.	- Non-interference with worker unionization	- Worker health and safety.	- Governmental re-organizations of sick industries.	- Wage and price control.	
- Property rights superior to worker rights.		- Equal employment opportunity.		- Profit-sharing.	
		- Minimum wage.		- Obligatory employee ownership.	
				- Governmental involvement in capital investment financing.	

TRANSITIONAL SPECTRUM OF GOVERNMENT INTERVENTION

FIGURE 5:1

Of the other nations characterised by this sort of all-of-one-piece approach to governmental intervention, Japan is probably the most prominent.

Elsewhere, however, the form of governmental intervention in the economy has emerged and continues emerging from a transitional process ... and not necessarily a smooth, orderly one but instead one more commonly characterised by fits and starts. The different stages usually most visible in this transitional process are depicted in Figure 5.1.

Governmental policy in any country may, of course, span a variety of such stages. But the stage involving the greatest amount of current activity, controversy, and attention is the clearest indicator of where a country may stand along the spectrum. Brazil, for example, is at the lower end, while the United Kingdom is moving rapidly toward the upper extreme. France and Germany would be positioned strongly toward the upper end although most observers would not place them in the "mixed economy" category since governmental ownership of productive industry (for example, Renault, Saabergwerke) has been oriented more toward preserving large and sick employers than toward thrusting the government into industrial ownership. In both countries there is some evident diffusion of management control - in France a fairly modest sort involving national economic planning, but in Germany a major and growing version based upon concepts of industrial democracy and co-determination.

Although movement along the interventionist spectrum is usually sequential, some governments adopt policies that skip over certain stages along this spectrum. Such countries as Spain and Mexico have created mixed economies, often because the state represents the only available national mechanism for certain very large forms of investment. Nonetheless, in the sectors remaining entirely in private hands there are very few of the instrumentalities which invade management control.

Whether the solution for the individual business is to fight the tendency for more involvement, or to co-operate, is a matter for individual decision. There are, of course, weapons available to business to help it resist increasing intervention, notably political lobbying, public relations and trade association pressures. But the fact that the trend is a worldwide one makes resistance a less viable strategy for the long run. Modification through co-operation might be more beneficial: some intervention policies leave business with no option but to resist, and few managers would advise the British Banking and Insurance industries to abandon their counter-attack against announced nationalisation intentions; despite respites offered by changes of government.

The Emerging Pattern in the U.K.

Figure 5.2 gives one way of looking at the techniques of government intervention. Segments 1-4 are concerned with the ownership and control of the factors of production, and it is in the first two of these segments that there has been enormous movement in recent years. Segments 5 and 6 might have been generally termed protection of the citizen: either his health, his legal rights or his safety. Environmental control does go wider than the individual and is usually an attempt to balance the needs of the present and future community as a whole. Segments 7 and 8 are concerned with social trends (some would say including the protection of the individual's right to have a job) and the role of labour vis-a-vis capital.

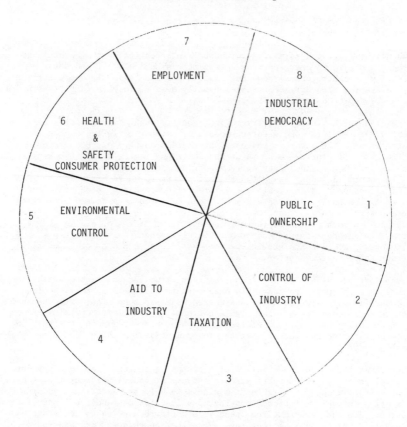

Fig. 5.2. Techniques of Government Intervention

This way of looking at things is by no means perfect, and is not intended to do
more than provide a framework against which a few of the issues can be considered.
Those issues selected for discussion include some of the most important, but by
no means cover all the factors that would be required in a comprehensive study.
And the analysis is partial, in both senses of the word, in that it does not
relate growing Government involvement in business to all of the many other
developments in social and political beliefs and attitudes.

Let us start with two sets of data which show how government involvement in the
economy has been increasing, at least in the two dimensions illustrated. Figure
5.3 shows total public expenditure as a percentage of gross domestic product.
This shows that despite the fluctuations (at least partly due to changes of
government and the fortunes of the two main British political parties) the long
run trend has been for government to increase at the expense of the private
sector. This reflects an increasing involvement in society as a whole, of which
business is a part. Whether the actions of the new Conservative Government will
have any long term affect on this trend has yet to be seen.

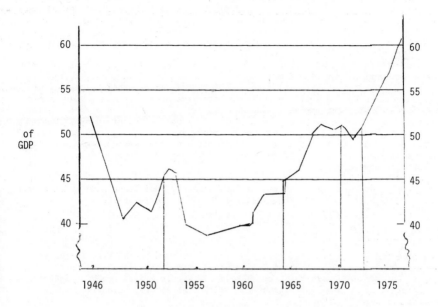

Source: Annual Abstract of Statistics

Fig. 5.3.   Total Public Expenditure as % of GDP in the
United Kingdom

	1965		1975	
	Employment	GDP	Employment	GDP
Private Sector	76	75	71	68
Public Sector	24	25	29	32
Of which public corps.	8	10	8	11
Central Govt.	7	7	9	8
Local Govt.	9	8	12	11
GDP £ Million		31221		93146
Employment '000	25192		24968	

Source: Annual Abstract of Statistics

Fig. 5.4.   % of GDP and National Employment

Another dimension is illustrated in Figure 5.4. Here a direct increase is illustrated in the public sector's contribution to gross domestic product and direct employment. Points to consider are the fact that percentages in 1975 are high partly because the private sector bore the brunt of the recession: job security is largely a luxury of only the civil and local government services.

In addition the figures for public corporations are misleading, since publicly owned enterprise is included when it is called a corporation, but excluded when it has the word company in its name. Thus the extent of public ownership is not fully revealed by these figures. There have also been changes of view during this period, with enterprises which in 1965 were classified as private sector despite their public ownership being counted as public sector in subsequent years. All businesses in which Government has a shareholding of under 100% are also classed as private sector: this distortion becomes increasingly significant as the National Enterprise Board develops its role of a Government owned investment company.

It should also be mentioned that the public sector includes mining and railways, both of which have faced a long spell of labour force reduction.

Nationalisation

The pace and extent of nationalisation have increased in the U.K. in the post war years. On Figures 5.5(a) and 5.5(b) a crude attempt has been made to trace the way in which the pattern has been changing. Figure 5.5(a) looks at industries which might be termed "infrastructure" and 5.5(b) studies industries which fall outside of these trends.

Time is measured along the horizontal axis, and the charts show the history of nationalisation since 1920, with a scenario for 1990. Although there is no significance in the thickness of the bars between industries, within each industry sector an attempt has been made to give an impression of the extent of public ownership. In most cases this is a crude estimate and should be interpreted accordingly in terms such as a little, about half, significant, nearly all and all. Even the last category is not always accurate enough for the purist: for example, there is some open cast coal mining by private enterprise outside of the National Coal Board; the Post Office postal monopoly does not extend to parcels; there is one part of the telephone system at Kingston on Hull which is operated by local government, and there are also internal telephone systems which are outside the monopoly. It is the overall picture that is important, and the impression given by the figures is fair.

A distinction has been made between types of government ownership: national or local government. This may affect how the enterprises are managed, and where the statisticians classify them, but in either case they are in public ownership.

Also excluded is the recent wave of partial government ownership of companies, with the exception of British Petroleum where the government shareholding is 51% (although there was a short period when it rose to 70%) and of the oil sectors generally. The reason for this is that the BP holding is of very long standing, and was originally for national strategic reasons which had little to do with political doctrine. The new wave of government share participation has a different basis.

The charts show definite periods in the history of nationalisation. Before the second world war, public ownership fell into three categories. There were the Post Office services which were largely a matter of history: a history copied

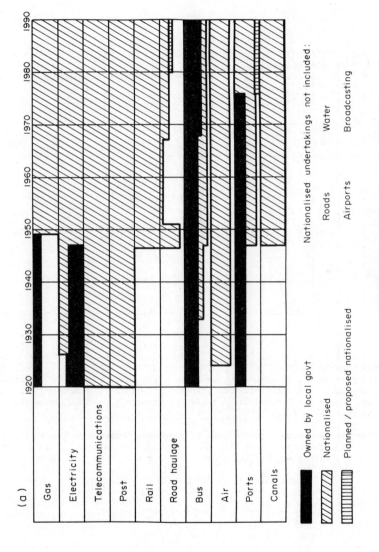

Fig. 5.5(a) Development of Public Ownership – Infrastructure

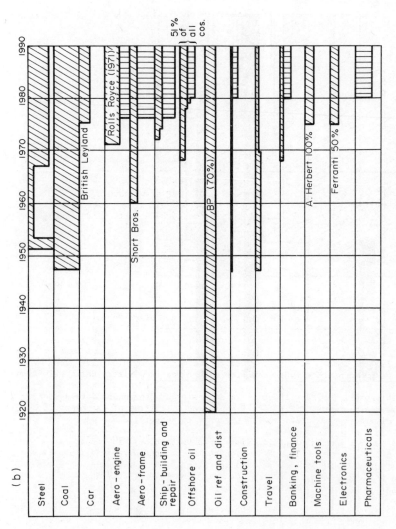

Fig. 5.5(b) Development of Public Ownership

through the world, at least as far as the post is concerned.   The starting point
of this, and many of the other activities on the chart, was long before 1920.

Next came a group of activities that were largely operated by local authorities:
gas, buses, electricity and ports.

The last group consists of the two special cases of airlines and the interest in
BP. Neither of these represented any intention to start a trend.

With the exception of oil, all the pre-war public undertakings were in the
category of infrastructure. They were not generally the result of nationalisation,
and tended to be in public ownership because this is how they started. Even at
this time the Labour Party had definite, but unrealised, policies for public
ownership. Their chance came in the second period, the immediate post war years.

The first phase after the war was also largely directed at the infrastructure,
sometimes as an amalgamation of local government interests, and sometimes as a
direct act of nationalisation. Exceptions to the infrastructure rule were coal,
steel, and travel. There were some special circumstances around coal, although
steel was an act of political dogma rather than a need to rationalise for market
or economic reasons.

At that time steel was an efficient industry.   The travel business was
largely an accident, in that the private railways had owned some travel interests.
Thomas Cook and Sons, for example, were vested in Southern Railways at the time
of nationalisation.

The infrastructure phase lasted until the mid-seventies. During this period
steel was unscrambled and returned to the private sector, with the exception of
one company for which buyers could not be found. The reversal of political
fortunes in the late 1960s led to the re-nationalisation of most of the steel
industry.

Similarly de-nationalisation of road haulage left a number of vehicles in
Government hands which could not be disposed of and which were therefore kept as
a going concern. With subsequent additions this grew into the National Freight
Corporation, although for some time major road transport undertakings were
operated by British Rail. Further private road haulage companies have been
moved into the public sector by acquisition rather than compulsory nationalisation.

The N.F.C. is unusual in that it trades in competition with the private sector,
and has no monopoly status. (The retail appliance activities of the Electricity
Boards also operate in competition with the private sector).

In the 1970s two new phases of nationalisation developed, all in companies
outside the infrastructure. The motivation of the two phases were different: the
first was expediency, the second political doctrine. The expediency phase was
the era of lame ducks, when a number of organisations had to be rescued by
injections of public funds and came into the Government portfolio. Among these
were British Leyland, Rolls Royce (1971) and others. Political doctrine led to
the nationalisation of the aero-frame business, ship building and repair, and to
the British National Oil Corporation and its activities.

This period also saw the establishment of the National Enterprise Board which in
some ways represents yet another stage in the history of nationalisation. The
N.E.B. was set up to acquire shareholdings in profitable undertakings in the
private sector. It requires the consent of the Secretary of State if it wishes
to acquire more than 30% in any one company. In addition to this investment role

it was envisaged as a new source of funds for industrial investment, a provider of finance for industrial restructuring, and an assister of lame ducks. It was immediately made the repository of some of the lamest of the ducks in the Government portfolio.

Whether the N.E.B. is seen as good or bad probably depends on one's political viewpoint, and is not a relevant question for this book. The actual result of the N.E.B. is a new method of Government intervention or involvement in the private sector; it sets the U.K. on a very different path for the future.

It is too early to evaluate whether the policies of the 1979 Conservative Government will set a permanent trend for divestment of public ownership.

Control of Industry. It is not always necessary for government to own industry in order to control it. Recent years have seen a significant interest in the legal mechanisms by which industry can be manipulated to government policy. These have been accompanied by a growing social responsiveness on the part of business, and changing social views of the roles of government and business. Although the legislation makes another step in the U.K.'s regression to the right hand side of Figure 5.2, and is certainly not supported by all sectors of the community, it is not far out of step with public opinion.

Business may be controlled by a variety of legislation. Perhaps the price control mechanisms are among the most significant because they restrict the ability of the company to use price as a means of increasing profits. Although introduced for the control of inflation, the measures have the potential for use for other purposes. Periods on and off price control have been a feature of the past 15 years.

With less general impact, but of more potential long term interest, are the moves to obtain a greater government and union involvement in the plans of selected individual companies? There are two mechanisms for this - planning agreements and the industrial strategy initiative of NEDO.

Planning agreements are stressed to be a voluntary mechanism whereby Government agrees the plans of selected major companies, and in return guarantees to hold the grants on which the plan was based. Unfortunately the political origins of planning agreements mean that the whole concept was viewed with distrust by much of private enterprise, and the aims of the concept were confused. It seemed partly designed to bring industry closer to government, and partly to encourage industrial democracy and union involvement. The initiative also assumed that companies have corporate plans to agree with government: not all do.

Although planning agreements may be interpreted as a genuine desire by government to co-operate with industry, they were not always viewed in this light, and were largely unsuccessful. It is probable that a Conservative Government would take little interest in them.

The industrial strategy initiative, on the face of it, appears to be more successful in bringing government and industry closer together. Here the mechanism is for representatives from industry to join NEDO working parties and help define an overall strategy for an industry sector. This enables both sides to influence each other's thinking without the political and emotional overtones of individual planning agreements. The National Economic Development Office is a well-established mechanism for government/business/trade union collaboration, and the industrial strategy initiative is an extension of this.

Government attempts to manipulate industry include control of the location of industry, and methods of driving industry to regions which are considered

desirable for development in the national interest. This is achieved by control
of new industrial building, financial incentives, and publicity. Office location
is also controlled on a similar but less intensive way.

Through the Manpower Services Commission and the Training Boards Government
intervenes in employment policies, by giving incentives to encourage business to
employ people they do not need, and - by creating what is effectively an
additional tax structure for those who do not co-operate - ensuring that employees
are trained to the standard government considers to be desirable.

Monopolies and mergers have long been subject to government control, as indeed
they are in many countries.

The most recent method, which may be only a temporary phase, but which could be
the start of a new era, is control by blacklist. In 1978 "voluntary" wage control
norms were enforced by Government partly through the price control mechanism, and
partly through putting transgressors on a blacklist. Firms on this list became
ineligible for certain forms of government assistance, and were no longer able to
act as contractors to government and its agencies.

Taxation and aid to industry. To a certain extent taxation and industry aid may
be considered together, since the aid is frequently given in the form of a tax
deduction. Tax is often used as a means of manipulating industry into following
government policies: for example, on the location of industry.

In addition to tax linked aid and incentives there are numerous ways in which
Government tries to aid industry. Substantial sums of money have been made
available as capital grants to specific industries as part of the industrial
strategy initiative. Among the sectors to benefit have been machine tools, wool
textiles, ferrous foundries and clothing.

Real assistance is given to exports through the export credits guarantee scheme,
grants for export market research, and from the provision of export intelligence.
Additionally, the pattern of exports is linked to Government trade policies, a
good example of an area where industry and government need to work closely
together.

Capital is made available through various methods: the National Research and
Development Corporation makes loans or participates in joint ventures for new
innovations, the National Enterprise Board is available (as has already been
mentioned), and the Bank of England has a stake in Finance for Industry Limited.
The pattern seems to be for an increasing amount of government finance, as
capital or grants, to be made available to private industry.

Environmental Control, Health and Safety, Consumer Protection. In a democracy
it is reasonable for public concerns over pollution, health and safety at work,
and the rights of the consumer to find their way into Government legislation.
Certainly the last decade has seen a spate of this, with considerably more
government regulation in areas as widely diverse as the disposal of wastes to the
protection of credit card users. There is an inevitable relationship between
public concern over issues of this type, government restrictions and regulation,
and frequently special administrative procedures within the company. The Health
and Safety at Work Act provides a good example of this: although the extra costs
borne by industry, directly on administrative costs, and indirectly through
increased government expenditure are deplorable, it is difficult to fault the
basic intent behind the legislation. From the point of view of business the
problem of adhering to all the legislation is considerable, and is likely to get
bigger. This is even more clearly illustrated in the field of employment law.

Employment.   There are at least two pressures which will lead to an ever
increasing involvement by government in the employment affairs of the private
sector. The first is the dynamic nature of social attitudes, and the rapid
changes that are taking place in the expectations of people. Employees have a
different view of their relationship with their employers to that held even as
short a period as a decade ago.

Society no longer accepts that employers have an undisputed right to hire or fire
at will, to force individuals to adhere to norms of behaviour which they find
repugnant, or to give blind "loyalty" to a faceless corporation. So-called
"loyalty" is seen as a two-way door, with the employee now expecting more from
the company than he himself is prepared to give: a complete reversal of the
attitudes of many companies. The Bullock Report summed up the change as "the end
of the deferential society", and this force is enough to lead to political activity
to give more statutory protection to the individual employee.

Parallel with this is the influence of the E.E.C. which through its directives and
regulations forces certain common threads of employee legislation through its
member countries. Although time is given for countries to change, and directives
are binding as to ends and not means, a realistic forecast of trends in U.K.
labour legislation can be made by studying the draft directives of the E.E.C.

The programmes of the E.E.C. are directly influenced by the Governments of its
member countries, but this is not the only influence. New initiatives come from
many quarters, one of the most significant being the international trade union
movement which speaks through the European Trade Union Confederation and is
represented on the Economic and Social Committee. The British Trade Union Council
is represented through its membership of the International Confederation of Free
Trade Unions which is in turn a member of the E.T.U.C.

The Confederation of British Industry also has a voice through its membership of
an international body represented on the same committee. However, it is the trade
union movement which is more likely to initiate "social legislation".

U.K. labour legislation has become increasingly complex over the last decade.
Among other things the Employee Protection Act establishes the right of the
employee to his job. It covers such aspects as contracts of employment, fair
dismissal, damages for unfair dismissal, redundancies, collective bargaining and
union relations. In this last area there is also other legislation, establishing
the closed shop.

In addition to forcing organisations to involve government and unions in certain
decisions, for example, redundancies, the laws give negotiating unions the right
to certain information. The importance of the legislation is not so much what it
requires companies to do, but the fact that it is considered necessary to have
legislation to force companies to do it.

There is considerable body of law in addition to the acts discussed above,
varying from fair wage legislation to anti-discrimination measures. Each piece
of legislation, however justified, represents one more step in government
involvement with private business, a reality which looms larger every year.

Industrial Democracy.   At the time of writing it is difficult to see the U.K.'s
path to industrial democracy, though undoubtedly there will be such a path. It
would be difficult for the U.K. to resist the E.E.C. 5th Directive on company law,
which requires moves to employee participation in company boards, even if there
were no other forces demanding such moves.

In Europe as a whole, the pattern of industrial democracy varies considerably between countries. Many establish the Works Council as a key part of the system of participation, giving it a legal role, and defined rights for co-determination, consultation and information. Others also add a two-tier board system, with worker participation in the supervisory board. Patterns vary widely, from parity of worker elected directors (who need not be employees) in Germany, to the Dutch system which does not have employees on the Board, but ensures that the Board consists only of people who are acceptable to shareholders and workers.

Related to this issue are the increased rights of union representatives of employees to information for collective bargaining purposes. Both the Industry Act and the Employee Protection Act extend the information rights of employees, but even this lags behind the legal rights of employees in most other European countries. Also the bias of British law is to information for collective bargaining: German law seems more inclined to facilitating employee involvement in the successful operation of the business. France now has a requirement for companies to file a "social balance-sheet", and there are moves in the U.K. for more information to be called for on matters concerning employment and the social aspects of business.

Whatever the direction of future legislation, there are two realities for management, and therefore planning, today. The first is a growing recognition that an enlightened company should both inform employees and explain that information. In this way it is possible to win considerable benefits in motivation and involvement, and to avoid the dangers of distortion of facts, deliberate or otherwise, by those whose interest in the business is political, mischievous, or misguided. A positive internal communications policy is now a recognised part of management in many companies, and includes training all employees in the basics of business. It is no good trying to hide the annual returns from the employees on the basis that "they won't understand them". If employees cannot understand the figures that is the fault of management.

The second reality is that planning will become more participative. Certainly this is already an essential at middle management level, and the case histories in this book suggest approaches to this problem.

Participation to shop floor level presents more difficulties and is affected by the industrial democracy laws in each country. In the U.K. a minority of companies has begun to advise their shop stewards of the contents of their corporate plans. One of the duties of the National Enterprise Board is to promote industrial democracy in its companies. In many ways it is easier to develop an argument for planning participation at plant level through a more effective form of works council, than for worker involvement in total corporate planning. The danger is a bureaucracy of workers' advisory committees, in hierarchical relationships, which could easily sterilise all action.

It is interesting to speculate whether the new 1979 Government in the U.K. will halt the country's movement to more intervention, turning back to an earlier stage in Figure 5.1. Or will it turn out to be a temporary bleep in an otherwise continuing trend?

Chapter 6

STRATEGY FORMULATION AS A POLITICAL PROCESS*

Andrew M. Pettigrew

School of Industrial and Business Studies, University of Warwick

The formation of strategy in organizations is a *continuous process*. Specific dilemmas within the firm, or in the firm's environment, may raise the organization members' consciousness of strategy and allow us, as analysts, to think of strategy formulation as an intentional process built around certain discrete decisions; but strategy is being formed implicitly all the time. Choices are made and acted upon in processes involving individuals and subgroupings, at various organizational levels, that develop into the pattern of thinking about the world, evaluating that world, and acting upon that world that we call *strategy*. Study of the process of strategy formulation therefore involves analyses of both discrete and identifiable decision events and of the pathways to and outcomes of those decision events, together with the connections between successive decisions over time.[1]

Strategy formulation is *contextually* based. Strategy may be understood as a flow of events, values, and actions running through a context. Part of the context is the location of strategy in time. Yesterday's strategies will provide some of the pathways to and inputs for today's strategies; and today's strategies will have a concept of the future built into them. The consequences of the implementation of today's strategies will provide part of the context for tomorrow's strategies. But time is but a segment of the context: context also includes the culture of the organization; its environment and the rate of change or stability thereof; the organization's task, structure, and technology; and the leadership and internal political system of the organization.[2] At any point in time, the focus for strategic choices will be environmental and intra-organizational *dilemmas*; and the process of resolving those dilemmas will be influenced by organizational, cultural, task, leadership, and internal political factors.

Author's note: This paper has been written with theory development in mind. It is also very much a personal statement, although the discerning reader will see that I have been influenced by Bachrach and Baratz (1970), Cohen, March, and Olsen (1972), and Easton (1965).

* Originally published in *International Studies of Management and Organisation*, Summer 1977, volume VII, number 2.

This context affects the process of strategy formulation. The implementation of any outcomes of the strategy-formulation process in turn become the new contextual background for resolving future strategic dilemmas. The existing context can provide the enabling conditions for new strategies or the dynamic conservatism to sustain existing definitions of what the organization's core dilemmas are, and therefore to maintain the existing strategies for resolving those dilemmas. Out of the context come the dilemmas or issues that do or do not receive organizational attention. Out of the partial resolution of those dilemmas evolves *strategy*.

The subject matter and analysis of the process of strategy formulation include the following:

(1) identification of the set of dilemmas faced by an organization over time;

(2) analysis of the dilemmas that become a focus for organizational interest *and* of those that are suppressed;

(3) specification of the individuals or subgroupings that seek to define alternative dilemmas as worthy of organizational attention;

(4) study of the *demand* by those individuals and sub-groupings that certain dilemmas be discussed, and of the attempts to mobilize *power* in support of those demands;

(5) specification of the outcomes of these processes of demand-generation and power-mobilization and their implementation as the patterns of thinking about, evaluating, and acting upon the world, i.e. as strategy;

(6) finally, consideration of the relationship between strategy formulation and strategy implementation[3] and of the impact of the implementation of strategy on the formulation of future strategy.

STRATEGY FORMULATION AS A POLITICAL DECISION-MAKING PROCESS

The present assumption is that strategy formulation can be understood as a process of political decision-making. This process will include debate about which dilemmas should receive organizational attention *and* the choice of which alternative courses of action should be adopted to resolve those dilemmas. Strategies emanate from the decision processes about which dilemmas and which modes of resolution will be selected. In these processes of bringing new dilemmas to the organization's attention or holding existing dilemmas at the forefront of attention, certain demands are made by various parties in the organization. The demands may be precisely that certain dilemmas move from the strategic wings to the strategic stage, or that the old dilemmas stay on stage. But the analytical issue is not just what demands are made but how the parties making the demands mobilize power around their various demands.

A demand is politically feasible only if sufficient power can be mobilized and committed to it. The study of the *"political"* in the process of strategy formula-tion therefore involves the isolation of two analytically separate but empirically interdependent processes. The first concerns the demand-generation process, including the sources of the disparate demands in the strategy-formulation process; the second deals with the processes of power mobilization in association

with each demand. In what follows I shall briefly delineate the theoretical
language system, in order to unravel the above two processes; but first let us
consider the issue of why one expects political behaviour to occur in the process
of strategy formulation.

Political processes in organizations evolve at the *group* level from the division
of work in the firm, and at the *individual* level from associated career, reward,
and status systems. Subgroupings develop interests on the basis of specialized
functions and responsibilities, whereas individual careers are bound up with the
maintenance or dissolution of certain types of organizational activity and with
the distribution of organizational resources.

Political behaviour is defined as behaviour by individuals or - in collective
terms - subgroupings within an organization that makes a claim against the
resource-sharing system of the organization. Decisions about the formulation of
new strategy or the maintenance of the old are, to a greater or less degree,
likely to threaten the existing distribution of organizational resources as
represented in salaries, in promotion opportunities, and in control of tasks,
people, information, and new areas of a business.

Bringing a new dilemma to attention and having that dilemma at least partially
resolved may induce sufficient organizational change to unscramble current
distributions of resources. Additional resources may be created and appear to
fall within the jurisdiction of a department or individual who previously had not
been a claimant in a particular area. This department or its principal representative may see this as an opportunity to increase its/his power, status, and
rewards in the organization. Others may see their interests threatened by the
focus on the new dilemma and its resolution, and needs for security or the
maintenance of power may provide the impetus for the release of political energy.
It should be clear, then, that the release of political energy during the
strategy-formulation process is concerned not just with aggrandizement or the
acquisition of power but also with security and thus the maintenance of power.

POLITICS AS THE GENERATION OF DISPARATE DEMANDS

In this view of strategy formulation as a process of political decision-making,
the choices will focus on which dilemmas receive attention and how those dilemmas
are resolved in further choice behaviour. The political decision process can be
understood in part as the resolution of conflicting demands from various interested
individuals and groups. The analytical question therefore centres on why there is
a disparity in demand. Why is individual A or subgrouping B demanding that a
certain dilemma be brought to the decision-making table and other demands, made by
other individuals or groups, removed?

At the stage at which dilemmas are or are not discussed, the disparities may come
from the functional responsibilities and intra-organizational and environmental
search behaviour of different functional units. Different parts of an organization,
because of their interaction patterns and modes of problem solving and information
processing, may see the problems and opportunities of the organization differently.
Indeed, it may be the explicit task of certain development and planning groups to
bring emerging organizational dilemmas to debate. Whether the existing power
structure screens out such attempts at strategic influence is likely to be a key
question. Dilemmas are likely to be pushed forward for discussion and decision
on the basis of firmly held value positions about the organization's future
direction or in the belief that the debate and resolution of those dilemmas will
have a consequential effect on individual or subgroup distributions of activities,
roles, and power.

Once a dilemma receives organizational attention, the process of its partial resolution may also stimulate disparate demands from various individuals and groupings. The extent of the disparities will be conditional on:

1. The *structure* of the decision unit dealing with the dilemma, whether, for example, the structure was relatively complex. One would expect greater disparities in a decision unit that was both vertically and horizontally differentiated than in one that was structurally simple, i.e. composed of people from one vertical level or one horizontal unit.

2. The *complexity* and *uncertainty* of the dilemma. On simple-complex and static-dynamic dimensions, one would expect the greatest room for disparities in the complex-dynamic case, the situation in which the dilemma was both a complex and ever-changing problem.

3. The level of *salience* of the dilemma for various parties and the system repercussions of the dilemma will also affect the propensity of individuals or groups to intervene in the process with demands.

4. The existence of specific and publicly stated *value positions* and of exclusive *styles of language use* and *problem-solving style* will also add to the disparities in the demand-generating process.

5. Additional fuel may be added to the conflicts about demands by the selective and/or sporadic intervention of *external pressure* on the decision unit.

6. Finally, the *history* of relationships, and thus of personal likes and dislikes, among individuals in the decision process will affect the extent of the disparities in demands.[4] It may be a case of "If he's for it, I'm against it!"

POLITICS AS THE MOBILIZATION OF POWER AROUND DEMANDS

If one key aspect of strategy formulation as a political decision process is the process of demand generation, the other linked process concerns the mobilization of power around those demands. Demands are generated and processed in the context of social structures in which individuals are differentially located and have, by implication, access to varying amounts of the resources that are the bases of power. A demand is politically feasible only if sufficient power can be mobilized and committed to its support. Decisional outcomes evolve from the processes of power mobilization attempted by each party in support of its demand. But in the context of strategy formulation, what is power?

A *power relation* is a causal relation between the preferences of an actor regarding an outcome and the outcome itself. Power involves the ability of an actor to produce outcomes consonant with his perceived interests. From this viewpoint, the analysis of organizational power in the context of processes of strategy formulation requires some attempt to map out the distribution and use of certain power resources and the ability of individuals or groups to produce outcomes consonant with their interests. The assumption is that in a competitive demand-generating process, the decisional outcome will not necessarily be a product of the greater worthiness or weight of the issues ranged to uphold one or other demand in the dispute, but may result from the differential awareness of, possession of, control over, and tactical skill in using certain power resources.

The analysis of power therefore does not just entail specifying that because of structural position, an individual or group *possesses* certain power resources. Individuals may indeed possess certain power resources, but not be *aware* they have them. Without awareness, such resources can hardly be marshalled, controlled, and put to use. This view of the resource theory of power suggests that the analysis include data on individual or group: (1) awareness of power resources, (2) possession of power resources, (3) control of power resources, (4) tactical use of power resources – assuming the individual or group possesses the resource and is aware of that possession and can control it.

In previous research (Pettigrew, 1972, 1973, 1975), I have indicated the kinds of power resources that may be crucial in having one's demands met. These include:[5] system-relevant expertise, political access and sensitivity, control over information, assessed stature, and group support.

POLITICS AS THE MANAGEMENT OF MEANING

Earlier in this paper I suggested that one way to analyze strategy formulation as a political decision-making process was to focus on processes of demand-generation and power-mobilization. The bare outlines of such analyses have been presented above. But there is also the issue of the connections between the demands people make in the strategy-formulation process and their capacity to mobilize power for those demands. In presenting a demand that a dilemma be considered for discussion or that it be resolved in a certain way, one usually encounters a question about that demand's legitimacy in its particular institutional context. There is clearly a point at which any particular demand may be unsupportable, and the issue becomes not one of mobilizing power for the pre-existing demand, but determining how the existing demand can be modified so that its power requirement can be assembled.

In considering *what* demand is presented and *how* it is presented and later modified, issues of *legitimacy* are likely to be crucial. Legitimacy is a highly diffuse and movable resource, but one whose significance and unequal distribution can structure decisional outcomes. Politics concerns the creation of legitimacy for certain ideas, values, and demands – not just action performed as a result of previously acquired legitimacy. The management of meaning refers to a process of symbol construction and value use designed both to create legitimacy for one's own demands and to "delegitimize" the demands of opponents in a political decision-making process. Therefore, a fundamental factor in the life history of a demand in a strategy-formulation process will be the answer to the question: "What does that demand *symbolize*, what does it *mean* to the various interested parties in the process?"

Key concepts for analyzing this process of the management of meaning are symbolism, language, belief, and myth.[6] Language is not just a means of expressing thoughts, categories, and concepts: it is also a vehicle for achieving practical effects. Language is a carrier not only of information but also of meanings. Presentation of a demand involves the choice of language to describe it and the stylistics of language use. Stylistics may include the use of dialectic forms of presentation and the use of metaphors and myths – the latter being devices for simplifying and giving meaning to complex issues that evoke concern. Myths serve as ways of legitimizing the present (demands) in terms of a perhaps glorious past, of reconciling apparent dilemmas, and of explaining away the discrepancies that may exist between what is happening and what ought to be happening. As such, myths provide part of the social cement that links old strategies with new strategies and that justifies the very existence of the new strategy.

But the temporal connecting role of language, beliefs, and myths in linking old strategy and new strategy takes us back to the opening statement that strategy formulation is a continuous process. Part of politics as the management of meaning is to legitimize after the fact a strategy that has been implicitly formulated through action yet never placed before the organization as a dilemma for consideration. Much of what is known in organizations as strategy is the reconstruction and relabelling of old ways of thinking about, evaluating, and acting upon the world. In this way, through time, organizations deal with their members' and their environment's needs for both continuity and change.

NOTES

1. See A. Pettigrew (1973) for such a time-based analysis.

2. Culture includes the language and other symbolic systems of the organization, including the organization's ideology, beliefs, rituals, and myths. See A. Pettigrew (1976) *The Creation of Organisational Cultures*, paper presented to the Joint EIASM-Dansk Management Centre research seminar "Entrepreneurs and the Process of Institution-Building", Copenhagen, 18-20 May, 1976.

3. One treatment of the issue of implementation of strategy is provided by Mumford and Pettigrew (1975).

4. See Pettigrew (1973) for detailed empirical examples from a research study of these six factors.

5. See Pettigrew (1973) for detailed definitions of these concepts and empirical examples.

6. See Pettigrew (1976) (note 2 above) for a more extended theoretical discussion of these concepts and their relevance to entrepreneur-follower relationships in organizations.

REFERENCES

Bachrach, P. and Baratz, M.S. (1970) *Power and Poverty: Theory and Practice*, New York: Oxford University Press.
Cohen, M.D., March, J.G. and Olsen, J.P. (1972) "A Garbage-can Model of Organizational Choice", *Administrative Science Quarterly*, 17, 1-25.
Easton, D. (1965) *A Systems Analysis of Political Life*, New York: Wiley.
Mumford, E. and Pettigrew, A. (1975) *Implementing Strategic Decisions*, London: Longman.
Pettigrew, A. (1972) "Information Control as a Power Resource", *Sociology*, 6(2), 187-204.
Pettigrew, A. (1973) *The Politics of Organisational Decision-Making*, London: Tavistock.
Pettigrew, A. (1975) "Towards a Political Theory of Organisational Intervention", *Human Relations*, 28(3), 191-208.

Part 3

PLANNING AND INNOVATION

Chapter 7, by Bernard Taylor, surveys recent thinking and practice in corporate development. It introduces the modern use of life cycle theory, explains the controversial experience curve concept, and contrasts a number of approaches to top level corporate strategic analysis.

Many of the approaches to strategic portfolio analysis, considered by many to be essential to orderly planning for innovation in modern complex companies, are of a proprietary nature. Enough information is provided to demonstrate their uses, but often insufficient data is given on how to develop them.

The detailed descriptions by John Robinson and his colleagues from Shell Chemicals which appear in Chapter 8 are therefore a welcome supplement on how to develop a portfolio analysis technique. In this case it is the Directional Policy Matrix, initiated within Shell Chemicals, and offering a much more sophisticated approach than that in some at least of the proprietary packages.

In Chapter 9 David Hussey explains how the Directional Policy Matrix was applied in three large organisations and adds a third dimension to give a view of risk from environmental changes.

Chapter 7

MANAGING THE PROCESS OF
CORPORATE DEVELOPMENT*
Bernard Taylor

1. THE PROBLEM OF REGENERATION

These days you can hardly pick up a newspaper without being reminded that British
industry is in decline. The regeneration of British industry is a central subject
for national debate and the remedies proposed include:

> (1) the injection of public money into ailing industries
>   and bankrupt companies and the use of the National
>   Enterprise Board to rationalize and restructure
>   fragmented industries;
> (2) the introduction of industrial democracy by the
>   appointment of employee directors, the establishment
>   of works councils and greater worker participation on
>   the shop floor;
> (3) improved collaboration between public servants, business
>   leaders and trade union officials through 'planning
>   agreements' between the government and large companies
>   and through tripartite discussions about whole industries
>   in National Economic Development Committees.

The implication seems to be that British industry has declined because:

> (1) management has not invested enough money in new plant
>   and equipment;
> (2) management has not been able to motivate the work force
>   and therefore productivity is low and we have a poor
>   industrial relations record;
> (3) government, management and unions are not working
>   together and planning together to make British industry
>   more competitive.

It is difficult to quarrel with these suggestions. British industry has invested
too little in new equipment, manufacturing productivity is low in Britain
compared with other developed countries, and Britain has had a record of poor

---

* Originally published in *Long Range Planning*, June 1976. c B Taylor (1976)

industrial relations. Also government, industry and unions do not seem to
collaborate in Britain as well as they do in some other industrialized countries.

Industrial Development

But is this the way companies grow and businesses are built? Through government
subsidies, debates in Works Councils and industrial planning committees? In fact
how do businesses grow and prosper? What are the key factors which enable one
company to survive and make good profits when another, in the same industry and
in a similar society becomes a dependent of the state?

What is the role of the entrepreneur? Does he have a place in modern business,
or must he be replaced by the company bureaucrat working through committees?

What is the scope for creativity - new products, new processes, new personnel
policies, new marketing ideas and how can we foster innovation in large
monopolistic concerns?

Are we right to see the salvation of British business in the creation of larger
and larger enterprises with bigger, more powerful, union bosses and more
government involvement?

To produce sensible policies for the development of individual companies and
whole industries we need to have an understanding of how businesses rise and
fall. Is there a life-cycle and a life-cycle for each stage in the cycle? Are
there times when formal planning is vital and other times when it is destructive?
Are there occasions in the history of a business when building a larger operating
unit is the only way to survive and other situations where concentration into
large units could destroy the very quality and service on which the business is
based? Is there a time for employee participation and another time for
charismatic leadership? Our instincts say there must be different strategies
for different situations.

In this chapter I would like to summarize recent thinking and practice about
Corporate Development and to offer a basis for policy-making in the individual
business and at national level, and it certainly is a shade more sophisticated
than the general panaceas which are the subject of national debate at present.

2.   THE CORPORATE LIFE-CYCLE

The Product Life-Cycle

An assumption which is fundamental to modern business thinking is the belief
that products and technologies, though inanimate, have a 'life'. They are
introduced, they grow, they reach a saturation level and then they fall out of
favour or are replaced by other products. A technology is said to have a
'switch-over point', when the new technology takes over from the established
technology. A range of products, or an individual brand may be taken off the
market when it reaches a minimum level of distribution or when servicing becomes
too expensive. Figures 7.1 - 7.3 give a number of real-life examples of the
product life-cycle.

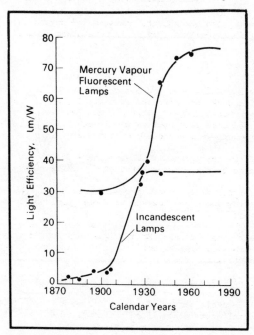

Fig. 7.1 Technological Obsolescence - Technical Capability
          Trends.
          Source: Gordon Wills *et al.*, *Technological
          Forecasting & Corporate Strategy*, p.5, Crosby
          Lockwood, London (1969).

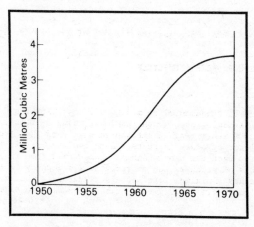

Fig. 7.2 The Product Life-Cycle - Ready-Mix Concrete,
          Holland (1950-1970).

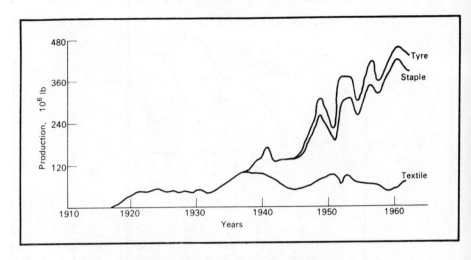

Fig. 7.3 The Product Life-Cycle - Viscose Rayon.

Source: Quoted by Peter Ward in *The Dynamics of Planning*, p.54, Pergamon Press, Oxford (1970)

Market Segments

Another basic concept is that large markets are not usually homogeneous but should be viewed as a collection of smaller markets. In fact each customer's needs may be quite individual. More commonly, markets may be divided into sections or segments according to customer usage and attitude, the distribution channels used, or the geographical location. Also as countries and regions vary in sophistication, products may become obsolete in one market and still be appropriate in a less developed or less affluent area. Figure 7.4 shows the way that black-and-white television sets have been introduced in different countries - a sequence of product life-cycles, or rather a similar product life-cycle occurring at different times in different markets.

Stages of Corporate Development

Harvard Business School's studies of the administration of large industrial enterprises in the U.S.A. and Western Europe suggest that companies, too, tend to pass through phases of growth.

    (1) The owner-entrepreneur with a single product and an informal organization acts as the pioneer.

    (2) If the sales of his product grow, he eventually has to delegate control to departmental managers and he usually divides his business by functions, e.g. engineering, production, sales and service.

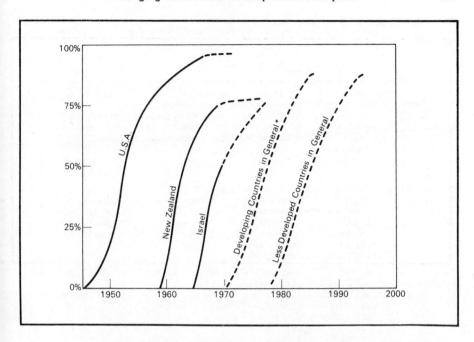

Fig. 7.4   The Product Life-Cycle in Different Markets.
           Percentage of Households with Television Sets*

* Actual figures for the years 1946-1970 (U.S.A., New
Zealand and Israel).   Projections are estimated.
Z.Z. Shipchandlar, Diffusion Patterns of Consumer Durables
in International Markets, University of Indiana, Fort Wayne.
Categories relate to average GNP *per capita* (industrialized
$3700, Developing Countries £1500, Less Developed Countries
$160).

(3)   Often the first product becomes obsolete and others
      are added; the company offers a series of related
      products and it is normal at this stage for the
      enterprise to adopt a divisionized organization with
      a number of semi-autonomous businesses based on
      different products or product groups.

(4)   Later, businesses may be added which are not connected
      with the original technologies or markets; at this
      point it may seem more appropriate for the central
      management to work through an industrial holding
      company regarding the businesses largely as investments.

Table 7.1 shows one version of the theory of corporate development by Malcolm
Salter, Figure 7.5 illustrates the evolution of the organization structure through

different stages and Figures 7.6 - 7.8 illustrate the progress of diversification and divisionalisation in large manufacturing companies in the U.S.A. and in Britain.

TABLE 7.1 Stages of Corporate Development

	Stage I	Stage II	Stage III	Stage IV
Structure of Operating Units	Single unit managed by a sole proprietor	Single unit managed by a team	Several regional units reporting to a corporate HQ each with structure I or II	Several semi-autonomous units reporting to corporate HQ each with structure I, II or III
Product-Market Relationships	Small scale, single line of related products, 1 market, 1 distribution channel	Large scale, single line of related products, 1 market, 1 distribution channel	Each region produces same product line, single market, multiple channels	Each unit produces different product line for separate markets, multiple channels
Top Management	One man operation, very little task differentiation	Responsible for single functions e.g. production, sales, finance	Regional units performing several functions	Product divisions performing all major functions
Quantitative Measures of Performance	Very few, personalized, not based on formal criteria	Operating budgets for each function	Operating budget, return on sales, ROI	Return on sales. Return on investment

Adapted from Malcolm S. Salter, Management Appraisal and Reward Systems, *Journal of Business Policy*, 1(4), 44 (1971).

Phases of International Expansion

Parallel investigations by other Harvard researchers suggest that there are characteristic stages of development associated with international expansion:

(1) initially the export business is a small proportion of the total and is handled through an international department or division;

(2) as the export business grows a new organization is needed:

- if there is a simple product line and many markets the tendency is to set up geographic divisions or national companies;
- if there are a number of different products and technology is complex, world-wide product divisions may seem to be more appropriate;

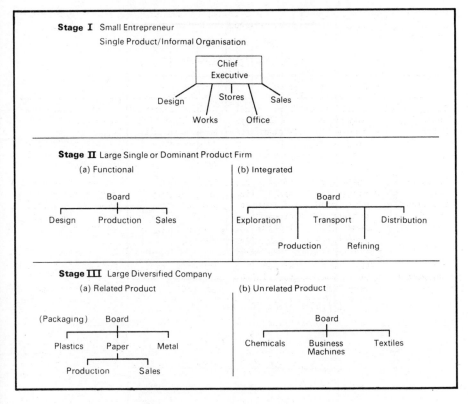

Fig. 7.5 Stages of corporate development

Source: D.F. Channon, *The Strategy & Structure of British Enterprise*, chapter 1, London (1973)

    (3) further growth will probably result in a matrix or
         'grid' organization with product divisions, geographi-
         cal units, and functional groups.

Figure 7.9 illustrates the phases of growth which the research suggests that a business typically goes through as it expands geographically.

3. DEVISING A CORPORATE STRATEGY

A central tenet of teaching and research in Business Policy over the past decade has been that, to avoid becoming victims of technological obsolescence and changing markets, companies should have a Corporate Strategy – defined by Igor Ansoff as 'the concept of the firm's business – which provides a unifying theme for all its activities', to provide a basis for strategies in the functional areas, to act as a guide for operational planning, and to guide the choice of products and markets and the types of businesses they enter.

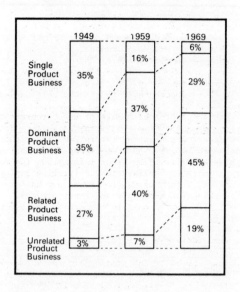

Fig. 7.6   Product diversification (U.S.A.)

Source: R.P. Rumelt, *Strategy, Structure & Economic Performance*, Harvard
University (1974)

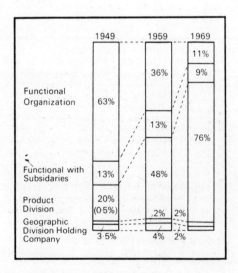

Fig. 7.7   Formation of product divisions (U.S.A.)

Source: R.P. Rumelt, *Strategy, Structure & Economic Performance*, Harvard
University (1974).

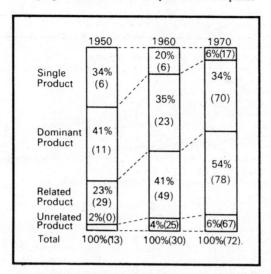

Fig. 7.8 Diversification and multidivisional structures (U.K.)
(Figures in brackets refer to the percentage of
multi-divisional structures in each category)

Source: Adapted from a table in D.R. Channon, *The Strategy & Structure of British Enterprise*, p.67, Macmillan, London (1973)

In attempting to put this idea into effect, senior managers and planners are invited to ask a number of fundamental questions such as:

   (1) What are the objectives to be achieved and how should
        we define the scope of the business?

   (2) What limits are set on these objectives by our personal
        values and social responsibilities?

   (3) On which strengths can we build, and what are the
        weaknesses which need to be compensated for?

   (4) What opportunities are to be taken advantage of and
        what threats should be avoided?

   (5) What are the main decisions to be taken and to what
        major courses of action must we commit ourselves?

   (6) What resources will be required and where will these
        resources come from?

   (7) What are the risks in this strategy and what contin-
        gency plans are required?

In practice, business strategies seem to evolve as the business develops. The original entrepreneur starts with a simple concept of the business. As the business grows he has to share it with others, and it becomes modified to suit

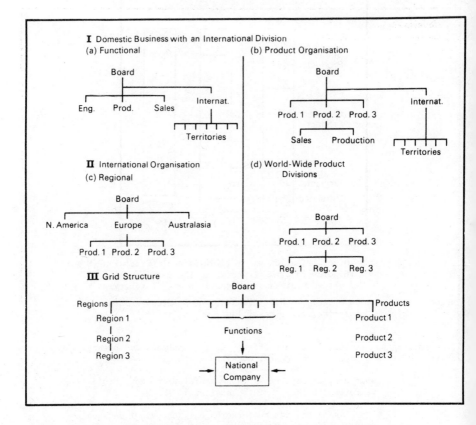

Fig. 7.9 Developing the international business organization

Source: Adapted from John Stopford and Lewis Wells, *Managing the Multinational Enterprise*, Longman, London (1973).

changing conditions. What was once one man's inspiration, becomes a set of flexible guidelines to be applied variously in different fields of operation.

Often the business out-grows its original strategy but this concept of the business is assiduously imposed as 'company policy' or 'the way we do things around here', until a market failure, competitive action or government intervention cause a crisis. Frequently the ruling coalition has to be replaced before a new strategy can be evolved.

In recent years, academics and consultants have applied considerable efforts to selling the idea that strategies should be written down and regularly reviewed as part of a Corporate Planning process. Figure 7.10 describes a typical procedure for strategy-making and planning. Table 7.2 lists the main elements in the Corporate Planning process and Figure 7.11 and Table 7.3 indicate the kind of annual cycle which companies frequently establish in an effort to engage top

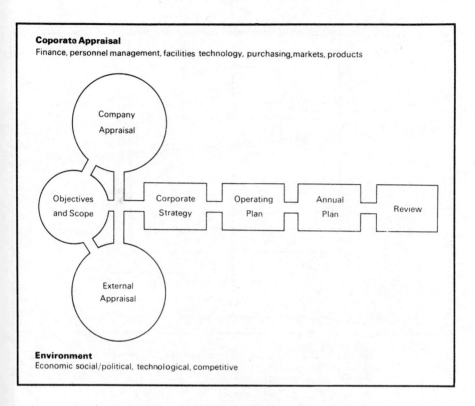

Fig. 7.10 Basic steps in corporate planning

TABLE 7.2 Essential Elements of Corporate Planning

---

1. Specific objectives (company, division, function)
2. Environmental Appraisal
3. Company Appraisal
4. Assumptions and Forecasts
5. Alternative Strategies
6. Integrated Plan
7. Action Programmes
8. Budgets
9. Review

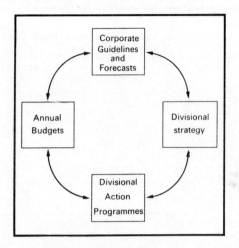

Fig. 7.11   The corporate planning cycle

TABLE 7.3   The Corporate Planning Cycle

   I. Divisional Strategy
       Corporate and Divisional Executives discuss Key
       Strategy Issues, tentative allocation of resources
       and new corporate projects

  II. Divisional Action Programmes
       Divisional and departmental executives discuss
       alternative programmes, new divisional projects
       and resources required

 III. Divisional Budgets
       Departmental staff and divisional staff discuss
       detailed 5-year and annual budgets

---

management, central staff specialists, and the general managers of product
divisions and national subsidiaries in regular discussions about strategies and
plans.

Increasingly, the dialogue occurs in three stages:

   (1) a discussion about the forecasts, assumptions and the
        broad policy guidelines on which the company's plan
        will be based;

   (2) an examination of the key issues involved in the
        divisional development plan, including the new
        facilities to be built, new programmes for market
        development, new business ventures, acquisitions,
        divestments and closures;

(3) a consideration of the operating plan and budget for
     the year ahead.

The idea of having an explicit corporate strategy seems to be widely accepted but
not so generally implemented. In practice, Boards of Directors find it difficult
to agree on a broad strategy - except in the most general terms. Chief executives
often prefer, for their own political reasons, not to discuss alternative
strategies with other executives, and they are even less forthcoming in the
presence of government officials and trade union leaders. Also, as numerous
studies have revealed, senior managers are usually too busy to formulate a comprehensive strategy; they are much more likely to take decisions in a piecemeal
way as important issues arise. This is not to say that they are necessarily
unaware of the longer-term implications of the commitments they are making. They
may simply feel that formalizing the process of analysis and decision-making is
likely to introduce a spurious sense of science and rationality into what is a
fundamentally intuitive and entrepreneurial process.

4. STRATEGIES FOR GROWTH

A good deal of the early literature on Corporate Development was concerned with
helping companies which were threatened with obsolescence to plan their way into
new businesses. As the Harvard research has shown, the 1960s were a time when
large numbers of companies recognized that they had limited prospects for growth
in their present businesses and they began to expand into new products, new
markets - including overseas markets and entirely new businesses outside their
usual areas of activity.

Igor Ansoff's analysis of alternative directions for growth served to emphasize
the importance of expansion and diversification (see Table 7.4).

TABLE 7.4 Directions for Growth

Mission	Product	
	Present	New
Present	Market penetration	Product development
New	Market development	Diversification

H. Igor Ansoff, *Corporate Strategy*, p.109, McGraw-Hill, New York (1965).

Figure 7.12 shows the Gap Analysis approach made popular by Stanford Research
Institute. Management is invited:

(1) to set an objective, e.g. in terms of sales revenue,
     return on investment, or cash flow;

(2) to forecast the 'momentum line', i.e. the level of
     achievement to be expected assuming no new initiatives;

(3) to plan to 'fill the gap' between the objective and
     the momentum line with projects for:

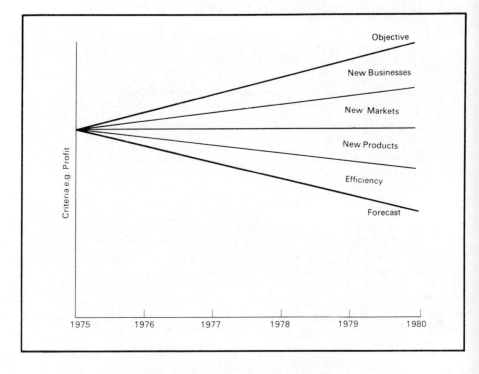

Fig. 7.12 Directions for growth - gap analysis

- *increasing efficiency*, e.g. by raising the level of
  performance in the present business up to the best
  in the industry, through reducing costs, increasing
  prices, increasing market share, etc.;

- *expansion*, e.g. through the introduction of new
  products, new applications of present products, and
  entry into new markets, including export markets;

- *diversification*, e.g. through internal research and
  development, by licensing other companies' inventions,
  by buying up customers, suppliers or competitors, or
  through acquiring companies in quite unrelated fields.

Stanford Research Institute also proposes that the Corporate Plan should contain
two types of Strategic Plans: Product-Line Strategic Plans for the present
businesses, and Corporate Development Plans designed to fill the planning gap
with new projects, ideas for mergers and diversifications etc.

In many companies, even in the affluent sixties, the problem of growth was not so
much a shortage of projects and ideas but lack of cash for investment. The
planners and consultants at this point set about analysing the negative gap, i.e.

possible ways of increasing funds. This would start with a forecast of cash flow
from the present business compared with the cash which might be required for new
projects. One might then examine the possibility of reducing cash tied up in
stocks and debtors, selling off certain assets, reducing dividends, obtaining
loans, issuing more shares etc. Figure 7.13 illustrates the idea of a negative
gap analysis.

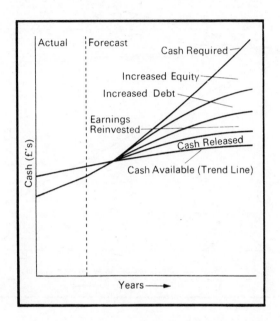

Fig. 7.13   Analysis of cash available for new investments

The Experience Curve

In more recent years, another American consultancy organization, the Boston
Consulting Group, has emphasized the need for companies to 'invest in growth and
cost reduction' in existing businesses which have a growth potential.

The argument is based on the assertion that as industries grow, and experience
increases, companies are able to benefit from economies of scale through bulk
purchasing, mass production high volume distribution, mass marketing, etc., and
so costs may be reduced by as much as 20-30 per cent every time the cumulative
sales volume doubles.

This gives substantial competitive advantages to the market leader in an industry
and enables the dominant company to reduce its prices and at the same time make
good profits.

Some major Japanese industries seem to have followed a strategy of 'market
penetration' and they have obtained a commanding position in world markets for
steel, ships, motor cars, motor cycles, radios, television, cameras, etc.

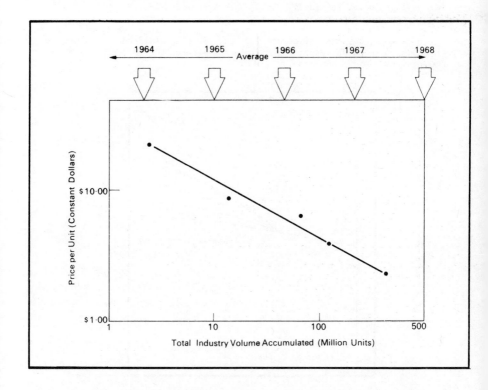

Fig. 7.14 The Experience Curve - integrated circuits

Prices decline as volume and experience accumulates (log-log scale shows a
constant relationship).
Source: The Boston Consulting Group, *Perspectives and Experience*, p.75, Boston
        (1972). Electronics Industry Association data.

Figures 7.14 - 7.16 which are based on Boston Consulting Group analyses, show the
dramatic effects that rising industry volumes have had on prices of integrated
circuits, gas cookers and black and white television sets.

It is only fair to say that the Experience Curve is a subject of much controversy.
Those who contest the theory argue that:

       (1)   There is only limited evidence that expanding volume
            in an industry or in an individual firm can produce
            these dramatic falls in total costs and there are
            certainly areas where costs per unit of volume seem
            to rise because of large scale working, especially in
            labour intensive operations where turnover and
            absenteeism, and industrial stoppages may increase.

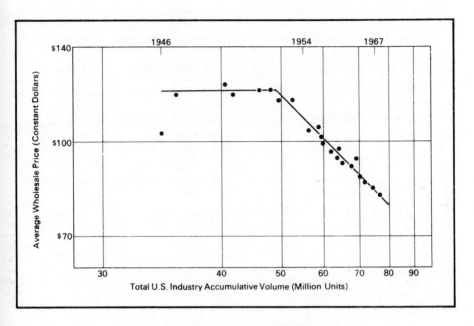

Fig. 7.15 The Experience Curve – gas cookers

Source: The Boston Consulting Group, *Perspectives and Experience*, p.94, Boston
(1972). Electronics Industry Association data.

(2) Where companies commit themselves to long runs and
     high volumes of standard products – as Henry Ford did
     with his Model 'T' – the organization may lose its
     flexibility and the firm may become vulnerable to a
     competitor which, like General Motors in the 1920s,
     chose to compete not on price but on product perfor-
     mance.

(3) Even if the Experience Curve does apply, there is no
     guarantee that management will be able to reduce costs
     in line with the curve. We have numerous examples in
     Britain of companies which have grown in size and
     where management have not been able to reap the profits
     from higher volumes.

(4) The Experience Curve theory invites companies to commit
     more and more funds to a few large products in limited
     market areas. This concentration may increase the risk
     to the business in the case of a change in technology
     or market. The heavy commitment of the Japanese ship-
     builders to large oil tankers and their huge over-
     capacity after the energy crisis illustrates the danger
     of over-specialization.

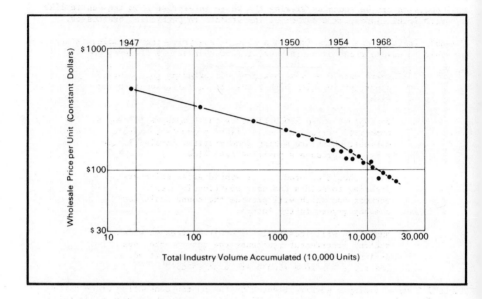

Fig. 7.16   The Experience Curve - television receivers (monochrome)

Source: The Boston Consulting Group, *Perspectives and Experience*, p.92, Boston
(1972).   Electronics Industry Association data.

(5)   The theory assumes a competitive market, whereas in
many markets prices are controlled by monopolies, by
price controls and by government intervention.

These arguments do not, of course, invalidate the theory, which has many adherents
particularly in high technology industries, but they do emphasize the need for
care in applying the concept, e.g. in defining the product, the market segment,
and the stage in the life-cycle, and in ensuring that management have the capacity
to realize the potential cost savings, and at the same time maintain a high rate
of product innovation.

5.   THE BUSINESS AS A PORTFOLIO OF INVESTMENTS

The companies which expanded and diversified in the 1960s and early 1970s are now
trying to sort out the businesses which were created or acquired into some kind
of sensible pattern.   The usual approach is to create various groups or subsidiary
companies around which the various activities can be collected.   The next stage
is to centralize those operations which seem likely to benefit from economies of
scale and to decentralize those functions where transportation and distribution
costs or customer service are an important factor.   Then an attempt has to be
made to find a reasonable method for allocating resources, i.e. management effort,
skilled personnel, and scarce materials, as well as capital for investment.

Priorities must be set and decisions must be made about acquisitions and mergers, the allocation of capital, the closure of unprofitable business etc. A basis for this decision can be found by viewing the whole enterprise from the centre like a portfolio of shares, as a number of investments in particular businesses.

Valuable insights can emerge from this kind of analysis. For example, it seems sensible to have a range of businesses at different stages of development:

-   there should be some new projects offering good profit opportunities with high risks, and a large appetite for cash;

-   to support these new businesses the company will need a number of solid, well-established products in mature markets, which are making good profits, involve little risk, and produce a positive cash flow;

-   there should be products or subsidiaries which are fighting to hold a dominant position in growth markets and which will provide the sound basis for company growth in the future;

-   and there will inevitably be other businesses which are due for 'retirement', because the total market has declined, the products have become uncompetitive, or the risks for some reason are unacceptable.

Table 7.5 shows a simple matrix produced by the Boston Consulting Group which is commonly used as a starting point for discussions about the 'product portfolio'.

TABLE 7.5   Portfolio Management

Industry Growth	Market Share	
	High	Low
High	Strong growth businesses	Weak businesses with potential
Low	Strong businesses in stable or declining markets	Weak businesses in stable or declining markets

Attributed to Boston Consulting Group.

Another approach is to balance the portfolio of investments by type of industry. Management may be worried about the fact that their basic business is too cyclical. This could mean that earnings are variable and the share price is unstable. A number of companies finding that their traditional businesses were too closely tied to the capital investment cycle - or to government purchasing, have diversified into industries which have a more stable pattern of demand or a different cycle of trade. Tube Investments have stabilized their pattern of earnings by expanding into consumer markets such as bicycles and cookers. Rockwell International have combined an aerospace business, which is a cyclical business heavily dependent on U.S. defence policy, with electronics, automobile

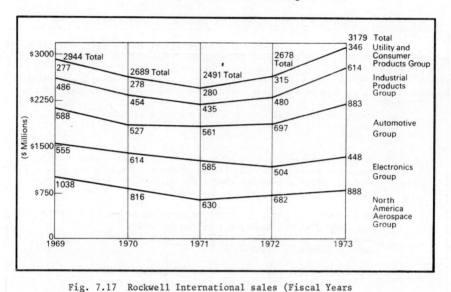

Fig. 7.17   Rockwell International sales (Fiscal Years
1969-1973, to 30 September)

Source: W.F. Rockwell, Jr., Management of Multi-industry Business, *Journal of General Management,* Spring (1975).

components, printing and textile equipment and household appliances. Figure 7.17 shows how the demand cycles experienced by the different marketing groups have, to a large degree, cancelled each other out with consequent improvement in stability for the whole enterprise.

Geographical diversification is another way of achieving a spread of risk and opportunity. Here again, the objective is not to be too dependent on one national or regional market, or on one type of market.

The advantage of a geographical spread in producing a steady stream of earnings is evident with companies such as Metal Box. Profits from Britain are stable but unexciting; on the other hand overseas markets yield higher profits but are subject to higher risks from wars, expropriation etc. UAC International (formerly the United Africa Company) which had a dominant position in West African trade, and Fiat which has two-thirds of the Italian automobile market, are typical examples of companies which have seen a clear need to expand geographically to 'diversify their portfolio'.

For the purpose of analysis, it is helpful to display the pattern of a company's business in diagrammatic form. Figure 7.18 is an example of a two-way matrix of products and national markets, as used by a firm based in Scandinavia. Figure 7.19 shows a three-dimensional matrix used by a number of multi-national companies as a means of displaying the shape of their operations. Both matrices provide a useful basis for discussion between central staff and divisional management. For example, they might ask: 'Why is it that we can achieve a 50 per cent share of the market in Product C in Norway when in Sweden our share is less than 1 per cent?' or 'We sell Product A to the textile industry in Germany. Why don't we sell it for the same applications in France or Britain?'

Product \ Market	Italy	France	Finland	Denmark	Sweden	Norway	W. Germany	England	Holland	Rest of Europe	Other Exports
A	0	0	0	0	1	1	1	1	1	0	0
B	1	0	0	2	3	1	3	1	0	0	0
C	0	0	0	0	0	4	1	0	0	0	0
D	1	3	0	1	4	1	0	0	0	0	0
E	0	0	1	3	3	1	1	1	0	1	0
F	1	0	0	3	4	1	0	0	0	0	0
G	0	0	3	4	0	0	1	1	1	1	0
H	0	0	1	3	0	1	1	1	1	0	1
I	0	0	0	3	0	3	3	0	0	0	0

Fig. 7.18 A European company's territory – an analysis by
products and markets.*
*Figures represent market shares, e.g. 0 = up to 1 per cent, 1 = 1 to 10 per cent,
2 = 10 to 25 per cent, 3 = 25 to 50 per cent, 4 = 50 per cent or over.

Source: E. Rhenman, Organisation Theory for Long Range Planning, p.123, Wiley.
London (1973).

These kind of questions are likely to lead to discussions about the allocation
of resources by product and by region. In general one expects that there will be
a correlation between the business potential and the resources provided.
Sometimes, however, certain markets, e.g. overseas markets, do not receive an
appropriate level of support. Table 7.6, from a recent survey of British
exporting practice, shows the extent to which some companies have neglected the
growing sales potential of overseas markets.

The idea of the business as a portfolio of investments is a helpful analogy to
use in allocating resources but of course businesses do not consist merely of
money which may be transferred at will from one business to another. They

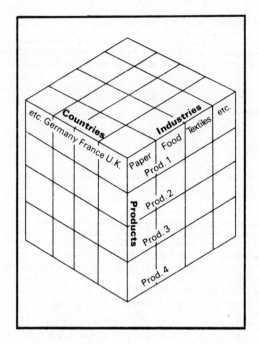

Fig. 7.19   Analysing the pattern of business - an interim
            Company.

TABLE 7.6   British Salesmen in Overseas Markets - 1975*

Companies chosen at random.

| | No. of Salesmen | | Overseas Sales | |
Company	Home	Export	% of Total Sales	Value £m
Textiles	31	1	55	1.25
Light Engineering	4	1	80	7.20
Electrical	70	1	60	3.00
Chemicals	10	6	58	6.00
Pharmaceuticals	60	8	57	5.10
Earthenware	30	20	62	14.00
Publishing	14	3	60	6.60
Engineering Tools	22	1	60	7.20
Light Engineering	30	3	62	6.80
Electrical	27	1	70	57.40
				114.55

* *Concentration on Key Markets, A Development Plan for Exports*, p.30, ITI Research
  (1975).

involve managers and workers with very specific knowledge, skills and attitudes, investments in raw material reserves, property and equipment which are useful in certain businesses but not in others, long-standing commitments to suppliers, customers' local communities and public bodies. It is natural therefore that management should search for more comprehensive and more realistic forms of analysis.

The Business Screen

Figure 1.8 in Chapter 1 showed one of a number of analyses used by General Electric (U.S.A.) in deciding on the allocation of resources between different businesses. Other elements discussed include risk and sensitivity to changes in assumptions about the future state of the environment. In this chart, however, attention centres on an attempt to evaluate and rank each business in relation to both industry attractiveness and business strengths, in terms of market size and growth, competition, profitability, technical and other factors. The matrix is used to enable division general managers to develop a dialogue first with the corporate planning group and then with top management about key strategic decisions. The business plans are checked against the priorities for the business as a whole, e.g. to develop world-wide strength in certain specified 'businesses of the future'. The businesses' plans are also considered against their previous track record as shown in a Quality of Earnings matrix which ranks the estimates from hard to soft. In the Business Screen, businesses are divided broadly into three groups. Businesses in the 'green' category are given the highest priority for investment. These include:

- businesses with high market shares or the possibility
  of achieving market dominance in growing industries;

- businesses which are in areas which the corporation
  regards as its present or future 'prime territory';

- ventures which offer very high earnings or cash returns
  in the short-term.

Businesses in the 'yellow' area are often stable or declining and the policy is to be very selective when making further investments in them. Businesses falling into the 'red' area are those which management is worried about - because of poor earnings, high risks, vulnerability to competition, etc. The guideline for these activities is to reduce investments and possibly to sell off the assets or the whole business.

Profit Impact of Market Strategy

Another strategic approach, which came originally from General Electric, is known as PIMS - Profit Impact of Market Strategy. This is now marketed as a research programme. The programme at present includes 300 items of data taken from 700 businesses in different industries (mainly in the U.S.A.) over a 3-5 year period. And the intention of the programme is to find the answers to two basic questions:

(1) what factors influence profitability, i.e. return on
     investment in a business, and by how much?

(2) how does the return on investment change in response
     to new policies and trends in the environment?

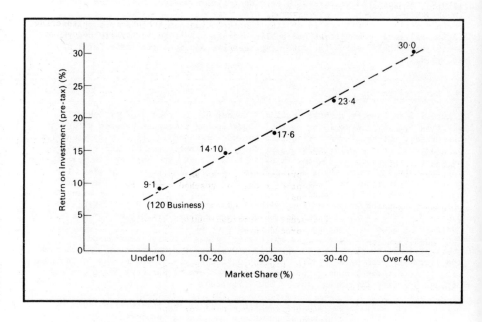

Fig. 7.20 Market share and return on investment.
Study of 600 U.S. businesses 1970-1972.
Source: The Strategic Planning Centre, Manchester Business
School.

These analyses, like the Experience Curve studies, indicate that there is a
strong relationship between a product's market share and its return on investment.
Figure 7.20 displays the results of an investigation based on 600 U.S. businesses
over the period 1970-1972. Products with under 10 per cent market share averaged
9 per cent return on investment, whereas those with over 40 per cent share
produced a 30 per cent return on investment.

Other factors having a critical effect on return on investment are:

-   *market share compared with competition* - especially in
    the 'mature' phase of a business, and particularly with
    consumer durables and capital goods;

-   *product quality compared with competition* (a subjective
    judgment); high quality products and services are the
    most profitable and usually achieve a dominant market
    position;

-   *'investment intensity'*, i.e. a high ratio of investment
    to sales tends to depress the return on investment. As
    investment intensity rises, profitability declines;

- *high marketing expenditures* seem to be harmful to profits
  when the product quality is low, and disastrous when
  combined with high levels of capital investment.

Cash flow analyses confirm the need to balance the product portfolio as Boston
Consulting Group suggest. Products with a high market share relative to
competition produce large positive cash flows and products in rapidly growing
markets are big users of cash - particularly in capital intensive businesses.

On reflection, the initial results from these computer analyses are not
surprising - and up to now the results are based almost entirely on businesses
in the U.S.A. An important benefit of the system, however, is that it encourages
management to ask what are the critical factors affecting profitability in their
different businesses - product quality, research into new products, the level of
capital investment, market share, the level of marketing expenditure, and so on.

6. A WIDER VIEW OF STRATEGY

The Stakeholder Approach

Much of the writing on strategy during the 1960s by Igor Ansoff, Peter Drucker
and Theodore Levitt, emphasized the need for a marketing orientation to correct
the traditional focus on production and productivity which largely ignored the
changing needs of the customer.

A viewpoint more typical of the 1970s is expressed in the 'Stakeholder Approach'
(see Figure 7.21).

Fig. 7.21 The stakeholder analysis
Source: Stanford Research Institute.

The stakeholder theory suggests that a firm has obligations not only to shareholders and customers but to all the individuals and organizations with which it
has transactions and relationships:

    (1)   suppliers of raw materials, components and services;

    (2)   employees, the leaders of trade unions and professional
           associations;

    (3)   private shareholders, institutional investors and
           banks;

    (4)   private and industrial customers;

    (5)   distributors, agents, wholesalers and retailers;

    (6)   competitors and collaborators in the same industry,
           and officials of industrial and trade associations;

    (7)   public servants in local and national government, and

    (8)   members of the communities in which the company's
           offices and factories are located.

This modern view then is that management cannot afford to focus their attention
on satisfying the needs of the customers, or meeting the demands of the shareholders, whilst ignoring the claims of other powerful groups. In practice it is
usually necessary at any one time to give priority to the needs of one interest
or another – depending on the problems of the business. There may be a shortage
of raw materials, labour problems, or a need to raise capital. But a prudent
management team is aware that all of the stakeholders have the power to damage or
help the business. They are therefore continually monitoring and promoting these
stakeholder relationships – often using marketing research and other marketing
techniques which were initially developed for use in selling products, to market
the company and its policies to employees, shareholders, local communities,
suppliers and governments (see Figure 7.22).

In effect, management is recognizing that Corporate Strategy is concerned not
simply with producing a return on the shareholders' capital and delivering
satisfactory products to customers, but also achieving social acceptance in the
community, ensuring a continuing and uninterrupted supply of key raw materials
and components, influencing government policies, and of course ensuring that the
work force and the whole management team are motivated and committed to the
company and its policies.

The 'stakeholder approach' suggests that management should be searching for a set
of policies for research, production, marketing, finance, personnel and 'public
affairs' which are compatible with each other and which manage to satisfy the
minimum requirements of the stakeholder groups, giving priority to those interests
which, for various reasons, seem to merit more attention than the rest. Some
firms seem to manage this – Marks and Spencers and IBM for example appear to have
evolved satisfactory relationships with suppliers, customers, shareholders,
employees and the community.

Another consequence implied by the stakeholder view of business, but by no means
fully worked out, is the recognition that Corporate Strategy cannot be stated
simply in terms of products and markets – as was widely believed in the 1960s.

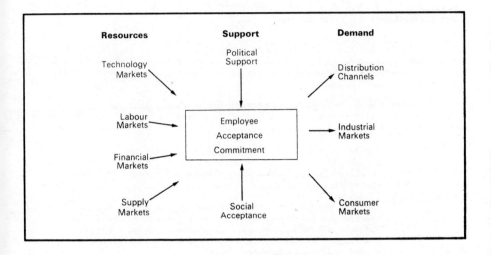

Fig. 7.22 The firm and its markets

Now the key management decisions may be concerned with worker and trade union participation, relationships with governments, securing supplies of key raw materials from Third World sources, and how to maintain a positive cash flow in conditions of hyper-inflation.

The arena for debate about Corporate Strategy still centres on the development of products and the penetration of markets but there is increasing recognition, particularly in Europe, that the supply of resources cannot be taken for granted and nor can the reactions of society or of employees. In consequence there is a growing interest in public affairs and 'societal strategy', in strategies for supply markets and strategies for involving employees more in decision-making.

7. THE DEVELOPMENT OF MANAGEMENT SYSTEMS

An important trend in recent thinking about Corporate Strategy is the suggestion that businesses at different stages of development require different organization structures, different management systems and different styles of leadership.

The Harvard research into Stages of Corporate Development mentioned earlier appears to have established that a company's organization structure is related to the spread of products which it sells and the range of markets which it serves; and as they grow, firms tend to move through the various phases, e.g.:

(1) a small one-product company with an informal organization structure;

(2) a large firm with a single or dominant product, having
an integrated or functional organization, often sub-
divided into regions;

(3) a large business with a range of related products, using
a product division organization;

(4) a multi-industry company with a conglomerate structure.

Some of the Harvard researchers into the Stages of Corporate Development theory
also found indications that companies at a particular phase of development tend
to have characteristic management systems, e.g. performance measurement and
reward systems for management.

In view of this work it has been suggested, for instance, that the use of product
divisions and profit centres in diversified companies in Britain has been far less
effective than in the U.S.A. because:

(1) British management were reluctant to install the necessary
systems of performance measurement, with the associated
penalties - e.g. management salaries and incentives based
on profit performance;

(2) they did not have at their disposal the large numbers of
trained general managers which are required to manage such
a decentralized system, i.e. executives with an understanding of all facets of a business and the ability to
manage a diverse management team;

(3) they had little experience in using formalized planning
systems which are required to co-ordinate policy-making
and resource allocation in complex diversified businesses.

Strategy Centres

Figure 7.23 illustrates one of the most ambitious attempts to associate management
systems with businesses at different phases of development. This type of analysis,
known as the 'Strategy Centres Approach' is being marketed by Arthur D. Little
for use by diversified companies in developing management systems for their
various subsidiaries or divisions.

This approach suggests that in a diversified business there should be strategy
centres as well as profit centres:

(1) for purposes of strategy and resource planning,
diversified businesses should be divided into Strategic
Business Units (a term coined by General Electric) - i.e.
a unit of the company with its own mission and its own
competitors, and capable of developing an independent
long-term strategy. These units usually differ from the
existing divisions and profit centres.

(2) strategic planning should be concerned with the allocation of managerial as well as financial resources.
This means in effect having a 'portfolio' of managers
of different types to allocate to different types of
businesses:

- entrepreneurs, sophisticated professional staff,
careful administrators and experts in 'turn-around'
situations.

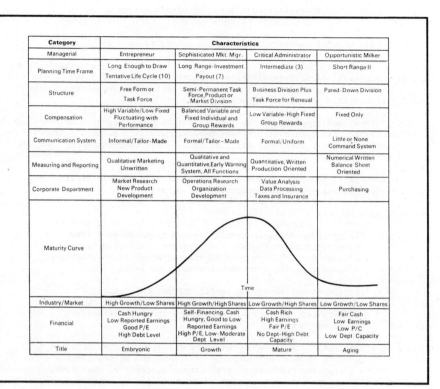

Category	Characteristics			
Managerial	Entrepreneur	Sophisticated Mkt. Mgr.	Critical Administrator	Opportunistic Milker
Planning Time Frame	Long Enough to Draw Tentative Life Cycle (10)	Long Range-Investment Payout (7)	Intermediate (3)	Short Range II
Structure	Free Form or Task Force	Semi-Permanent Task Force,Product or . Market Division	Business Division Plus Task Force for Renewal	Pared-Down Division
Compensation	High Variable/Low Fixed Fluctuating with Performance	Balanced Variable and Fixed Individual and Group Rewards	Low Variable-High Fixed Group Rewards	Fixed Only
Communication System	Informal/Tailor-Made	Formal/Tailor-Made	Formal/Uniform	Little or None Command System
Measuring and Reporting	Qualitative Marketing Unwritten	Qualitative and Quantitative,Early Warning System, All Functions	Quantitative, Written Production Oriented	Numerical Written Balance Sheet Oriented
Corporate Department	Market Research New Product Development	Operations Research Organization Development	Value Analysis Data Processing Taxes and Insurance	Purchasing
Maturity Curve			Time	
Industry/Market	High Growth/Low Shares	High Growth/High Shares	Low Growth/High Shares	Low Growth/Low Shares
Financial	Cash Hungry Low Reported Earnings Good P/E High Debt Level	Self-Financing. Cash Hungry, Good to Low Reported Earnings High P/E, Low-Moderate Dept Level	Cash Rich High Earnings Fair P/E No Dept-High Debt Capacity	Fair Cash Low Earnings Low P/C Low Dept Capacity
Title	Embryonic	Growth	Mature	Aging

Fig. 7.23   The strategy centres approach

Source: R.V.L. Wright, *Strategic Centers - A Contemporary Managing System*, p.9, Arthur D. Little, Cambridge, Mass. (1975)

(3) the emphasis in the managerial system should also be tailored to the stage of development in the business.

    (a) New ventures will require entrepreneurial manage-
ment, a flexible organization structure, informal
systems for information, communication, performance
measurement and control, and the financial resources
to enable them to develop and introduce new products
into a rapidly growing market.

    (b) Businesses which have passed the introductory stage
require professional management to install more
formal systems to improve communications within
the growing organization, and to keep control of
costs, production, sales etc. They are likely to
be self-financing but they need to make use of

sophisticated management techniques such as
operational research and organization development.

8. DEVELOPING THE COMPANY AS A SOCIAL SYSTEM

Recent research in large diversified companies by Joseph Bower* and others
suggests that resource allocation systems such as capital budgeting provide most
inadequate controls for top management.

In a divisionalized company, by the time a project for a new product or a new
facility reaches the main Board, it has normally acquired so much commitment on
the way up the organization that it is difficult to arrange a proper consideration
of other options.

For the most part, the top management team has to rely on less direct methods of
influencing thinking within the organization.

The influence process is likely to involve:

> (1) *periodic discussions with operating management about
>   divisional strategy*, to ensure that various options are
>   considered before a particular approach becomes embodied
>   in a specific development plan or project;
>
> (2) *the establishment of profit centres and 'strategy
>   centres'*, to ensure that managers are held accountable
>   both for operational performance and for business
>   development;
>
> (3) *changes in the whole management system*; better informa-
>   tion on new technology, competition and market trends;
>   improved measures of performance in terms of cash flow,
>   and profit contribution by products and by customer
>   groups; salaries and bonuses which reflect achievement
>   as well as seniority; the recruitment and promotion of
>   managers with potential, and the early retirement of
>   others who are no longer effective.

Staff Development

Another important way for top management to exert influence in a large organization
is through getting other people to grow, learn and develop.

Operating managers are primarily concerned with the day-to-day running of the
business and frequently the senior management team has the main responsibility for
ensuring the 'self-renewal' of the organization – in terms of management development and succession as well as through innovation in products and services, in
production processes and in marketing and distribution.

This entails recruiting and training managers with potential for promotion, placing
them in appropriate positions and planning the succession for key appointments. As

---

* Joseph L. Bower, *Managing the Resource Allocation Process*, Harvard Business
  School, Boston (1970).

is suggested in the Strategy Centres approach, the chief executive and the Board are in a position to manage a 'portfolio' of executives and relate their various strengths to the needs of different parts of the business and the stages of business development provide a useful guide to the classification of managers: individuals may be suited to starting new ventures, developing systems in growing enterprises, the administration of established businesses, or the stabilization and exploitation of declining markets.

Organization Development

Also, of course, top management has the possibility of influencing the business organization as a social system. In a large company there are severe limits to what can be achieved by direct personal leadership. The chief executive exercises his influence largely through the impact which he has, or does not have, on standards of performance, levels of morale and on the ideas and attitudes which become accepted and are approved within the organization.

In a modern diversified company with different parts of the organization at different phases of development, some highly innovative, others very stable and set in their ways, it is natural that there will be tensions.

The top management of the company has to reflect these different points of view and the chief executive may require exceptional skill to resolve the conflicts and to produce a coherent company philosophy and a set of business strategies which are internally consistent and are also consistent with changes which are occurring in the external environment.

If he and his team are successful, the original business idea and the accompanying value system will evolve in line with the changing needs of the business and with developments which are occurring outside the company. Also, innovation will be fostered at an appropriate level - but the company will not be overcommitted to new ventures. If the management are unsuccessful in marrying the different cultures and value systems, there will be a kind of organizational schizophrenia as incompatible strategies are put together. Different factions will develop and management may spend too much time on lobbying and internal politics. In extreme cases the inconsistencies will be made explicit, through operational problems, poor morale and increases in stoppages, absenteeism and labour turnover.

The notion of Strategic Management, coined by Igor Ansoff, links together Strategic Planning, Staff Development and Organization Development and serves to emphasize that these are key elements through which the top management team can influence and control in a diversified, decentralized corporation. Occasionally these functions may be put together in a co-ordinated programme which can be extremely effective in changing the culture of an organization, fostering innovation and building morale. More frequently, the integration of these policies for Corporate Development has to occur - if it happens at all - on an informal basis, through collaboration between corporate staff groups, or through the initiative of individual managers at various levels in the organization.

CONCLUSION

The purpose of this chapter was to review recent thinking and practice in Corporate Development. We suggested that organization for regeneration and renewal is a central problem of management.

Products and services eventually become obsolete and the organizations which sell them may disappear with them, unless new businesses are added.

One approach is for top management to develop an explicit or implicit Corporate
Strategy against which they can review the organization's progress periodically.

Additionally, they may analyse the opportunities for growth through increasing
the profitability of existing products and by expanding into new products and
markets.

The business may be analysed as a portfolio of assets or investments which must
be 'balanced' to achieve a spread of risk and opportunity.

It is also possible to analyse the various factors affecting the profitability of
various businesses.

In the present challenging social climate it is clearly advisable for management
to examine the social and political consequences of different strategic moves.

Management should consider how they might best change the attitudes of staff and
promote innovation within the organization through the development of staff as
individuals, and in groups.

Also it is important to employ appropriate leadership styles and management
systems for businesses at different stages of development.

Finally, it would seem sensible for top management and central staff groups to be
clear about how they propose to promote Corporate Development or Corporate
Renewal as an activity in the organization. This will probably require a
co-ordinated approach - involving initiatives in strategic planning, marketing
and product planning, organization and staff development.

THE REGENERATION OF INDUSTRY

This chapter has focused then on the managerial problems involved in resuscitating
declining industries. A review of recent thinking and practice in the field of
Corporate Development suggests that the solution to industrial problems may lay
partly in:

> (1) the encouragement and rewarding of innovation within
> the firm - not only in technology but in production,
> marketing and distribution;

> (2) the formulation by top management of broad strategies
> and plans for the future development and growth of the
> enterprise as a whole and the review of these plans
> with divisions and subsidiaries on a regular basis;

> (3) the establishment of organization structures and
> management systems which invite managers to set
> challenging goals and provide rewards and sanctions
> which relate to performance;

> (4) the selection, training and development of managers who
> know how to operate the large, complex decentralized
> systems which have been set up. This involves learning
> to manage on the instruments rather than managing an
> operation directly by personal contact.

Finally, the analysis suggests that top management need to view their organizations or organisms at various stages of growth - rather than machines which are amenable to the application of tools or techniques. We seem to be on the verge of discovering the management styles and cultures which best suit organizations at different stages of maturity.

Meanwhile a great deal must be left to the individual manager's flair and his ability to match his style and his systems of management to the particular needs of the organization.

Chapter 8

THE DIRECTIONAL POLICY MATRIX — TOOL FOR STRATEGIC PLANNING*

S. J. Q. Robinson, R. E. Hitchens and D. P. Wade**

In diversified business organizations one of the main functions of the management is to decide how money, materials and skilled manpower should be provided and allocated between different business sectors in order to ensure the survival and healthy growth of the whole. Good management allocates resources to sectors where business prospects appear favourable and where the organization has a position of advantage.

In a reasonably stable economic environment the normal method of comparing the prospects of one business sector with another, and for measuring a company's strengths and weaknesses in different sectors, is to use historical and forecast rates of return on capital employed in each sector to provide a measure of the sector's prospects or the company's strength. This is because a sector where business prospects are favourable and the company's position is strong tends to show higher profitability than one in which business prospects are less attractive and the company's position is weak. But records and forecasts of profitability are not sufficient yardsticks for guidance of management in corporate planning and allocation of resources.

The main reasons are:

  (a) They do not provide a systematic explanation

    (1) Why one business sector has more favourable
        prospects than another.

    (2) Why the company's position in a particular sector
        is strong or weak.

---

* The basic concept behind this chapter was discussed in the publication *Planning a Chemical Company's Prospects*, Shell Briefing Service, December 1975. This chapter was originally published in *Long Range Planning*, volume II, June 1978.

** John Robinson is in the Corporate Planning Division of Shell Chemicals U.K. Ltd; Bob Hitchens is with Shell International Chemical Co. Ltd; David Wade is in the Planning and Economics Division of the same company.

(b) They do not provide enough insight into the underlying dynamics and balance of the company's individual business sectors and the balance between them.

(c) When new areas of business are being considered, actual experience, by definition, cannot be consulted. Even when entry to a new area is to be achieved by acquiring an existing business the current performance of the existing business may not be reliable as a guide to its future.

(d) World-wide inflation has severely weakened the validity and credibility of financial forecasts, particularly in the case of businesses which are in any way affected by oil prices.

Corporate managements which recognize these shortcomings bring a variety of other qualitative and quantitative considerations to bear on the decision-making process in addition to the financial yardsticks. These are described in the following sections.

OUTLINE OF TECHNIQUE

In building up a corporate plan, a company will normally have available a number of plans and investment proposals for individual business sectors. These will include historical data on the company's past financial performance in the sector, and financial projections embodying the future investment plans. Such projections will reflect the expectations of those responsible for the company's business in that particular sector in relation to:

(a) Market growth;
(b) Industry supply/demand balance;
(c) Prices;
(d) Costs;
(e) The company's future market shares;
(f) Manufacturing competitiveness;
(g) Research and development strength;
(h) The activities of competitors; and
(i) The future business environment.

The basic technique of the Directional Policy Matrix is to identify:

(a) the main criteria by which the prospects for a business sector may be judged to be favourable or unfavourable; and

(b) those by which a company's position in a sector may be judged to be strong or weak.

Favourable in this context means with high profit and growth potential for the industry generally.

These criteria are then used to construct separate ratings of 'sector prospects' and of 'company's competitive capabilities' and the ratings are plotted on a matrix. It is convenient to divide the matrix into three columns and three rows, but other layouts are equally feasible. The ratings can be plotted in various

Business Sector Prospects

	Unattractive	Average	Attractive
Weak			× Pesticides
Average		× Chemical Solvents × Chlorinated Solvents	× New Chemical Business
Strong	× Detergent Alkylate	× Dyestuffs	Engineering Thermoplastic ×

Company's Competitive Capabilities

Fig. 8.1 Positions of business sectors in a hypothetical
          company's portfolio.

ways. Figure 8.1 displays the position of a number of different sectors in a
hypothetical company's portfolio. Alternatively, the matrix can be used to
display all the competitors in one particular business sector, since the method
lends itself to evaluating competitors' ratings as well as those of one's own
company.

DETAILS OF TECHNIQUE

Scope of the Analysis

The detailed techniques have been developed by reference to the petroleum-based
sector of the chemical industry, but the general technique is applicable to
almost any diversified business with separately identifiable sectors. It could
be applied to a diversified shipping company where the separate business sectors
might be different types of cargo, or to an engineering company offering a range
of products and services. In most cases there is no difficulty in identifying
a logical business sector to analyse. In the chemical industry business sectors
can generally be identified with product sectors, since these form distinct
businesses with well defined boundaries and substantial competition within the
boundaries.

Any particular geographical area may be defined for study. For the majority of
petroleum-based chemicals it has been found most convenient to consider economic
blocs (e.g. Western Europe) since there is generally greater movement of chemicals
within these blocs than between them.

The time scale of assessment is the effective forecasting horizon. This will
vary according to the business growth rate and the lead time needed to install

new capacity or develop new uses.   For most petroleum-based chemicals a time
scale of 10 years has been found appropriate.

Analysis of Business Sector Prospects

There are four main criteria by which the profitability prospects for different
sectors of the petroleum-based chemical business may be judged. These are:

(a) Market growth rate;
(b) Market quality;
(c) Industry feedstock situation; and
(d) Environmental aspects.

Some of these criteria are not applicable to other industries and other criteria
have to be introduced.   Industry feedstock situation, for example, would not be
of significance in evaluating sectors of the engineering industry. Market growth
and market quality, however, are fundamental to any analysis of business sector
prospects.

The significance of these four criteria and the way in which they are rated is as
follows:

Market Growth. Sectors with high market growth are not always those with the
greatest profit growth. Nevertheless market growth is a necessary condition for
growth of sector profits even if it is not a sufficient condition.   It has
therefore been included in the rating of sector prospects on the basis of an
appropriate scale.   For sector analysis in the chemical industry the scale given
below is the one used in Shell chemical companies. The centre point, or average
rating, corresponds roughly with the 5 year average growth rate predicted for the
heavy organic chemical industry in Western Europe.   A star rating system gives
more visual impact than a display of numerals.

sector growth rate per year	market growth rating	
0 - 3 per cent	*	(minimum)
3 - 5 per cent	**	
5 - 7 per cent	***	(average)
7 - 10 per cent	****	
10 per cent and over	*****	(maximum)

When applying this rating system to another industry it would be necessary to
construct a different scale with a centre point appropriate to the average growth
rate for that industry.

The other criteria are used to qualify the basic forecast of growth of demand so
far as their effect on growth of profits is concerned.

Market Quality. Certain sectors of the chemical industry show a consistent record
of higher and/or more stable profitability than others. These differences can be
ascribed in part to differences in the quality of the markets which the various
sectors serve. For example, in some sectors, notably those of a commodity type,
profitability can be highly variable as profit margins contract and expand over a
wide range as market conditions swing between under- and over-supply. This
problem is often most severe in the case of commodity type products with a large
number of producers. Again some sectors may have a chronically poor profitability
record because the market is dominated by a small group of powerful customers who
are able to keep prices down.

Other sectors remain profitable even in depressed periods of the economic cycle. This may be due to a variety of causes. For example, the market may be supplied by a few well entrenched producers who are content to let sales fall when demand goes down, rather than reduce prices. Or it may be that the consuming industry, able to add a high value, and having a prospect of further substantial growth accepts the need for suppliers to earn a reasonable living. Or, again, the determining factor may be the high technical content of the product, the performance of which has been carefully tailored to the needs of the consumer.

Market quality is difficult to quantify; in order to arrive at a sector rating it is necessary to consider a number of criteria in relation to the sector and try to assess their impact. The following are some of the more important questions:

(a) Has the sector a record of high, stable profitability?

(b) Can margins be maintained when manufacturing capacity exceeds demand?

(c) Is the product resistant to commodity pricing behaviour?

(d) Is the technology of production freely available or is it restricted to those who developed it?

(e) Is the market supplied by relatively few producers?

(f) Is the market free from domination by a small group of powerful customers?

(g) Has the product high added value when converted by the customer?

(h) In the case of a new product, is the market destined to remain small enough not to attract too many producers?

(i) Is the product one where the customer has to change his formulation or even his machinery if he changes supplier?

(j) Is the product free from the risk of substitution by an alternative synthetic or natural product?

A sector for which the answers to all or most of these questions are Yes would attract a four or five star market quality rating.

Industry Feedstock Situation. Normally in the chemical industry, expansion of productive capacity is often constrained by uncertainty of feedstock supply. If this is the case, or if the feedstocks for the sector in question have a strong pull towards an alternative use, or are difficult to assemble in large quantities, this is treated as a plus for sector prospects and attracts a better than average rating.

Conversely if the feedstock is a by-product of another process, and consumption of the main product is growing faster than the by-product, pressure may arise, either from low prices or direct investment by the by-product producer, to increase its consumption. This would attract a lower than average rating.

Environmental (Regulatory) Aspects. Sector prospects can be influenced by the extent of restrictions on the manufacture, transportation or marketing of the product. In some cases the impact of such restrictions is already quantifiable and has been built into the forecasts of market growth. If it has not, it must be assessed if there is a strongly positive or negative environmental or regulatory influence to be taken into account for the product.

Analysis of a Company's Competitive Capability.   Three main criteria have been identified by which a company's position in a particular sector of the chemical business may be judged strong, average or weak. With suitable adaptation they can probably be applied to the analysis of companies' positions in almost any business sector. The three criteria are:

> (a) Market position;
> (b) Production capability; and
> (c) Product research and development.

The significance of these criteria and the ways in which they are rated is shown below. In general it is convenient to review the position of one's own company in relation to that of all the significant competitors in the sector concerned, as this helps to establish the correct relativities.

Normally the position being established is that of the companies *today*. Other points can be plotted for one's own company to indicate possible future positions which might result from implementing alternative investment proposals and product strategies.

Market Position. The primary factor to consider here is percentage share of the total market. Supplementary to this is the degree to which this share is secured. Star ratings are awarded against the following guidelines:

***** Leader. A company which, from the mere fact of its pre-eminent market position, is likely to be followed normally accompanied by acknowledged technical leadership. The market share associated with this position varies from case to case. A company with 25 per cent of West European consumption in a field of ten competitors may be so placed. A company with 50 per cent in a field of two competitors will not be.

**** Major Producer. The position where, as in many businesses, no one company is a leader, but two to four competitors may be so placed.

*** A company with a strong viable stake in the market but below the top league. Usually when one producer is a leader the next level of competition will be three star producers.

** Minor market share. Less than adequate to support R & D and other services in the long run.

* Current position negligible.

Production Capability. This criterion is a combination of process economics, capacity of hardware, location and number of plants, and access to feedstock. The answers to all the following questions need to be considered before awarding a one to five star production capability rating:

Process economics. Does the producer employ a modern economic production process? Is it his own process or licensed? Has he the research and development capability or licensing relationships that will allow him to keep up with advances in process technology in the future?

Hardware. Is current capacity, plus any new capacity announced or building, commensurate with maintaining present market share? Does the producer have several plant locations to provide security to his customers against breakdown or strike action? Are his delivery arrangements to principal markets competitive?

Feedstock. Has the producer secure access to enough feedstocks to sustain his present market share? Does he have a favourable cost position on feedstock?

Product Research and Development. In the case of performance products this criterion is intended to be a compound of product range, product quality, a record of successful development in application, and competence in technical service. In other words, the complete technical package upon which the customer will pass judgment. In awarding a one to five star rating, judgment should be passed on whether a company's product R & D is better than, commensurate with, or worse than its position in the market.

In the case of commodity products, this criterion is not relevant and is not rated.

ASSIGNMENT OF RATINGS - PLOTTING THE MATRIX

The most straightforward method of assigning ratings for each of the criteria is discussion by functional specialists. They should be drawn from the particular sector of the company's business which is being studied and assisted by one or two non-specialists to provide the necessary detached viewpoint and comparability with other sector assessments.

Although members of the group may differ in the initial ratings which they assign, it is usually possible to arrive at a set of consensus ratings. Where there are still unresolved differences, a representative rating can generally be obtained by averaging. More sophisticated methods of sampling opinion have been designed, using computer techniques, but experience shows that the group discussion method was to be preferred as the end result is reached by a more transparent series of steps which make it more credible both to those participating and to management.

Simplified System

In the simplified form of the technique each of the main criteria is given an equal weighting in arriving at an overall rating for business sector prospects and for company's competitive capabilities. This system of equal weighting may be open to question in comparing certain business sectors but has been found to give good results when applied to a typical chemical product portfolio.

In converting star ratings into matrix positions it is necessary (in order to avoid distortion) to count one, two, three, four and five stars as zero, one, two, three, four points respectively. One star is thus equivalent to a nil rating and a three star rating scores two points out of four and occupies a midway position where three points out of five would not.

It is also convenient in practice to quantify the criteria in half star increments so that there are effectively eight half star graduations between one star and five stars. Half stars are shown as: (*).

The working of the system is illustrated by the hypothetical example in Table 8.1. In this, the technique is being used to assess the competitors in a particular business sector. In general it is desirable to record the arguments and supporting data in considerable detail but in this case the results of the matrix analysis are summarized in highly abbreviated form.

TABLE 8.1 Examples of Simplified Weighting System

Product sector: Product X is a semi-mature thermoplastic suitable for engineering
  industry applications. There are two existing producers in Western Europe and
  a third producer is currently building plant.

Sector prospects analysis (Western Europe, 1975-1980)

		Stars	Points
Market growth	15-20% per year forecast	*****	4
Market quality Sector profitability record?	Above average		
Margins maintained in over-capacity?	Some price-cutting has taken place but product has not reached commodity status.		
Customer to producer ratio?	Favourable. Numerous customers; only two producers so far.		
High added value to customer?	Yes. The product is used in small scale, high value, engineering applications.		
Ultimate market limited in size?	Yes. Unlikely to be large enough to support more than three or four producers.		
Substitutability by other products?	Very limited. Product has unique properties.		
Technology of production restricted?	Moderately. Process is available under licence from Eastern Europe.		
Overall market quality rating:	Above average	****	3
Industry feedstock	Product is manufactured from an intermediate which itself requires sophisticated technology and has no other outlets.	****	3
Environmental aspects	Not rated separately	-	-
Overall sector prospects rating			10

(Contd.)

TABLE 8.1 Examples of Simplified Weighting System (contd.)

Companies competitive capabilities analysis
(Competitors A, B and C)

	A	B	C	A	B	C
Market position Market share	65%	25%	10%	*****	***	***
Production capability Feedstock	Manufactures by slightly out-dated process from bought-in precursors	Has own precursors. Feedstock manufactured by third party under process deal	Basic position in precursors. Has own second process for feedstock			
Process economics	Both A and B have own 'first generation' process supported by moderate process R & D capacity		C is licensing 'second generation' process from Eastern Europe			
Hardware	A and B each have one plant sufficient to sustain their respective market shares		None as yet. Market product imported from Eastern Europe			
Overall production capability ratings				****	***	**(*
Product R & D (in relation to market position)	Marginally weaker	Comparable	Stronger	****	***	**(*
Overall competitors' ratings				10/12	6/12	4/12

Weighting System

In certain businesses it is unrealistic to suppose that each factor is equally important, in which case an alternative method of analysing company's competitive capabilities can be used, introducing objectively determined weightings.

An example of such weightings is given in Table 8.2. This is taken from a particular study on speciality chemicals, in which the four functions

        (a) Selling and distribution;
        (b) Problem solving;
        (c) Innovative research and development; and
        (d) Manufacturing

were considered to be the most important.

TABLE 8.2   Example of Weightings on Company's Competitive Capabilities Axis

| | Businesses | | | |
	W	X	Y	Z
Selling and Distribution	2	3	6	3
Problem Solving	2	4	3	1
Innovative R & D	4	1	0	1
Manufacturing	2	2	1	5
	10	10	10	10

In addition to giving a more refined approach to the company competitive axis, the set of weighting factors is useful in its own right, indicating what sort of organizational culture is most apt in this particular business.

INTERPRETATION OF MATRIX POSITIONS

The results of the hypothetical example in Table 8.1 can be plotted on the matrix as shown in Figure 8.2.

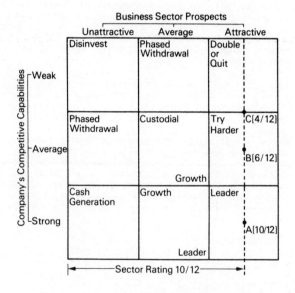

Fig. 8.2   Comparison of competitive capabilities - Product X

Since the various zones of the matrix are associated with different combinations of sector prospects and company strength or weakness, different product strategies are appropriate to them.   These are indicated by the various key words which suggest the type of strategy or resource allocation to be followed for products falling in these zones.

The zones covered by the various policy key words are not precisely defined by the rectangular subdivision arbitrarily adopted for the matrix.   Experience suggests that:

     (a)   The zones are of irregular shape;
     (b)   They do not have hard and fast boundaries but shade
           into one another; and
     (c)   In some cases they are overlapping.

The most appropriate boundaries can only be determined after further practical experience of comparing business characteristics with positions plotted in the matrix.

Matrix Positions in the Right Hand Column

Leader. Competitor A, the largest producer with the lowest unit costs and a commanding technical situation, is in the highly desirable position of leader in a business sector with attractive prospects. His indicated strategy is to give absolute priority to the product with all the resources necessary to hold his market position. This being a fast growing sector he will, before long, need to install extra capacity. Although in all probability he is already earning satisfactory profits from Product X his current cash flow from this source may not be sufficient to finance a high rate of new investment. In that case the cash must be found from another sector of his business. Later, as the growth rate slows down Product X should be able to finance its own growth and eventually to become a net generator of cash.

However, in this hypothetical example, competitor A's position on process and feedstock economics is threatened by second generation processes. This suggests that he may need to strengthen his process R & D. A production capability of one star below market position reflects A's slight weakness in this area.

Try Harder. Competitor B is in this position. It implies that products located in this zone can be moved down towards at least an equality position by the right allocation of resources. However, competitor B does not appear to have any very special advantages in this sector and unless he can strengthn his position by, for example, licensing one of the new processes, he may be condemned to remain No.2. This is not necessarily an unacceptable position in the short term but is likely to become increasingly vulnerable with the passage of time.

Double or Quit. This is the zone of the matrix from which products that are destined to become the future high fliers should be selected. A company should not normally seek to diversify into any new sector unless the prospects for it are judged to be attractive. Only a small number of the most promising should be picked for doubling and the rest should be abandoned. Competitor C, on the strength of his successful feedstock process development and his licensing relationships with Eastern Europe for the X process has already decided to double, i.e. invest in a commercial plant. He is therefore on the borderline of the Double or Quit and Try Harder zones: his production capability and product R & D ratings are both higher than his present market rating. Competitor C faces a more uncertain prospect of reaching a viable position in this sector than if he had been first in the field like competitor A.

Matrix Positions in the Middle Column

Business sectors falling in the middle column of the matrix are in general those in which market growth has fallen to around the average for the industry. In many cases they are the high growth sectors of a decade or two previously which have now reached maturity. Sector prospects can range, however, from 0.33 (below average) to 0.66 (above average) according to market quality, industry feedstock situation and environmental considerations. The significance of the key words in this column is as follows:

Growth. Products will tend to fall in this zone for a company which is one of two to four major competitors (four star market position) backed up by commensurate production capability and product R & D. In this situation no one company is in a position to be a leader and the indicated strategy for the companies concerned is to allocate sufficient resources to grow with the market in anticipation of a reasonable rate of return.

Products in this zone will in general be earning sufficient cash to finance their own (medium) rate of expansion.

Custodial. A product will fall in the custodial zone of the matrix when the company concerned has a position of distinct weakness either in respect of market position (below three star), process economics, hardware, feedstock or two or more of these in combination. Typically, custodial situations apply to the weaker brethren in sectors where there are too many competitors. The indicated strategy in these situations is to maximize cash generation without further commitment of resources.

Experience shows that for any individual company's portfolio there tend to be more products in the centre box of the matrix than in any other, and that these products do not just fall into the custodial and growth zones but also occupy intermediate positions between the two. In such cases the matrix gives less clear cut policy guidance but the relative positions of the sectors still enable a ranking to be drawn up for resource allocation.

Matrix Positions in the Left Hand Column

Business sectors falling in this column are those in which a growth rate below the average for the industry as a whole is combined with poor market quality and/or weaknesses in the industry feedstock situation and environmental outlook. A typical case would be a sector in which the product itself is obsolescent and is being replaced by a quite different product of improved performance and environmental acceptability or one in which the product is serving a customer-dominated industry which has fallen into a low rate of growth.

Cash Generation. A company with a strong position in such a sector can still earn satisfactory profits and for that company the sector can be regarded as a cash generator. Needing little further finance for expansion it can be a source of cash for other faster growing sectors.

Phased Withdrawal. A company with an average-to-weak position in a low-growth sector is unlikely to be earning any significant amount of cash and the key word in this sector is phased withdrawal. This implies that efforts should be made to realize the value of the assets and put the money to more profitable use. The same policy would apply to a company with a very weak position in a sector of average prospects.

Disinvest. Products falling within this zone are likely to be losing money already. Even if they generate some positive cash when business is good, they will lose money when business is bad. It is best to dispose of the assets as rapidly as possible and redeploy more profitably the resources of cash, feedstock and skilled manpower so released.

In general, unless the prospects for the sector have been completely transformed as the result of some rapid technological or environmental change, it will be rare for a well managed company to find that any of its business sectors lie within the disinvest area; it will be more usual for a company to be able to foresee the decline in sector prospects in the phased withdrawal stage.

THE SECOND ORDER MATRIX

The second order matrix enables one to combine two parameters of an *investment* decision. This is distinct from examining the parameters of product strategy, the object of the first order matrix. In this instance we are relating the product strategy parameters with our priorities in non-product strategy notably location and feedstock security aspects.

Table 8.3 shows a classification of the business sectors in Figure 8.1, in order of priority for resources. It will be noted that new ventures and double or quit businesses only receive attention after those with proven profitability or cash generation have been allocated sufficient resources to get the best advantage from existing commitments.

TABLE 8.3   Classification of Business Sectors in Order of
                        priority

Criteria	– Matrix position – Profit record – Other product related criteria – Judgment
Category I	Hard core of good quality business consistently generating good profits. Example: Engineering thermoplastic
Category II	Strong company position. Reasonable to good sector prospects. Variable profit record. Examples: Dyestuffs. Chlorinated Solvents.
Category III	Promising product sectors new to company. Example: New Chemical Business
Category IV	Reasonable to modest sector prospects in which the company is a minor factor. Variable profit record. Example: Chemical Solvents
Category V	Businesses with unfavourable prospects in which the company has a significant stake. Example: Detergent Alkylate

Table 8.4 shows a list of non-product strategic options. These will usually have been developed at the corporate level and the company management will have a clear idea of relative preferences.

TABLE 8.4 Non-product Strategic Options

Category
1 - Joint venture to make olefins with petroleum company having secure feedstocks.
2 - Make maximum use of land and infrastructure at existing sites.
3 - Develop new major coastal manufacturing site in the EEC.
4 - Develop a foothold in the US market.
5 - Reduce dependence upon investment in Europe in order to spread risk. Develop manufacturing presence in, *inter alia*, Ruritania.

These two desiderata can then be combined in the second order matrix shown as Figure 8.3. It will be noted that three of the businesses appear twice, as their future development can be used to satisfy alternative non-product priorities, whereas three of them do not appear at all.

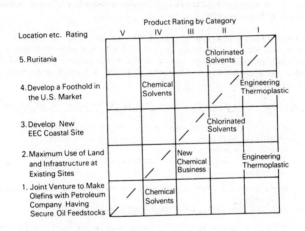

Fig. 8.3   Second order matrix.

This matrix gives a very convenient method of presentation of priorities and feasible alternatives, from which the most appropriate decisions can be more easily resolved.

OTHER USES OF THE DPM

In addition to the applications described, the Directional Policy Matrix can be used in several other ways.

Analysing the Dynamics and Financial Balance of the Portfolio

The general shape of the product matrix plot for a diversified business will give an insight into its financial position. Thus a company in which the majority of products plotted fall in the mature phase (cash generator or custodial) may be expected to generate more cash than it needs to pursue its total strategy. If so it must either seek new areas of business in the double or quit or try harder areas, or else act in effect as a banker to other businesses.

Conversely, a company that has the majority of its individual product sectors in the double or quit, try harder or leadership areas will need more cash if it is to pursue the opportunities open to it.

Ideally the overall strategy should aim at keeping cash surplus and cash deficit sectors in balance, with a regular input or promising new business coming forward from research or to take up the surplus cash generated by the businesses already in or moving into the mature phase.

Building up a Picture of Competitors

The DPM can also be used to build up a qualitative picture of the product portfolios of other companies. Some insight into competitors' market positions, production capability and product R & D is in any case a prerequisite to arriving at one's own company's ranking in a particular sector. The matrix analysis will perform a useful function in codifying this information and high-lighting areas where more needs to be obtained.

Once competitors' matrices have been plotted, and assuming that competitors will base their investment decisions on broadly the same logic, one can gain an insight into their likely future moves. For example, the matrix analysis will identify the points at which a competitor's production capability is weaker than his market position and hence will indicate that he is likely to lose market share unless he strengthens his position by further investment in manufacturing plant. Conversely it will also identify where production capability is stronger and a competitor is likely to seek to gain market share.

BIBLIOGRAPHY

Planning a Chemical Company's Prospects, published by the Royal Dutch/Shell Group of companies.

Perspectives: The Product Portfolio. The Growth Share Matrix. The Boston Consulting Group.

Barry Hedley, Strategy and the 'Business Portfolio', Long Range Planning, 10, February (1973).

Chapter 9

PORTFOLIO ANALYSIS: PRACTICAL EXPERIENCE WITH THE DIRECTIONAL POLICY MATRIX*

David Hussey

EXPERIENCE WITH THE DIRECTIONAL POLICY MATRIX

In November 1975 Shell Chemicals caused a stir of interest in the planning world when they published details of a technique of portfolio analysis called the Directional Policy Matrix.[1] This was described more recently in an article by Robinson, Hitchens and Wade which appeared in the April issue of Long Range Planning.[2]

The original booklet included the statement that although designed for petro-chemicals '... the general technique is applicable to almost any diversified business with separately identifiable sectors. It could, for example, be applied to a diversified shipping company where the separate business sectors might be different types of cargo, or to an engineering company offering a range of products and services'.

At the time I first read this booklet, early in 1976, I had just started planning assignments with both an engineering company offering a range of products and services and the largest transport undertaking in Europe (not quite a shipping company, but very close in many ways).

The way I was working with both of these clients in a 'process' role (see, for example, Young and Hussey[3]) meant that I was well situated to introduce them to the new technique, to share in the practical problems which arose (and in some of the solutions), with the added benefit that the style of working meant that the adaptation of the technique was the result of a genuine partnership with my clients, drawing heavily on their skills and efforts. The initial experiments moved in very different directions in each company.

The main thrust of this chapter is based on experience with Rolls Royce Motors, whose products include cars, diesel engines and shunting locomotives, and the National Freight Corporation.

The NFC has far more products than the casual observer might guess, including parcels services, tanker services, household removals, express road services,

---

* Originally published in Long Range Planning, volume 11, August 1978.

freight forwarding, warehousing, refrigerated storage and numerous others. With
Rolls Royce Motors the need was to view the company from a different perspective
and to ensure that the corporate plan, although strongly influenced by the
Divisions, was more than a consolidation and summary of the Divisional plans.

The NFC need was much closer to the traditional reasons for applying portfolio
analysis – the problem of 'sorting out' numerous subsidiaries and products from
a strategic view point, in relation to development, investment, and cash flow
contributions.   DPM was examined as a potential approach to the analysis, but at
that early stage the Corporation was anxious to concentrate, as a significant
element of its marketing strategies, on the creation and maintenance of a low
level of risk.   It was therefore a first priority to develop a meaningful definition of risk in terms of its causal factors.

A method of risk analysis using a portfolio analysis philosophy and owing much to
the DPM was produced.   Currently the DPM is being adapted for use in the NFC,
with the risk approach remaining an important adjunct to it.

At Rolls Royce Motors we used the DPM but added to it a technique developed by
Harbridge House inspired by the work of Mike Sweet of the NFC in developing their
approach to risk analysis.   Our new technique, risk matrix (RM), effectively
converts the two dimensional DPM into a three-dimensional matrix, and opens the
door to a number of exciting concepts.

Parallel with this involvement, another client, Arthur Guinness Ltd., had
independently begun to apply the DPM to their business which includes sweets,
holidays, plastics, and retailing interests as well as lager and Guinness stout.
Their experience has been made available to me for this chapter.

In addition we have twice used the DPM in senior management education programmes.
The first was spontaneous, as a reply to a problem which developed from a
marketing case study: how do you evaluate competitors? It made an interesting
diversion from the traditional methods.   The second programme, for an oil
distributing group, dealt with top management development and included strategic
planning.   We adapted the questions in the DPM and used it as a classroom
exercise, evaluating two of the company's products.   Two noteworthy things came
out of this experience: the first was the need to pay attention to the weightings
of some of the sub-questions; the second was that both sessions of the course,
with different participants in each, reached the same consensus view of the matrix
position of the products.   Both of these points will be returned to later.

                    DESCRIPTION OF THE DPM

A full description of the technique will be found in the Shell booklet and the
article, both of which have been referenced.

In summary the DPM is a nine box matrix with two axes.   One measures 'prospects
for market sector profitability' and the other 'the company's competitive position'.
A series of questions (Table 9.1) are asked about factors relevant to each axis,
are scored and weighted, and the answers plotted on the matrix.   The position in
which the answer falls provides an indicative strategic guidance.   An example of
the matrix, slightly modified from the Shell original in the titling of the matrix
positions, appears in Figure 9.1.

It is interesting that in the management programme discussed above we started
with a blank sheet of paper, and asked the experienced managers present to say
what they considered important in evaluating a business opportunity. We cheated

TABLE 9.1   Questions for the DPM

Market Sector prospects analysis	Companies' competitive capabilities analysis
Market growth	*Market position* Market share, Western Europe

Market quality
  Sector profitability record?
  Margins maintained in over-capacity?
  Susceptible to commodity pricing?
  Customer to producer ratio?
	Production capability
	Feedstock

High added value to customer?	Process economics
Ultimate market limited in size?	Hardware
Substitutability by other products? Technology of production restricted?	
Overall market quality rating: Industry feedstock	*Product R & D* (in relation to market position)
Environmental aspects	

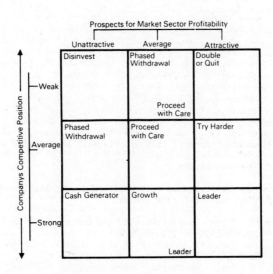

Fig. 9.1   Example of D.P.M. (note the minor variations of labelling between this and Figure 8.2)

only by separating the list into two groups, corresponding with the two axes. All the key items included in the Shell booklet – market growth; profitability; ease of entry; stability of profits; competitive position, supply position *vis-à-vis* competitors, etc. were readily identified by the managers.   This, I think, points to one of the advantages of the technique: it deals in terms and questions familiar to managers, and does not move explicitly into concepts such as product life cycles or complex mathematics as some other techniques do.

The meanings of the labels in the matrix boxes may be summarized as:

* *Disinvestment*

    Products falling in this area will probably be losing
    money - not necessarily every year, but losses in bad
    years will outweigh the gains in good years. It is
    unlikely that any activity will surprise management by
    falling within this area since its poor performance should
    already be known.

* *Phased Withdrawal*

    A product with an average to weak position with low un-
    attractive market prospects, or a weak position with
    average prospects is unlikely to be earning any significant
    amounts of cash. The indicated strategy is to realize the
    value of the assets on a controlled basis to make the
    resources available for redeployment elsewhere.

* *Cash Generator*

    A typical situation in this matrix area is when the
    company has a product which is moving towards the end of
    its life cycle, and is being replaced in the market by
    other products. No finance should be allowed for expansion,
    and the business, so long as it is profitable, should be
    used as a source of cash for other areas. Every effort
    should be made to maximize profits since this type of
    activity has no long term future.

* *Proceed with Care*

    In this position, some investment may be justified but
    major investments should be made with extreme caution.

* *Growth*

    Investment should be made to allow the product to grow with
    the market. Generally, the product will generate sufficient
    cash to be self-financing, and should not be making demands
    on other corporate cash resources.

* *Double or Quit*

    Tomorrow's breadwinners among today's R & D projects may
    come from this area. Putting the strategy simply, those
    with the best prospects should be selected for full backing
    and development. The rest should be abandoned.

* *Try Harder*

> The implication is that the product can be moved towards
> the leadership box by judicious application of resources.
> In these circumstances the company may wish to make
> available resources in excess of what the product can
> generate for itself.

* *Leader*

> The strategy should be to maintain this position. At
> certain stages this may imply a need for resources to
> expand capacity with a cash need which need not be met
> entirely from funds generated by the product, although
> earnings should be above average.

These descriptions are close to those developed by Shell: the key-words in the
centre box 'Proceed with care' equate with the terms 'Custodial' used by Shell
which we found unsuitable at Rolls Royce Motors. Interestingly, Guinness also
found problems with the original word, and use the term Keep/watch in their
model.

PRACTICAL PROBLEMS

The questions/criteria developed by Shell for both axes presented certain
problems, and in turn led to a number of other queries around the practical
application of the technique. Some were answered, but others remain. Briefly
the main tasks and problems found in using the technique were:

(1) The need to change the questions to suit different
    markets.

(2) The problem of weightings.

(3) The treatment of 'environmental' factors.

(4) How broadly to define businesses and markets.

(5) Value of the star scoring system.

(6) Market growth scores.

(7) Competitive position scores.

(8) Validity and reliability of the approach.

THE NEED TO CHANGE THE QUESTIONS

It was immediately obvious that the concepts of market growth, quality and supply
made sense to all of the businesses for which the technique was considered.
Certain specific criteria were patently not valid, and there were obvious omissions
of criteria critical to specific businesses. The competitive concepts of market
share, supply and support raised more problems and were not universally valid.

These extracts from an internal Guinness document summarize some of the problems
of adaptation:

(1)   Are there/should there be different criteria for
      different businesses in the portfolio?

(2)   How to decide on the criteria?
      - is one type of analysis better/more reliable than
         another?
      - should the analysis concentrate on a small number
         of parameters ... or a large number?
      - how is it possible to prove that the right factors
         have been used? How scientific can one be?

In practice it was found that the problem of different criteria could be solved
by simply not scoring questions that had no relevance to the product. This
seemed to work well for the market axis, but problems occurred with the competitive axis over certain types of business. For example, it is very difficult to
see the relevance of most of these criteria to even a large horticultural business:
strict application of them by all the nation's farmers would mean that everybody
would be guided by the matrix to get out of farming, since all the producers are
in a 'weak' competitive position. This is not an empty example, as many companies
have interests in activities where size and market dominance are not of great
significance to success. Examples include secretarial services, and consultancy.

The criteria developed for Rolls Royce Motors are:

		Max. score
Market axis		
(1) *Market growth*		4 points
(2) *Market quality*		4 points
2.1	Stable profitability	
2.2	Margins maintained in over capacity	
2.3	Brand loyalty	
2.4	Customer/producer ratio	
2.5	Degree of substitutability (of the product, not of the brand)	
2.6	Restriction of technology	
2.7	Generation of after sales business	
(3) *Market supply*		4 points
	Are there major supply difficulties in the industry?	
Competitive axis		
1	*Market position*	4 points
1.1	Market share (or approx. ranking in market)	
1.2	Captive outlets	
1.3	Dealer network	
1.4	After sales service network	
2	*Production capability*	4 points
2.1	Production economics	
2.2	Capacity in relation to market share	
2.3	Component availability	
2.4	Ability to handle product change	

> Market axis   Max. score
>   3 Engineering and support services
>   3.1 Capability in relation to market position
>   3.2 Production innovation ability
>   3.3 Product quality

Guinness took a slightly different approach to the market axis:

Market axis	Rating points	Maximum rating
(1) Quality of profitability		4
Excellent prospects (high return on capital/secure)	4	
Good prospects (high/not so secure or average return/secure)	3	
Average prospects	2	
Poor prospects (relatively low return/insecure)	1	
Likelihood of loss	0	
(2) Growth		4
Excellent growth prospects (over 12 per cent per annum)	4	
Good growth prospects (8-11 per cent per annum)	3	
Average growth prospects (4-7 per cent per annum)	2	
Poor growth prospects (0-3 per cent per annum)	1	
Declining market (less than 0 per cent)	0	

(3) Supporting factors   4
    Rate each business on a scale from 4 to 0 (or
    negative) taking into account:

Price elasticity:	inelastic	positive
	elastic	negative
Substitutability of type of product/service:	hard to substitute	positive
	easily substituted	negative
Openness of market:	hard to enter	positive
	easy to enter	negative
Extent of government control:	not much	positive
	a lot	negative
Economic/political stability:	stable	positive
	unstable	negative

Other Factors (e.g. threat of nationalization) add to or subtract
from score as relevant.

(4) Overall rating   12

THE PROBLEMS OF WEIGHTINGS

There are really two sets of related weighting problems. The first basic issue
is whether each of the three groups of criteria in each axis should have the same
weighting, as in the Shell system. Robinson, Hitchens and Wade[2] give examples of
situations where other weightings are determined and used. But if, in a conglomerate, you apply different weightings to every product or business area, are the
resultant matrix positions comparable?

The second problem is the need for sub-weightings to assess the value of each
sub-criteria. The original Shell method suggested an overall assessment taking
the sub-factors into account, and this is the way we used the technique at Rolls
Royce Motors. I cannot claim to have reached any more objective solution than
this, and am worried because of this.

THE TREATMENT OF ENVIRONMENTAL FACTORS

The original Shell description provided for a fourth factor in judging the
market, the environmental one, but omitted this from the worked example on the
grounds that it did not apply to 'Product X' on which the illustration was based.

The Shell notes on this factor state:

> Sector prospects can be influenced by the extent of
> restrictions on the manufacture, transportation or
> marketing of the product. In some cases the impact of such
> restrictions is already quantifiable and has been built
> into the forecasts of market growth. If it has not, it
> must be assessed if there is a strongly positive or
> negatively environmental or regulatory influence to be
> taken into account for the product.

The problem we found was the distorting effect of applying a factor on an
irregular basis. Logically, if there were no environmental influences on product
X, should it not receive top score, when compared with product Y on which the
environmental influence was severe? These theoretical examples show the effect
of a 'sometimes' rating on matrix positions.

	Product A		Product B	
	A1	A2	B1	B2
Market growth	4	4	2	2
Market quality	2	2	0	0
Market supply	2	2	3	3
Environment	0		4	
Total	8	8	9	5
Out of	16	12	16	12

This shows how the inclusion or exclusion of a rating on the environment can
change the position of product A versus product B.

It was also apparent that the environmental factor dealt only partly with the
much wider question of risk. At the NFC the thinking moved much more to an
exploration of risk and the first attempt at analysis dealt only with this issue.
At Rolls Royce Motors we decided to ignore the environmental factor in the DPM,
but to use another technique to look at all environmental risk, and to use the
results of this as an aid to interpreting the DPM. This gave another dimension
to the use of the DPM, without the distorting effect mentioned above. (The risk
matrix approach is described towards the end of this chapter.)

HOW BROADLY TO DEFINE BUSINESSES AND MARKETS

Relevant definitions of businesses and markets are often harder to reach than
might be imagined. At Rolls Royce Motors we used a strategic business area

concept, for example, subdividing the car market into geographic dimensions. What were relevant areas were not too difficult to deduce.

Less simple, is the answer to the question what is a market? Is the market for the Rolls Royce car all motor vehicles, an upper crust of a few competing high value makes, or is the car truly unique? The answer is important, because not only does it affect market growth rates, but also the competitive rating: market share, for example, could vary from 100 per cent to a minute figure depending on the definition used.

Guinness faced similar problems. For example, should they consider their main product as part of the beer market or part of the stout market?

It is probable that some of the exceptions to the DPM discussed earlier would fit if the strategic business area market and competition could be defined narrowly enough. The right answer might be a minute geographical area, or a finely drawn market segment.

The danger is that things can change. The strategic business area for many activities was once the boundaries of a small town; for most the boundaries have enlarged to cover an entire country, and for many national borders are no longer significant. What appears 'right' today may not remain so for ever, and an important lesson of the DPM is that one major strategic task is to continually watch, and test, the definitions of business area.

There may of course be more than one strategic business area for any one product.

An added complication comes when the company has one source of supply to several strategic business areas. A matrix position suggesting divestment in one may not be a simple decision unless the capacity can be diverted to a more profitable activity.

VALUE OF THE STAR SCORING SYSTEM

Shell suggested a star scoring system, converted to points on the basis that one star scored 0 points, two stars 1 point, etc. Universally this practice was found to have little value in all the companies with which we were associated (and Guinness independently) and we omitted the star step and moved directly to the assignment of points.

MARKET GROWTH SCORES

The scoring system for market growth used by Shell was:

0-4 per cent p.a.	0 points
5-7 per cent p.a.	1 point
8-10 per cent p.a.	2 points
11-14 per cent p.a.	3 points
15 per cent and over	4 points

This was based on chemical industry performance. Shell added the comment:

> When applying this rating system to another industry it would be necessary to construct a different scale with a centre point appropriate to the average growth rate for that industry.

Guinness did adjust the scale, as was shown in the example earlier. The real
problem comes when using the matrix in a true conglomerate - where portfolio
analysis is most necessary - when many industries each with different growth rates
are involved. Should the scale be based on the average of all industry, or of
those industries in which the conglomerate operates, or of the upper quartile of
industry (on the grounds that this is a desirable objective and can therefore
provide a good standard for all activity). One approach which seems wrong is to
use a different market scale for each strategic business area in the portfolio.

The solutions arrived at were essentially practical answers to fit the specific
companies, rather than a general principle applicable to all situations. My
tentative recommendation for a conglomerate is to construct a scale based on the
average for all their own industries: this differs from the Shell recommendation
in words, though possibly not in intent.

COMPETITIVE POSITION SCORES

Shell, very sensibly, move from the concept of market share, to one of market
leadership. The suggested ratings are:

4 points	Leader	- a company whose pre-eminent market position makes it price leader. The market share associated with this state is variable, and does not imply a majority share where there are many competitors.
3 points	Major producer	- where no one company is a leader, but where there may be a number of major producers.
2 points	Viable producer	- a strong viable stake, but below the top league.
1 point	Minor	- less than adequate to support R & D in the long run.

This concept fits most companies very well. The problem of the farming business
where the whole concept is irrelevant has already been mentioned.

The idea of relative market leadership position, rather than market share, also
fits the road transport business where in most sectors there are innumerable
competitors with small (and for practical purposes) immeasurable market shares.
Whether we will need to adjust the definitions to fit the road transport business
is still an open question.

VALIDITY AND RELIABILITY

The ultimate aim of any new technique must be to have both validity and reliability. Validity means the ability to measure what it sets out to measure:
reliability is the quality of consistency.

Probably the biggest worry any of us had in using the technique is that we could
prove neither validity nor reliability.

The tests which we have been able to make provide indicative evidence only:

      (a)   A measure of reliability was achieved at the management
            programme, where different groups reached the same
            answer. Whether this answer was also valid is another
            question.

(b) In one company, after making the matrix analysis, we
     examined major capital expenditure proposals from each
     area. If the matrix position and the evaluations were
     reasonably efficient, we postulated that a major project
     for a 'try harder' product would yield a higher expected
     d.c.f. rate of return than that for a 'proceed with care'
     product. This was borne out.

(c) We compared the individual matrix positions of various
     products with assessments made of them from their
     individual plans and studies. There were no surprises
     (and we do not think one set of expectations biased the
     other assessment).

DPM AS A BEHAVIOURAL TECHNIQUE

One way to judge the reliability of the technique is to use it as a participative
management tool. If different groups of managers consistently produce similar
answers this will at least demonstrate reliability.

But more than this, it will encourage thinking. There seems to me a tremendous
value in using the technique firstly to help managers to think as a group about
their markets, the competition and the relative strategic value of their portfolio to the company. Secondly, the portfolio approach provides a useful way of
communicating strategic guidelines to different business units.

Potentially, I would set the value of the use of the technique in this way as
about equal to its value as a tool of strategic analysis. Those wishing to bring
more real participation to planning could do worse than to use the DPM as the
medium.

THE RISK MATRIX (RM)

The remarks about validity and reliability, and the value as a group technique,
apply equally to the RM.

All businesses are subjected to influences outside the control of the company
but some are more affected than others. The risk matrix attempts to examine key
external influences and to evaluate the likely *adverse* significance of these on
the product portfolio.

A combined rating is obtained which may be compared with market sector prospects.
Figure 9.2 illustrates the matrix. Prospects for market sector profitability are
taken direct from the DPM and need no further description.

The position on the environmental risk axes is obtained by:

*   identifying the significant external factors (selection
    has to be made: it is impracticable to suggest that
    every factor should be studied).

*   assessing the impact that adverse changes could have on
    the product.

*   assessing the probability that the change will occur.

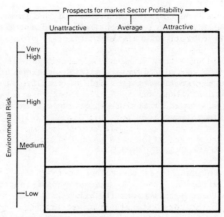

The Risk Matrix

◄──── Prospects for market Sector Profitability ────►

Unattractive   Average   Attractive

Environmental Risk: Very High, High, Medium, Low

Note: Ratings for Market Prospects Axis as in D.P.M.

Fig. 9.2 The Risk Matrix

Impact and probability are scored in the following manner –

Impact					*Probability*
Extremely high	6	A certainty	100 per cent	6
	5	Very likely	84 per cent	5
High	4	Quite possible	67 per cent	4
	3	As likely as not	50 per cent	3
Relatively low	2	Probably not	33 per cent	2
	1	Highly unlikely	16 per cent	1
None	0	Impossible	—	0

Scoring is impact x probability. For example:

Impact extremely high and *probability* a certainty: 6 x 6 = 36
         High   Very likely: 4 x 5 = 20
         Low   Very likely: 1 x 6 = 6

This exercise is carried out for each of the factors and for each product/
strategic business area. Scores are totalled by product/strategic business area
and normalized (to reduce the size of the numbers). The result gives a risk score
for each product which is entered on the RM.

When the technique was used by Rolls Royce Motors some 15 key environmental
factors were identified (not all applied to all products), examples are emissions
legislation, external industrial disputes, exchange rates and shortage of key
supplies.

The use of the RM in conjunction with the DPM effectively provides a third
dimension to the DPM. This is an interesting concept, which opens up new areas
for exploration. It is, of course, difficult to draw a usable three-dimensional

matrix, although it is easy to describe the results of one in narrative terms by using sub-headings.

At Rolls Royce Motors we used the risk matrix to explore this additional dimension, but presented the results as two, two-dimensional matrices, the lessons from which were intertwined in the narrative of the plan.

The possibility of building a three-dimensional matrix out of glass or plastic blocks has also exercised our minds, as a way of providing a visual view of the interaction of the two matrices. But this is for the future.

Also for the future are some additional developments of the 3-D matrix concept, to enable the company to examine its 'portfolio' against individual problems which the strategy might face: for example energy consumption, manpower needs, capital needs, proneness to inflation, and no doubt many more.

CONCLUSION

There is every reason to be excited over the benefits that portfolio analysis techniques can bring to the corporate planning activities of any organization of any degree of complexity. There is also a need to end on two notes of warning:

(1) They are not push button, 'black box' techniques which
     tell a company what to do. They should be used with
     commonsense and in conjunction with other methods of
     analysis.

(2) By their nature they tend to rule out what might be a
     very profitable strategy of being a minority producer
     in *certain* markets. What they should do is to help the
     company to define that this is indeed a valid strategy
     it wishes to follow - and not a rationalization for
     poor performance.

ACKNOWLEDGMENTS

I am grateful for the help given by Bob Young and Tony McCann of Rolls Royce Motors Ltd., Dick Teager and Mike Sweet of National Freight Corporation, Mike Hatfield and Chris Trott of Arthur Guinness, Son and Co. Ltd., and John Robinson of Shell Chemicals. The chapter draws heavily on their knowledge and experience and without their active help in its preparation there would have been no chapter.

REFERENCES

[1] Shell International Chemical Co., *The Directional Policy Matrix - A new aid to corporate planning*. (1975)

[2] S.J.Q. Robinson, R.E. Hitchens and D. Wade, The directional policy matrix - tool for strategic planning, *Long Range Planning*, 10 (2), June (1978). (Chapter 8 of this book)

[3] R. Young and D.E. Hussey, Corporate planning at Rolls Royce Motors Ltd., *Long Range Planning*, 10 (2), April (1977). (Chapter 12 of this book).

Part 4

PLANNING AS A PROCESS OF
ORGANISATIONAL CHANGE

David Hussey provides in Chapter 10 an introduction to some of the aspects which should be considered in designing planning processes. He emphasises the importance of having a planning approach which matches the organisational style, and which takes account of structure and strategy. Planning is a change agent, but planning processes may well be changed by the strategies they bring about.

The relationship of planning and organisation change is taken further in two case studies. Chapter 11 by Nigel Freedman and Kees Van Ham describes a novel approach to planning used in parts of the Philips organisation. This represents a marriage between planning and O.D. thinking.

In Chapter 12 Bob Young and David Hussey show how planning was introduced to Rolls Royce Motors, again emphasising the importance of blending behavioural and analytical concepts.

Chapter 10

CORPORATE PLANNING AND ORGANISATIONAL CHANGE
David Hussey

Corporate planning is often claimed to be one of the most effective methods of
achieving organisational change, because it helps the company to understand what
changes are needed to achieve growth targets, to take advantage of opportunities,
and to respond to perceived movements in the business environment. This indeed
is one of the major reasons for undertaking corporate planning. The reality is
often far from the theory, largely I believe because of the way many managers
think about organisations.

If your view of an organisation is of a piece of white paper on which have been
written lines and boxes, you may be lulled into thinking that organisational
change is simply a matter of picking up a pen and ruler and altering the chart.
In fact the organisation chart represents only a tiny element of what is involved
in a process of organisational change.

Two factors give us grounds for concern. The first is the findings of a membership
survey of the Society for Long Range Planning (also referred to in chapter 3),
which showed that a majority of organisations which employed corporate planners
did not do organisational planning. Our own very wide contacts with planners in
all types of organisation lead us to believe that most corporate plans deal mainly
with market strategy, finance, to a lesser degree facilities planning, and hardly
at all with human resources, organisational change or implementation of the plans.

The second is that we still find managers who are searching for a universal
planning system that can be dropped into place in their own organisations. A
recent survey of readers of the journal *Long Range Planning* has revealed a demand
for even more "how I did it" articles. Some, no doubt because there is a value
in contrasting various practical approaches with the theory, but many we know
because they still seek the one true path to salvation. In fact, not only are
there several paths that might have value for the individual organisation, but the
ones that will work are dependent on the unique characteristics of the importing
organisation. The net result of this is that standard planning "packages" rarely
make sense even when backed by a reputable consultancy, or when they obviously
have worked in another company. This is not to argue that packages *cannot* work:
only that a better approach to ensure success is to study the company and design
an approach that meets its needs, starting from a set of concepts and principles,
rather than a firm commitment to a particular *system*.

There are a number of reasons why the universal solution is sought so avidly.
Many companies embrace corporate planning with much enthusiasm but little thought:
the purposes and aspirations of moving to a planning process are rarely made
explicit and indeed are seldom considered. A glance back to the diagram in
Figure 3.1 will give an idea of some of the numerous options there are for the
choice of planning system, each of which will produce a different effect on the
organisation.

In some of the older functions, such as accounting, there is a strong core of
professional expertise to guide top management and resist precipitate measures in
planning the number of experts is small. It is typical for a company to appoint
somebody to the post of planning director who has no previous experience or depth
of knowledge of planning. His brief is to introduce planning: the end product he
often sees as his task is, not unnaturally, plans. In fact, what are far more
important end products of a planning process are actions, flexibility, and the
adapting of the organisation to new circumstances which are expected to arise.
It is significant, but rather sad, that many planning systems stop short of any
formal method of ensuring that plans are actually implemented, and indeed
organisations frequently create a reward structure for management which encourages
hasty, short term actions, and gives no credit for far-sightedness, vision and
wisdom.

Perhaps the third reason for the search for the universal solution is that many
managers do not understand one of the basic realities of planning: that success
is rooted in analytical skill, decision-making ability *and* a recognition of the
numerous behavioural implications of planning.

While it is possible, and indeed sometimes desirable, to make organisational
changes in order to achieve a better planning process, it is rarely sensible to
drop in a system which will cause such changes without a proper decision being
taken in a full understanding of their implications.

One of the realities of successful corporate planning is that the chief executive
must have something more than the "commitment" stressed in the literature. True,
this is needed: but in addition he must be absolutely clear about what he expects
from corporate planning, and whether he is willing to pay the price. An effective
planning process is a way of management, and unless it becomes this it is not
worth having. Every change in the way a company is managed has a potential impact
on all the managers within the company. Some approaches to corporate planning
are likely to prove shattering to managers used to operating under completely
opposing management styles: whether it is the planning process or the managers
that shatter depends on the relative power and influence of the people concerned.

The most effective approaches to corporate planning, those approaches which fit
best the present tendancy to wider participation and more open management are
likely to be demanding of the chief executive's time, and will probably require
him to change many of his personal management practices. This is the sacrifice
he must be aware that he will have to make before he embarks on the planning
route. If he reneges on this contract with himself, once made, he is likely to
render ineffective any process of planning which he starts.

It is fairly obvious that the process of planning used by an organisation must
take account of business complexity and organisational structure, two factors
which will be returned to later. A third important influence is organisational
style, and in many ways the "fit" of planning approach and style are the most
important elements affecting the success or failure of planning efforts. Neither
are immutable, but at any one time in an organisation there will be a particular

style by which corporate management operates, and a particular process of planning.

In a large organisation it is possible for different organisational styles to maintain in the various units of an enterprise: despite the efforts of head office, there are frequently differences in overseas subsidiaries, or even within sub-units or departments within the same country.

Organisational style has certainly been recognised as an important determinant of the way in which different enterprises operate. It has been suggested as having an influence on the success or failure of planning although it has hardly featured in the research studies. Even more neglected as a research topic is whether different organisational styles require different approaches to corporate planning. Could some of the stages of planning evolution described in chapter 3 have at least part of their origins in a response to different organisational style situations? This is speculation, but we can say with more firmness that the organisational development style of planning described in the Philips case study in chapter 11 would have no hope at all of working in some of the companies we know. And the Rolls Royce case reveals a compatibility between the open style of the company, the intent of the chief executive and the process designed for the company. Involvement was not an ideal invented for Rolls Royce by the consultants: it was practised before the company began to give serious attention to a new planning initiative.

Although our own opinion is that a top-down "tablets from the mountain" planning approach is doomed to failure in the long run, and is certainly not the most effective of approaches in the short term, it is perhaps the only concept that will work at all in a company with an autocratic organisational style. Perhaps there is a fertile field of research here. (Another parallel area for investigation which has received some practical consideration, is the fitting of managers' personal characteristics to the different type of activity distinguished in the portfolio analysis techniques described in earlier chapters. Do we perhaps need a different set of management skills to do the right corporate task in, say, a declining business, a cash generator, a speculative entrepreneurial development or for the consolidation of a successful new development?)

The message for the top management team contemplating the introduction of planning for the first time, or analysing dissatisfaction with an existing planning approach, is study your organisational style. There may then be a decision about which to change, style or planning process, but at least this can be a rational decision which can be supported by a strategy for change, instead of the all too common assumption that things happen differently the minute a manager *thinks* he will make a change.

It also seems to us to be important that the chief executive carries his senior managers along with him if he wishes to make planning work effectively. It is considerably easier for him to do this, if he has worked through the other steps: when he knows what he wants, how it will affect him, and what problems will be caused by the organisational style of his enterprise.

Earlier we mentioned that the complexity of an organisation had to be taken account of in the design of an appropriate planning process. Complexity of product, market, resources and geographical scope are all factors which affect the planning process directly, as well as indirectly through their influence on structure. The size of the organisation is also significant, but only when related to the complexity issues. An enterprise employing 5,000 people making one product and operating basically in one market may need a considerably simpler planning system than is required for a company employing half that number, operating internationally, with four or five very different product ranges. To a

considerable extent these factors of complexity will also influence organisational
structure, another factor of vital importance in planning process design.

Many relatively simple businesses develop planning processes of almost unbelievable
complexity. Some of the articles and books suggest approaches to planning which
may contain ideal principles for many situations, but which are almost naive in
relation to the problems of complex multi-national operations. A typical example
is the planning model diagram, which suggests that strategic planning is a simple
choice of options arising from new or existing markets, influenced by strengths
and weaknesses and the impact of the external environment. The statement is
true, but not very helpful to the top management of the complex multi-national for
whom one of the products of planning must be a way of classifying and relating
the priorities for all the options open to them in all parts of the world. The
basis of this must be a technique such as portfolio analysis, which assists in
the understanding of the data, and provides a method of integrating it so that
sequential decisions can be taken within a framework of strategy. These
techniques are so important that they make up the major proportion of Part 3 of
this book.

Although vital for the complex multi-national, important for the multi-division
company, and possibly of value for the multi-product, multi-market company, these
techniques are absolutely valueless for the simple organisation.   They cannot
therefore be lifted from the pages of a text book, re-incarnated as a system,
and applied without attention to the unique characteristics of the organisation.

A typical problem in the design of planning processes is how to cater for the
different needs of head office, major division, and minor subsidiary. It is a
typical reaction to define a planning process which everyone has to follow, which
frequently means that the smaller units of a major company are drowned in an
approach which is too complex for their needs. Another problem, frequently
overlooked, is to design a timetable which gives all the units in the organisation
adequate time to apply participative planning approaches; if this is what they
seem to need.

It is by no means uncommon to find that the Board in a major multi-national
decides that a period of, for example, twenty six weeks might seem to be adequate
to prepare the corporate plan. What happens to this time when the task is
approached sequentially is something like this:-

	Preparation of Instructions	Consideration/Review
Head Office	2 weeks	4 weeks
Divisional Management	2 weeks	4 weeks
Regional Headquarters	1 week	3 weeks
Country Headquarters	1 week	3 weeks
Companies	1 week	3 weeks
Departments	1 week	1 week
	7 weeks +	19 weeks
	= 26 weeks	

In some types of planning process, the final "plan" is little more than a
consolidation of operating plans, with "guidelines" flowing down the organisation
through successive layers of management and plans eventually flowing up the other
way. The timing problem here is that although the values are smaller, the number
of managers participating in the process may be greater at the bottom end than at
the top, but the squeeze on time is usually applied in strict hierarchical order.

A temptation is to try to speed the process up by using a thick pad of forms. This aims to provide head office with data in a common format to facilitate consolidation. Unfortunately, it is about the best way of destroying creativity in planning than anything else I have ever come across. Filling in the little boxes receives a greater priority than actually thinking!

It is important that the scheme for preparing operating plans, of whatever time span, should follow lines of the organisational structure. By-passing a manager who carries responsibility for results, in the interests of speeding up the process, is a sure way of creating future difficulties.

For complex companies, the ponderous process outlined above will always either give inadequate time to people in some of the layers or will take so long to carry out that plans will not be produced within a realistic period of time. Of course the specimen timetable given above can be streamlined. It is possible for some work to be started in parallel, rather than sequentially as I have shown: it is also possible for those at the bottom of the process to start their planning work earlier, before formal instructions arrive.

An even better way is to consider a more formal separation of strategic from operational planning. Strategic planning need not necessarily mirror the organisational structure (and may think of the enterprise in terms of strategic business units), so long as guidelines from that activity can be spelled out in terms which do match the organisational structure.

The Rolls Royce case illustrates one way of structuring such a separation, and is based on a three stage planning process (strategy formulation, long range plan, annual budget plus other implementation tools). Each stage in the process is dependent on the preceding stage, but works to different "rules" and each stage goes to a deeper level of management involvement.

The strategy phase may be a momentary interruption and consolidation of studies and evaluations being carried out at corporate and divisional levels continuously throughout the year. It is an approach which blends smoothly with the concept of policy analysis discussed by Bernard Taylor elsewhere in this book.

It is also a process which allows a company flexibility to adjust the method of preparing the long range plans to the needs of the business units. There does not have to be an overall solution based on the needs of headquarters and the largest subsidiary: instead there may be a suite of two or three different approaches with common core, integrated under the strategy phase. Even the planning horizon may vary between business units, subject to a common core horizon needed for headquarters financial planning.

An alternative approach, which separates the definition of strategy and strategic guidelines from the annual review of, in this case, a five year plan, is practised by a Swiss based multi-national. Here, every few years, they bring together an international working party for each business area, consisting of staff from headquarters and the managing directors of their larger subsidiaries in that business. This working party reviews strategy, examines new options against the forecast business situation, and recommends the worldwide strategy the group should follow. Once accepted by the Board, this exercise provides the strategic guidelines on which the routine annual re-examination of the long range plans are based.

The approach is by no means perfect, but it has the merit of seeking the involvement of senior line management in the process of strategy development, and ensures that the plans are completed within a framework of strategy. (There is also an annual discussion about the actions each subsidiary will take which precedes the actual detailed compilation of the plan.)   The weaknesses of the approach are that:- it requires the same input from all subsidiaries regardless of their size or complexity; the five year plan format is a fat set of forms which never quite seem to fit the problems faced by the local subsidiary; the major planning information requirement is based on what fits the major business activity of the group, and is often not right for the other businesses it is in.

Enough has been said to emphasize that whether an organisation is good or bad at corporate planning can be the result of the way planning is approached. It is not just a reflection of the quality of individual managers, although there may be some correlation: but even organisations with managers of excellent quality are frequently very bad at planning. The chief executive should never forget that corporate planning is a major part of a total management process. It is not merely the way in which the planning element of the management task is performed, but is also an approach to all other elements, including organising, motivating, controlling and communicating. Because of this, the planning process should link up to and be compatible with other systems used in the organisation: project appraisal, budgetary control, management by objectives, personnel systems of appraisal and reward, and any other significant measures practised by the company. Thus the introduction of corporate planning should be undertaken with a full understanding of existing processes, and may cause these to change. It is a major error for any chief executive to view these tools by which he runs his company as discrete and unrelated activities.

Corporate planning is about management. Management is corporate planning plus a number of other factors. If you have good corporate planning you have good management: but you need more than capable managers to achieve good corporate planning. And success rarely comes from the ill-considered use of other people's approaches to planning. The universal solution does not exist.

Chapter 11

STRATEGIC MANAGEMENT IN PHILIPS*

Nigel Freedman and Kees Van Ham

N. V. Philips, Gloelampenfabriken, Eindhoven, Netherlands

1. INTRODUCTION

To support managers in their increasingly complex tasks strategic planning tries to systematically identify the issues and to support the decision making that determine the main directions of a business. Support frequently takes place in a variety of forms, for example the investigation of specific opportunities, the search for new products, technological forecasting, economic, technical or financial studies. Each or all of these are carried out in response to specific questions or identified problems (problem *solving*).

A broader approach is now recommended in Philips[1] and elsewhere. This involves an analysis of present business strategies and a search for new alternative strategies, to be developed by the confrontation of the results of systematic studies of the external environment and of the internal strengths and weaknesses of the organisation. The accent is then more upon the creative identification by a number of people of suitable opportunities and important threats, so highlighting the problem** areas. This represents an important move from support in problem *solving* to support in problem *identification*.

Perhaps the biggest difficult with this broader approach is that it is not at all a simple thing to introduce into an organisation. A comprehensive new way of reaching major business decisions cannot be switched in mechanically by staff departments. It must evolve by a development through several layers of the organisation that is properly planned, and that does not force managers abruptly to face major conflicts with the way they are used to working.

This chapter describes the first stages of one method that has been designed specifically for such a planned development. The underlying concept is such that

---

* This chapter was originally published by Philips under the title *An Approach to the development of strategic management.*

** "Problem" is used here in a broad sense to include for example opportunities. The word "issue" will be used instead to cover items that are of major importance to future development and therefore justify substantial management attention.

we want to concentrate more on how to help broaden the way of managing than on
the way of formalistic planning as such, while working on concrete business
issues.

To a great extent the success of any business will depend upon how well its
managers are themselves aware of and can deal with their changing environment.
Ansoff et al[2] refer to the sharp distinction between *competitive* (operating)
management and *entrepreneurial* (strategic) management.

- The former is concerned with making most use of the
  existing links to the environment, for example the
  efficient production and sales of goods and services.

- Entrepreneurial management seeks new patterns of relationships between the firm and its environment. It identifies,
  for example, new areas of business, divests old ones, and
  becomes increasingly important in *anticipating* social and
  political trends and assessing their impact upon the firm.

The skills, knowledge, attitudes and values needed for success in these two types
of management are quite different. For example, direct experience becomes of less
importance in anticipating and coping with changes in the environment than awareness, intuition and adaptability. For the continuity of the business in a
changing environment it is necessary to extend the capabilities in the firm while
developing new strategies for the external links.

Lately the term Strategic Management has come increasingly into use to describe
the following (see Figure 11.1):

a. Observing the environment and anticipating developments
   (economic, technical, social and political).
b. Changing the relationship with the environment (adapting
   externally: planning, negotiating and decision-making in
   connection with e.g. expansion, take-over, divestment).
c. Adapting the situation *internally* and developing
   appropriate capabilities (organisation, procedures,
   systems, skills, technology).

While we do not favour a formal switch to the term Strategic Management, the
Philips concept of Strategic Planning is fundamentally similar. We are concerned
not only with the creation of strategic plans, but with the development of
capabilities that will lead to better strategy *formulation*, together with the
necessary *implementation*. This implies improvement in three essential dimensions
describing aspects of management, namely:

a. Attitude, mentality, conduct, leading to better co-
   operation, environmental awareness, etc.
b. Procedures, techniques, instruments, planning technology.
c. Implementation skills (action planning, project working,
   delegation, etc.).

What follows is a description of the first steps of one particular approach to
the planned development of strategic management in a Product Division (PD) in
Philips. The division manufactures and sells consumer products on a world-wide
scale.

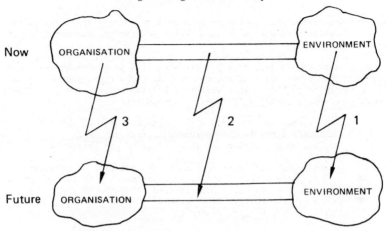

1. Observe and forecast changes
2. Change linkages
3. Change internal capabilities

Fig. 11.1 Strategic management in the changing environment

The distinguishing characteristics of this approach, which has been named the Strategic Orientation Round (SOR), are the following:

a. Main attention is directed to the identification of strategic issues that have to receive management's top priority.
b. By identifying the issues with a substantial group of managers, the issue will more readily become the "property" of the organisation.
c. Relationships have been sought between current major activities that contribute to the development of the PD and links have been actively encouraged. Thus an attempt has been made to stress the unity of the development of management, the development of organisation and the development of strategy (see Figure 11.2).

A dominating factor in the design of the approach was the strictly limited time to be allocated by the management team to formal strategic planning. Throughout the whole process it will be evident that a compromise has been sought between breadth and depth - thus between the development of insight into strategic problems and concrete output from the first introductory round (see also Figure 11.7).

A few main points about the background to the method are worth mentioning, to place it in perspective in the development of strategic planning activities in Philips. At a conference* attended by one of the authors in the United States in

---
* The proceedings of this conference are presented in H.I. Ansoff, R.P. Declerck, and R.L. Hayes (eds), *From Strategic Planning to Strategic Management*, John Wiley & Sons, 1976.

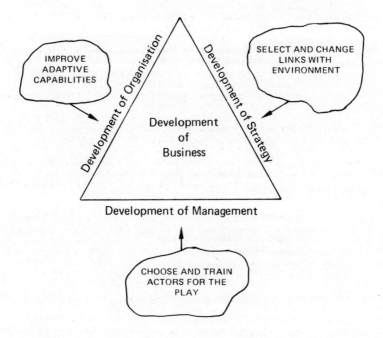

Fig. 11.2   Integral development of a business

1973 a method for developing strategic management was described by the Paris-based consultancy from Société Eurequip.[3]   This led to co-operation with Eurequip in designing and in implementing an approach in one of the Product Divisions. At about the same time one article group in the other Division concerned here began a project to examine its future strategy, with the initial co-operation of staff departments in Eindhoven including the new Corporate Strategic Planning (CSP) group. These events, plus the "Inventory of Present Strategies" project conducted by CSP,[4] have mainly provided the conditions whereby an appropriate methodology became available for an organisation that felt the need to develop strategic management at divisional level.

The authors are convinced that further development of this type of approach is valuable for the company's future. To stimulate this it will be necessary to encourage new activities and to communicate the experiences as far as possible in the concern. This is one of the essential tasks of CSP.

This chapter describes only a first step in a long process, a process that has recently been recognized as being a positive one in an external publication.[5]   Subsequent steps will involve more depth of analysis in selected areas, more attention to the development of clear objectives and goals, and explicit statements of strategies as these are evolved in the organisation. In this way meaningful strategic plans should be created together with the capabilities to implement them.

Future publications will report on aspects of the subsequent steps, as positive experience is collected in the programmes now in progress in diverse organisational units of the company.

2. MAIN FEATURES OF THE "STRATEGIC ORIENTATION ROUND" APPROACH

Structure

The PLANNING TEAM for the Strategic Orientation Round (SOR) comprised twelve managers including the directors of the product division.

To ensure coverage of the major functional areas of the business, the team members were grouped into seven ASPECT-GROUPS, for each of which one team member took responsibility, the ASPECT-CARRIERS (see Figure 11.3).

These were:

- Product/market
- R & D
- Production structure
- Personnel/social aspects

- Organisation and management
- Sales/Distribution/Service
- Financial/Economic aspects

A small SUPPORT GROUP assisted in preparing and guiding the process.

Procedure

In a series of seven monthly half-day meetings, the Planning-team worked systematically through the following seven steps:

I	Present Strategic Issues	The 10* priority problem areas initially considered to be the most typical of the present business situation.
II	External Appraisal	Selection of 10* major threats or opportunities in the business environment of importance for the next 5 years or so.
III	Internal Appraisal	Selection of 10* most important internal strengths or weaknesses.
IV	Synergy Study	Technique for stimulating creativity in the search for new ideas for appropriate opportunities or areas for concentrating attention, based on Steps II and III.
V	New Strategic Issues	Statements of the 10* most important strategic issues facing the management, based on new insight acquired in Step IV.
VI	Action Points	Translation of the ideas on WHERE to devote attention (strategic issues) into ideas on WHAT TO DO. About 10 actions, to be achievable within six months as a basis for further strategic decisions.

---

* To use the limited available time effectively, approximately 10 items were selected at each of these steps. Otherwise the subsequent complexity would have become too great for this first round.

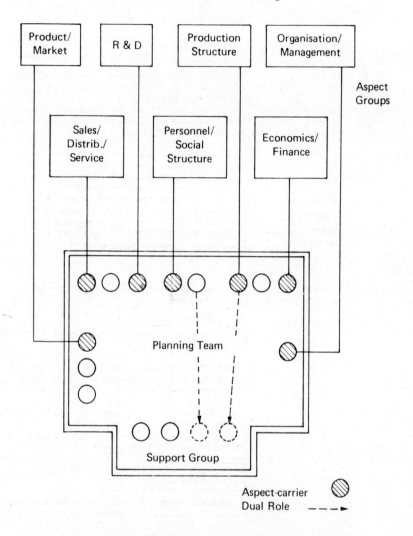

Fig. 11.3 Strategic orientation round team structure

(The planning team comprised the Product Division directors
plus managers representing the major functional departments
of the division. Input material for the first three planning
team meetings was supplied by the seven Aspect-groups, each
being responsible for discussing and selecting a limited
number of items for each step, generally but not exclusively
from the point of view of the aspects represented. In the
planning team meetings these inputs were reduced to a list
of about ten top-priority items, through combination,
reformulation and voting.)

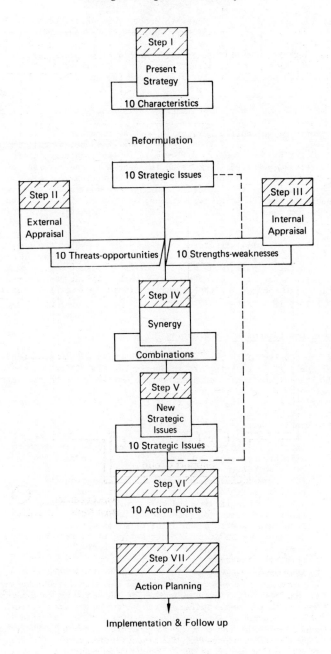

Fig. 11.4

VII   Action Planning   Specific project proposals, with clear statements
                                 of WHY, WHO, HOW, WHERE and WHEN.

In addition to these seven formal steps, a number of progress meetings were
arranged for the half-year following Step VII, to ensure that action projects
were being carried out effectively, still under the auspices of the total SOR-
team.

The total procedure is shown diagrammatically in Figure 11.4.

Each team meeting involved the members in working together as a group to establish
priorities and to distil strategically important items out of material generated
beforehand by the Aspect-groups. For example in the second step, from an input
of approximately 40 prepared items about influences in the external environment,
a list of about 10 agreed major threats and opportunities was obtained. To
prepare the input to the team meetings the Aspect-groups used knowledge and ideas
of individuals in the team, in the division, or from outside according to the
wishes of the man responsible for each aspect (the "Aspect-Carrier") (see Figure
11.5).

Each session was carefully structured to make maximum use of the very restricted
time available for the team meeting. To this end the Support-group provided a
considerable amount of background work, involving explanations, co-ordination and
reworking of the material to be submitted in each session, and ensuring adequate
communication with the rest of the organisation. One member functioned as
discussion leader in the team sessions.

Expectations, Limitations and Evaluation

In view of the novelty of this type of approach to strategic planning (inside and
outside Philips), it is essential to recognise the limitations of the method.
The very limited allocation of management time mainly affected the degree to
which it was possible to go into depth on any particular point; the whole project
must be clearly seen as being only a first round, a start to a longer-term process.

The expected benefits were:

          - Greater insight, individually and collectively, into the
             main problem areas or issues likely to confront the
             division in its changing environment.
          - For a wider cross-section of the organisation (team
             members and colleagues) a better insight and a sounder
             basis for a well-directed and co-ordinated approach to a
             restricted number of selected actions.
          - Acquaintance with a new "tool of management", a new
             decision-making process contributing to an increase in
             the quality of management and in the motivation for
             strategic management.
          - Increased awareness of the changing environment.

This focus on adapting the organisation to external developments is illustrated
in Figure 11.1

The first round was therefore not expected to lead *directly* to outputs involving
substantial new strategic decisions, or to a "strategic plan" as such, but rather
to help to define issues and to prepare for new strategies.

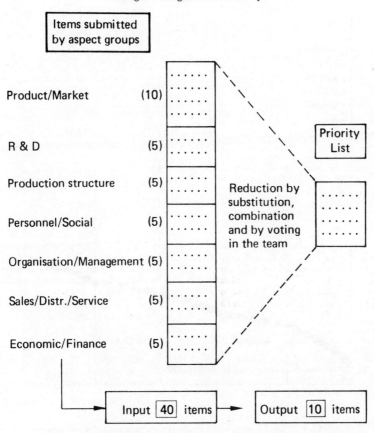

Fig. 11.5 Establishing priorities by group work in the
          planning team
(At Step I (Present Strategic Issues), at Step II (Threats
and Opportunities) and at Step III (Strengths and Weaknesses), the same principle was used to distil a set of
input items from the Aspect-groups, which provided the
starting material for the team work.

Typical outputs to be expected were actions relating to, e.g.:

        - information gathering
        - in-depth analysis of selected opportunities
        - competition studies/comparisons
        - new product/market studies
        - creation of new training activities
        - development of new relationships with outside bodies.

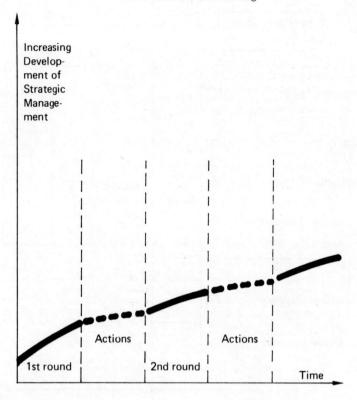

Fig. 11.6 Development of strategic management in an organisation

The foregoing goals and expected benefits are consistent with the conviction that
strategic planning will fail to support management if it is purely an instrumental,
analytical, ritual carried out only by staff specialists. The implication is that
the SOR is only a first step; it must be viewed in the context of further
development of the organisation by close involvement of other groups in subsequent
rounds, and with increasing range and depth of analysis, see Figures 11.6 and 11.7.

The extent to which the project matched the initial expectations, and led to
interest on the part of the participants in follow-up activities in strategic
planning, is indicated by the evaluation conducted at the end of process. The
voting results are given in Figure 11.8.

Communication Within the Organisation

The SOR is intended as a first stage in a longer term development of a more
strategic way of management. It is therefore crucial to the long term aims that
the group that is involved in this first orientation should not be isolated from

PRIORITIES:

. *Awareness of external trends and possible events*
. *Strategic problem/issue identification*
. *Management involvement*
. *Creation of a language for strategy*
. *Pace to maintain commitment*
. *Preparatory actions*

MISSING IN FIRST ROUND:

. *Detailed analysis*
. *Precision*
. *Specific objectives*
. *Use of specific planning tools and models*

SUBSEQUENT STEPS:

According to the specific needs of an organisation, follow-up from the first round should involve activities such as:

. *In-depth analysis of selected threats and opportunities*
. *Deeper analysis of the organisation's potential,*
  (strengths and weaknesses), more specifically related
  to business areas (product/market segments) and to
  competitors.
. *Further development of organisation structures, the*
  formal planning structure, and control of strategic
  change projects.
. *Development of explicit objectives and goals.*
. *Explicit statements of strategies as they are developed,*
  so that they become "living" guidelines for various
  levels.
. *SOR-type programmes involving other groups in the*
  organisation.
. *Involvement of allied divisions, National Organisations*
  and concern units in the strategic planning process.
. *Diversification/expansion analysis.*

Fig. 11.7   The strategic orientation round and subsequent
            steps

the rest of the organisation, since successively more people will become involved
in later phases.

The co-operation of the various business functions that occurs within the SOR-team
during the identification and the formulation of strategic issues should help
considerably in the implementation of the resulting action programmes.   Similarly,
it is important that other parts of the organisation are kept fully aware of the
nature and purposes of this approach to strategic planning, and where practicable
also of the results and experiences.

The danger of creating an isolated group should be avoided.

Further reasons for good communication in the organisation are the need to relate
to the various activities already running, and to try to prevent premature
decisions that could be costly or otherwise impede progress.

I   EFFECTS

1. I have learned nothing more about the environmental aspects that influence our business.

1	2	3	4	5
	1	1	9	

    I am now much more aware of the most important aspects in the environment that influence our business.

2. I have gained no further insight into the strengths and weaknesses of the P.D.

1	2	3	4	5
	1	2	7	1

    I have a much greater insight into the strengths and weaknesses of the P.D.

3. We are no further as a team in gaining collective insight into the main problems of the P.D.

1	2	3	4	5
		3	7	1

    We have developed as a team a good common picture of the main problems of the P.D.

4. The actions that were chosen were insufficient as outputs from the whole process.

1	2	3	4	5
		4	6	1

    The actions that were chosen were fully satisfactory, considering the amount of time allotted.

5. The implementation of the actions under the SOR-team was poor.

1	2	3	4	5
	1	6	3	1

    The actions were all carried out well under the guidance of the SOR-team.

6. The SOR had a disturbing influence on the actions to be taken in connection with the main problems of the P.D.

1	2	3	4	5
		2	5	3

    The SOR had a stimulating effect on the actions to be taken in connection with the main problems of the P.D.

II   TIME ALLOCATION

7. The SOR took far too much time.

1	2	3	4	5
		8	2	1

    Much more time should have been spent on the SOR.

8. Following the SOR I do not wish to spend any time next year on strategic planning.

1	2	3	4	5
	2	1	6	1

    Following the SOR I wish to devote a few days per month to strategic planning next year.

III   APPROACH

9. The SOR approach is much too general with too little depth.

1	2	3	4	5
	1		7	1

    I find the breadth of the SOR approach appropriate for a good introduction of strategic planning into an organisation.

10. The team-meetings did not go well.

1	2	3	4	5
		2	6	2

    The team-meetings went very well.

    (Number of votes)

Fig. 11.8 Final evaluation of the SOR by the participants

Steps taken by the Support-group to stimulate a good flow of information are
given below. In other organisations the local situation would probably demand
other methods of communication.

1. Publication of a short pamphlet describing the nature
   and purposes of the strategic planning activity, for
   distribution throughout the product division, in Dutch
   and in English.

2. Specially arranged talks to explain *the process* to the
   following groups:

   . Divisional Workers Council (GOR)
   . Workers Councils of several factories (OR)
   . Combined technical/commercial staff
   . Management staff of factories.

3. Feedback via team-members to colleagues at the various
   stages in the procedure.

In all cases the intention was to stimulate a two-way flow of information and
suggestions.

3. FURTHER INFORMATION ON THE APPROACH

Steps in the Procedure

The following survey of the seven individual steps of the SOR procedure will help
to give an indication of the planned progression from the initial questioning of
the present strategies, via the search for external and internal factors that
could lead to the recognition of new strategic issues, to the planning and
implementation of relevant action projects (see illustration, Figure 11.4).

Step 1: Present Strategic Issues

- A selection of 10 priority problem areas that the team
  initially considered to be most characteristic of the
  present strategy.

- Included mainly to give an initial orientation towards
  strategic topics, to develop terminology, and for
  inclusion and comparison with the results of the
  subsequent steps.

- Inputs were provided in advance by each Aspect-group, in
  the form of a list of about five points (ten from Product/
  Market), giving *characteristics* of the present business
  situation.   Formulation at this stage was in the form of:
  "The present strategy had lead to the situation that ..."

- To ensure that the points were appropriate for this step
  of the procedure, they were checked by the Support-group
  in order to weed-out items more suited to later steps, e.g.:

a. indications of external trends
b. suggested solutions
c. evaluation of potential.

The total list of points, in the form of 40 one-line
summaries of the input items, was reduced in the Planning-
team discussions by:

I   removing points clearly contained by another
II   combining similar points where appropriate
III   voting according to selection criteria, namely:

- does the point describe the present strategy well?
- does the point indicate an important strategic
  problem area?

The voting procedure followed that used in many such
programmes by Société Eurequip, and is described more
fully later in the chapter.

- The chosen priority items were reformulated, via team
  discussion and by the Support-group, into the form of
  Present Strategic Issues.

Examples of Formulation

Characteristic: Concentration of development expenditure is mainly around
product group XYZ.

Strategic issue: How should development expenditure be allocated to ensure an
appropriate balance of the product portfolio over the next 5 years or so.

Step II: External Appraisal

- A selection of approximately 10 events or trends in the
  Product Division's environment that were considered most
  likely to present opportunities or threats in the next
  5 years or so.

- Inputs were provided by the Aspect-groups, who each
  prepared a list of 5 items (10 for Product/Market).
  These were summarised into a total list of about 40 one-
  line statements by the Support-group, and distributed to
  all team members prior to the meeting.

- In the team meeting, the person responsible for each
  Aspect (the Aspect-carrier) gave a short explanation of
  each item submitted by his group. Following discussion,
  the list was reduced by successive combination and reformulation, followed by a voting process.

- In connection with the tight time schedule for the whole
  process, it was essential that about 10 priority items
  were obtained at each of the first three steps, so that
  the later stages would remain manageable. For this
  reason a voting system had to be employed, despite its

disadvantages for the group process. This is discussed
more fully later in the chapter.

Examples of Formulation

Opportunity: *Microcircuitry and "intelligent" products.*
The rapid improvement in Large Scale Integration technology provides countless
possibilities for building new functions into totally new or into existing
products. Replacement of mechanical by electrical elements can offer advantages
in price and in reliability, while the tendency to build "information" into
products is growing.

Due to the free availability of functional modules, there will be a shift of
emphasis from technical "Know How" to marketing "Know What".

Threat: *Political instability.*
Market area A where we achieve T% of our turnover is becoming politically more
unstable.

Local protectionism and/or higher tariffs are to be expected, and we do not have
production facilities there.

Step III: Internal Appraisal

- A selection of approximately 10 strengths or weaknesses
  of the Product Division, regarding the rest of the concern
  as being internal.

- Each Aspect-group submitted a list of 5 items (product/
  market 10). The Support-group checked them to ensure
  that the items complied with certain criteria for this
  step (for example that they did not propose solutions to
  weaknesses), and compiled from them a list containing 40
  one-line statements. This was circulated to all involved
  before the team meeting.

- Strengths and weaknesses were based upon comparisons
  with, for example, competitors or on an assessment and
  evaluation of "the state of art" in so far as this was
  known at the time. No detailed analysis was called for
  in the first round; instead the intention was to deal
  with the views of individual managers, as expressed
  through their preparatory Aspect-group discussions or in
  the team meeting.

- In the team meeting each Aspect-carrier explained the
  items submitted by his group. After some open discussion
  the 44 points were reduced to 10 by combination, by voting,
  and by reformulation.

- This process of working systematically on material arising
  from different perspectives on the business was an
  important factor in arriving at collective insight into
  business problems. Formulation and reformulation of the
  items was done carefully.

Examples of Formulation

Strength: *Product Innovation.*
We are known as innovators in the industry; this image is backed by a skilled development group with long experience of our present type of products and of mechanised production for large series.

Weakness: *Contacts with specialist outlets.*
Our traditional distribution channels in some major markets do not include good contacts with outlets that specialise in the important product lines P and Q.

Step IV: Synergy

- A creative search for relationships between the external threats/opportunities and the internal strengths and weaknesses, for subsequent attention by top management.

- The points from Steps II and III, each denoted by three or four key words, were entered into a very large board in the form of a matrix (see Figure 11.9). Taking one External point at a time, each participant went through the list of Internal points to select a maximum of 4 that for him suggested the most important relationships, based upon the questions:

  which *strength* helps us   and   which *weakness* hinders us
  directly to exploit   directly in exploiting
  this opportunity?   this opportunity?

  or which *strength* helps us and   which *weakness* hinders us
  directly to fight this   directly in fighting this
  threat?   threat?

- These individual selections were noted and the resulting total votes per cell entered into the matrix. The cells receiving most interest from the group were then made clearer by substituting large or small + or − signs as in Figure 11.9.

- Such a matrix, when filled in in this way, can lead to a vast number of ideas for further attention. Each participant was asked to study a copy of it, individually or in groups, in preparation for the next step, with the following guidance.

- Three classes of Strategic Issues (SI's) may be derived from such a matrix, namely:

  1. *Preparatory SI's*, obtained by concentrating upon the horizontal *rows* in which many cells have been given high priority (e.g. S2, W1 and W6 in Figure 11.9). The issues are typically,
     "how to *reinforce* a strength?",
     or   "how to *remedy* a weakness?".

  2. *Offensive SI's*, from a vertical column given by an *opportunity* for which there are many links with the

External			Opportunity						Threat			
Opportunity which *strength* helps us to exploit this opportunity which *weakness* hinders us in exploiting this opportunity	**Threat** which *strength* helps us to fight this threat which *weakness* hinders us in fighting this threat		Products P and Q becoming trend articles	Developing countries			Microcircuitry and intelligent products		Political instability in market area A	Raw material sources insecure		
			01	02	03	04	05	06	T1	T2	T3	T4
Industrial potential in W.-Europe		S1	+	+	**+**	+		+	–	+	+	+
Product Innovation		S2	**+**	**+**	+		+			+		+
		S3				**+**		+	**+**			+
Contacts with specialist outlets		W1	**-**		–	**-**	**-**	–			**-**	**-**
		W2	–	–	–					**-**		
		W3		**-**		**-**			–	**-**		
		W4				**-**	**-**	–				–
Expensive sales organisation		W5				–	–	**-**				–
		W6	**-**	**-**	**-**	–	**-**	**-**	**-**	–	**-**	**-**
		W7	–					–	–	–		

Votes	Sign
< 3	Blank
3 – 5	+,–
≥ 6	**+, -**

Fig. 11.9 Format of the synergy matrix (Step IV)

internal strengths/weaknesses (e.g. O1 in Figure 11.9),
typically the issues will be "how to *exploit* an
opportunity by working on our strengths and diminishing
our weaknesses?".

3. *Defensive SI's*, from a "threat column" (e.g. T2 in
Figure 11.9), typically the issue may be "how to
counteract a threat, by *using* our strengths and
eliminating our weaknesses".

In addition numerous more complex *Indirect Strategic Issues*
may be derived by seeking combinations of relationships
involving two or more rows or columns.

The Synergy step and its application in Step V are undoubtedly
the most complex parts of the approach, however they proved
to be a valuable stimulus in diagnosing strategic issues in a
creative way.

Step V: New Strategic Issues

-   In the previous step, the "synergy matrix" was generated
    as a way of stimulating creative thinking in identifying
    strategic issues. In the Product Division Planning-team
    many of the participants found a number of more complex,
    indirect issues, while others found for example simpler
    relationships between the weaknesses. The general
    experience seemed to be that much more time could be
    profitably spent in examining the matrix further.

-   It became increasingly clear that in order to be able to
    take proper advantage of *any* opportunity or to combat any
    threat, even in the longer term, the efforts would have
    to be focussed upon the internal weaknesses of the division.
    In the matrix the weaknesses severely dominated the
    strengths, in the light of the kinds of threats and oppor-
    tunities that had been generated. It was therefore
    recommended that attention should be restricted initially
    to seeking Preparatory Strategic Issues, so that a number
    of concrete action points could be found that were
    achievable within the agreed six months. *This did not
    mean that other ideas or issues would be completely lost;*
    they would have to be postponed until a later phase in
    the development process, unless urgent issues were
    discovered.

In the Strategic Orientation Round, a number of limitations
were necessary.

With limited time available, the goal was to select about
10 action points, on the basis of some 10 chosen strategic
issues.

The actions were not to be long-term, difficult ones, but
achievable within six months. (They could, however, be in
preparation for longer term activities.)

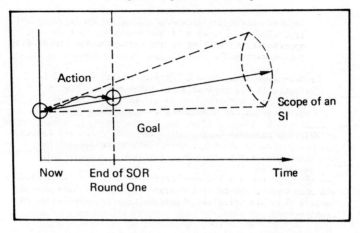

Fig. 11.10   Selection of appropriate SI's from the synergy
             matrix. Reasoning for concentrating upon
             preparatory issues.

A Strategic Issue indicates a direction - the *scope* of
the issue should not be too broad, else too much effort
would be required to move in the desired direction.

In the absence of any threats or opportunities that were
independent of the weaknesses, it was judged that priority
needed to be given to the formulation of strategic issues
that related to resolving those weaknesses.

- In connection with directing attention initially onto
  Preparatory SI's Figure 11.10 illustrates the reasoning
  that was used.

The issues selected were concerned with securing improvements
internally in a wide range of areas, for example:

1. Social policy.
2. The sales/distribution/service function.
3. Product creation procedures.
4. Management development.
5. Formalising the policy formulation process.
6. Agreements regarding profit targets.
7. Anticipation of societal developments.

Step VI: Action Points

- Participants were requested to work individually or in
  groups before Step VI, to suggest action points based on
  the Strategic Issues from Step V, also looking at those
  from Step I.

  - Criteria for selecting suitable actions were given as:

    - necessity
    - attainability with 6 months (a concrete project proposal
      must be possible)
    - effect upon results
    - relationship with existing activities.

  - 23 action points were submitted. These were each
    described by their originator, followed by some substi-
    tution/combination in the discussions.

  - A few action points lay close to actions already being
    undertaken in the PD.

  - Reduction was carried out further by voting; the group
    settled on a list of seven actions, one of which would
    be carried out directly under the PD management, outside
    of the SOR. These seven were felt to contain as much
    work as the PD organisation would be able to handle in
    the following 6 months.

Examples of Action Point Formulation

1. A typical action point, based on a strategic issue involving management
   development, could be:

   "The development of function profiles for key positions in the organisation,
   and the development of appropriate procedures for their subsequent creation,
   up-dating, and application. In addition a management development and
   recruitment programme for the next three years for these key positions".

2. Two strategic issues, relating to the scope of the business and to materials
   scarcity, could lead to one action point:

   "The investigation of diversification into the AB business, whereby our
   strengths in product development and technical know-how can best be exploited,
   and the over-dependence on material X can be reduced".

Step VII: Action Planning

  - The proposals for actions arising from the previous step
    need to be translated into concrete project proposals and
    plans, and then implemented under the sponsorship and
    guidance of the SOR-planning team. This translation is an
    essential part of the SOR-process.

  - A framework to be followed in the planning was provided in
    the following form:

    - Strategic issue(s) involved
    - Action point description
    - Task description
    - Problem definition
    - Method of approach
    - Planning (people, resources, meetings, organisation,

timing, reporting)

- The project leader who had been assigned to each of the
  action projects described his proposals to the team,
  along the above lines. A number of criteria were
  provided to assist the team in assessing and improving
  the proposals in the subsequent discussion.

  - Does the proposal sufficiently cover the SI?
  - Is it attainable in 6 months?
  - Is the approach an effective and efficient one?
  - Is there sufficient depth and breadth contained in it?
  - Does it fulfil our expectations?

- Meetings were arranged for subsequent reporting to the
  SOR-team, on progress and problems, over the following
  6 months.

Monitoring and Reporting of Projects

The planning of action projects, Step VII, took place in June 1976. Three
meetings of the full team were planned for the next half-year, for reporting on
progress, difficulties, etc., and to give the team the chance continually to steer
the actions for which it was responsible.

It is not appropriate in this chapter to give details of the projects themselves.
What is important, however, for the process of strategy development, is the fact
that most projects showed clearly the difficulties encountered when translating
ideas into actions. Nearly all projects took longer than was originally planned,
or were only partially undertaken, with the rest being altered or rescheduled to
be completed later.

Team Composition and Division into Business Aspects

To arrive at an appropriate composition for the Planning-team and the Aspect-
groups, the factors below needed to be taken into account:

- For a Product Division-level activity of this type, direct
  involvement of the directors was essential.

- A team of about twelve people would be a reasonable size
  to allow adequate discussion and voting possibilities.

- A good cross-section of the managers responsible for the
  major line and staff functions should be sought.

- Each team member would be expected to act as the link with
  his section of the organisation, in the channeling of
  information and ideas into and out of the Planning-team.

- In the first round, the numbers had to be limited. In
  later phases many others in the division would be expected
  to take part.

- Specific knowledge about an area would generally be brought

in by involvement of "experts" from inside or outside
the division, via the Aspect-groups.

- The division of the total business into the seven aspects
  used was based partly on experience gained elsewhere in
  strategic planning, and partly on the particular management roles of some of the team members. In practice, in
  the process of submitting items at the various steps
  there was little formality in the division into aspects.
  Similarly the meetings of the Aspect-groups were entirely
  informal, being at the discretion of the Aspect-carriers.
  (More formality is to be recommended, see later in this
  chapter.)

- Because of the balanced composition of the team, it was
  essential that all team members were present at all
  meetings. This required a high degree of discipline.
  Apart from illnesses, no major disturbance took place.

- It is important in activities of this type to take into
  account, in composing the team, the value of the group-
  process and the inter-disciplinary learning potential
  that is available, for example for new managers. The
  other side of the coin is the need to avoid disturbing
  influences.

Support Group Roles

To ensure that the process runs smoothly, the support-group can fulfil a wide
variety of tasks in connection with the procedures and in handling the material
to be discussed at each session.

Tasks. In the programme described here the following were involved (see Figure
11.3):

1. Planning and guiding the SOR-project.
2. Preparation and subsequent evaluation of the meetings of
   the Planning-team.
3. Leading the discussions in the team meetings.
4. Helping individuals and Aspect-groups with their
   preparation of items to be submitted at the various
   steps.
5. Checking and reformulating input items, to ensure
   appropriate consistency and to facilitate the presentations
   in the team meetings.
6. Two-way communication in relating the SOR-project to
   other activities, perhaps already running, in the Product
   Division (e.g. Organisation-change projects, personnel
   moves, 4-year planning, management training.)
7. Communication about the SOR with the organisation (in
   connection with content or process as appropriate), e.g.
   P.D.-management, staff-meetings, workers councils, other
   P.D.'s.
8. Suggesting the appointment of people to participate in
   the process.
9. Maintaining relationships with other company departments

in connection with strategic planning methodology, or
to bring in other specialist skills for example in the
action projects.

10. Ensuring continuity in the development of strategic
management in the division, through the planning of
appropriate follow-up to the SOR together with the
P.D.-management.

Composition. The support-group for the SOR consisted at the beginning of the
project of five people, whose main roles may be summarized as below. During the
project some changes in composition occurred due to personnel moves and to
conscious preparations for follow-up activities at other levels.

- Project leader/chairman
- Methodology/co-ordination
- Methodology/discussion leader
- Group process/communication within the organisation
- Observer/follow-up in the division and elsewhere.

Selection/Voting Procedure

It has been stated previously that the Strategic Orientation Round procedure
involves a number of compromises, in view of the limited amount of time that top
management as a group can reasonably devote to any one activity. Strategic
Management, and attempts to stimulate it, require that a very broad range of
management activities have to be dealt with in close relation to each other. This
results inevitably in a lack of depth in the treatment of many problems that are
discussed by the team.

To ensure that a broad range of topics could be handled in this first round, it
was necessary to use fairly strict procedures in the team meetings to use the
time effectively. In particular, for the selection of items to be passed on to
subsequent steps, a voting procedure was employed. Naturally there are disadvantages with voting, but without this it would have been extremely difficult to cope
with the complexity in trying to reach consensus, when distilling the top-priority
items from the input material that had been prepared by the Aspect-groups.

In most cases the voting system used was one which Société Eurequip had used with
success in a large number of interventions including one in Philips. The example
given below indicates the method used at several steps of the SOR. However, it
must be made clear that at all times a reasonable balance was attempted between
necessary and unnecessary voting, by making sure that no items were rejected
without good reason.

Any team member could veto any item that the voting procedure might have disallowed.

Examples of the Voting Process

- To select, say, 10 strengths/weaknesses from a total list
of 40 items, each participant had a sheet giving the
nature of each item in a single-line statement, plus a
more detailed description of the items which were also
explained verbally just before the selection step.

- Before any voting took place, the team reduced the list
as far as possible by reformulating some of the items,

and merging or substituting any that were too similar.

- In most cases one or more criteria were clearly stated,
  to give the basis for the selection.

- Each team member was asked to distribute a certain total
  number of votes amongst those items that he wished to
  select, with a maximum of two votes for any one item.
  In this way, each member had an *equal* voice in setting
  priorities, but could also indicate his weighting of the
  items over a small range.

- This total number of votes per person was calculated
  according to the number of items, the number of voters,
  and the average vote considered desirable to give
  reasonable "resolution" between the chosen and the
  rejected items.

- The voting scores were then examined and the group
  systematically looked at those items attaining the
  highest scores, until a reasonable number had been
  selected for that step. In every situation, the members
  were specifically requested to look carefully at the
  items being rejected, and any objections were discussed
  by the team to recheck the effects of the voting. Through
  combination and some reformulation, an attempt was made
  to select a good *set* of items from the material available.

The question of whether voting is a reasonable thing to do in such a group has
often been debated. There are many disadvantages, mainly in that it does not
allow the expert's opinion to be recognised above that of the less knowledgeable
person. On the other hand, it is important to realise that the kind of material
that is brought into the voting process frequently contains equally valid
interpretations, but seen from different viewpoints.

In addition, the items discussed are in fact always "packages" of ideas, briefly
summarized and where in any case every manager will have his own interpretation
of its implications. Thus a statistical justification of the voting process is
not to be attempted, since the items being voted for are not always straightforward objects or people.

The Eurequip voting system provides a very rapid method of highlighting the most
popular items, quickly removing a large number of low-priority items, allowing
attention and discussion to be focussed onto the middle-range where this is most
necessary.

4.   SUGGESTIONS FOR FURTHER DEVELOPMENT OF THE APPROACH

Introduction

The Strategic Orientation Round was designed to be a relatively simple way to
introduce strategic management to a particular organisation, where the amount of
time to be devoted to it by the top management was one critical factor in
selecting a method. In addition, there had been a positive experience beforehand
with strategic planning in one product group in the division, and help was available from corporate staff to bring in the first experience in Philips of this
type of group approach, from another division.

In any other set of conditions, it is appropriate to look carefully at the SOR procedure and to ask where, in the light of experience, it is advantageous to adapt the procedures.

The following contains some thoughts (and some experiences) of variations on the original theme. It is not appropriate to describe here the follow-up phases, that will depend strongly on the issues and actions raised in a particular organisation. A few possibilities are listed in Figure 11.7.

Participants and Aspect-groups

A team of about 12 people, meeting for half a day per month, does not get a great deal of opportunity to go into depth on the subjects that very often desperately need it.

The idea of having Aspect-groups is to give more chance for discussion, as preparation for more effective use of the main planning team meetings.

By making these Aspect-group meetings much more formal, and scheduling them properly, it is possible to improve the whole programme considerably.

In particular it has been found possible, in subsequent projects, to work quite comfortably with a much larger group. Here the total group meeting becomes more of a plenary session, where the results from the smaller groups are handled.

The composition of the team will have a major bearing on the type of strategic issues that result from the process. It is worthwhile to look for a reasonable balance of people who represent the "WHAT" and the "HOW" aspects of the business. Here the "WHAT" means the basic Product/Market combinations, Product Technologies and Regional Strategies of the business; the "HOW" aspects are concerned principally with the resources that the firm uses - its people, financing, materials, equipment, organisation, etc.

Without an adequate balance, it is easy to miss major issues, particularly those concerning the scope of the business, which aspect is dealt with more fully in the following section.

Business Scope - Step I

In the foregoing procedures, Step I involved the selection of a number of issues that were felt by the team members to be of importance in the present situation, resulting from recent (implicit) strategies. The main intention was to focus attention, as a team, upon the potential strategic issues, but not explicitly upon strategies themselves.

In practice, the results were rather similar to the subsequent strengths/weaknesses analysis of Step III, or to some of the issues finally selected in Step V. As far as the process is concerned this was unimportant, but there are now other ideas for better use of the limited time available. The new version of Step I, given below, has given encouraging results in practice.

Perhaps the most fundamental question to be asked when starting with an examination of strategy, is "What Business are we in?".

This may be obvious, or even trivial. But experience shows that the variety of different managers' interpretations of the so-called Business Scope can give valuable insight into problems and into new business opportunities.

Although some managers are likely to have a good picture already of the business
scope, it will be a tremendous help in the process if *all* members of the team
gain a common perspective. The term 'business scope' can be more clearly
understood if we use the now common marketing philosophy, that the business is
here to fulfil certain *Customer Needs*. In effect the firm has decided or grown
to operate within some *Boundaries;* the environment or other divisions provide
most of the limits upon the scope or freedom of choice.

We may express the scope largely by making two lists, namely:

        a. WHOSE NEEDS do we satisfy?
        b. WHAT NEEDS do we satisfy?

When we have done this, we will have an idea of the PRESENT SCOPE. In doing the
exercise one inevitably thinks of new needs or new users that could reasonably
come within the scope. These can be consciously looked for, as a first step
towards broadening or redefining the concept of business scope. The subsequent
steps in the procedure involve looking systematically at the business environment
and at the firm's internal capabilities, in order to identify the priorities for
where management's attention should best be directed. The scope is a very useful
guide to help in identifying where the influences, positive or negative, are
coming from, and where one can have influence, so that the most relevant trends
and capabilities are sought.

A useful way of summarizing the business scope is shown by the matrix in Figure
11.11. It is necessary to find an appropriate level of detail for the needs and
for the users, i.e. to avoid too much generalisation while also maintaining enough
information that will lead to a good definition of the business and to new
potential business opportunities.

The scope analysis may thus provide inputs for the External Appraisal, it may form
the basis for a specific Strategic Issue at Step V, and may be used directly for
an Action point to be added to the list at Step VI.

Further development of this stage in the procedure, if time permits, can usefully
involve a more thorough survey of:

        . The competitive environment
        . Technologies being used
        . Life cycle/growth positions of products.

An action point, or a subsequent stage in which the scope of the business is to
be examined in depth, may take the form indicated later in this chapter.

Relationships Between Strategic Issues

It could help considerably in the development of an organisation if it were
possible to reach a good *set* of strategic issues, and subsequently to work on a
consistent *set* of action points.

Figure 11.12 is a simple attempt to indicate some of the relationships between
some arbitrary Strategic Issues. Here two elements are recognised, namely the
hierarchical (vertical) relationships, and the mutual (horizontal) relationships.
In other words, any work that is to be carried out in connection with related
issues will be affected by, or will contribute to, issues surrounding it in the

			PRESENT NEEDS THAT WE SATISFY						NEW	
	Business Scope Step I		Entertain-ment	Comfort	Informa-tion	"Having"	Time-saving	Present-giving	Nourish-ment	Exerci-sing
			N1	N2	N3	N4	N5	N6	NN1	NN2
Present users	House-wives	U 1	* (8)	* (3)	* (2)	* (16)	* (4)	* (9)		•
Present users	Hobby-ists	U 2				* (2)	* (2)			
Present users	Working Women	U 3	* (3)	* (2)		* (1)	* (2)		•	
Present users	Men	U 4	* (4)	* (2)	* (8)	* (6)	* (3)	* (3)		•
Present users	Travel-lers	U 5	* (1)	* (1)	* (3)			* (2)	•	
Present users	Children	U 6	* (1)		* (1)				•	
New	Infirm People	N U 1	•	•	•					
New	Sports-men	N U 2			•			•		•

* = Products supplied
(Y) = Number of product lines
• = Potential User/Need

Fig. 11.11 Example of business scope matrix

"relevance tree" of Figure 11.12. It can be helpful to draw up such a diagram before selecting action projects, to help with identifying priorities, resources, or people likely to be affected. (A similar diagram for the Action projects may also be useful.)

The upper level "Goals" in Figure 11.12 are very loosely defined here, simply to indicate the existence of multiple objectives for a business.

Diagnosis Stage

Where possible it is recommended that one or two members of the support group,

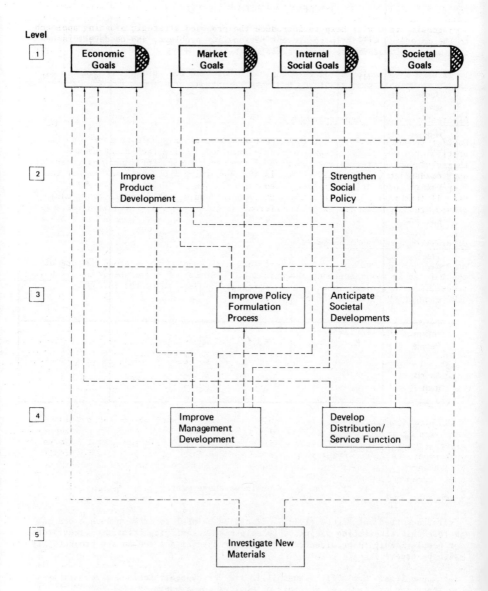

Fig. 11.12 Relationships between strategic issues

preferably from outside the organisational unit, should interview a number of managers throughout an organisation *before* the planning team is composed. Such a diagnosis stage will help to introduce the proposed strategic planning approach to the managers, will help to prevent personality problems, and to detect issues that may otherwise impede the progress of the work.

It is also a valuable way of ensuring that those who are guiding the process also have a reasonable picture of the business situation.

Alternatives to the Aspect-groups

Earlier it was suggested that the Aspect-group meetings should be more formalised, particularly when larger teams are to be involved. While the Aspect-groups themselves were selected for coverage of the basic management *functions*, they do not necessarily provide the best basis for generating the inputs for *all* of the Steps of the process. It is suggested that for Step I (Present Strategy) and Step II (External Appraisal), the participants should work in *multi-functional groups*, representing for example different Article Groups or Business Areas.

Diversification/Expansion Analysis

An orientation round such as that described here should give a broad picture of the main areas for management attention, and a number of actions that should help to determine a limited number of new strategies. Some suggested follow-up activities were given in Figure 11.7.

The approach used has not been specifically oriented towards what could perhaps be a fundamental problem, namely the scope or mission of the business. It may well be that due to a lack of focus upon fundamental objectives, or to insufficient depth of analysis of competitive position, that the product/market combinations may not be adequate to ensure continuity of the business in the long term.

As a sequel to the SOR, the following short stage may be carried out to examine diversification or expansion needs.

A full treatment of this subject requires far more attention than can be given here, and it is well covered in the literature. However the sequence of steps given below may provide a possible first stage for helping a management team to work towards a clear strategy for its future growth. The steps could be prepared beforehand by staff members, and discussed in a session of say two days with a small group of top managers.

Step 1 - Present Product/Market Strategy

An inventory of existing agreements, decisions, guidelines and goals, that determine the main directions in which the organisation conducts its product/ market policy. These can relate to:

- markets   - technologies   - co-operations
- products   - regions

Step 2 - Product Portfolio

Scheme indicating the relationships between existing and planned products with regard to their expected contributions to the total business in the coming years, based on:

- life cycles   - profit potential
- market growth   - cash flow
- market share

Step 3 - Scope Matrix

An indication of Business Areas, on the basis of Consumer Needs. A survey of present *Consumers* and of present *Needs* being satisfied, can give valuable insight into potential opportunities for growth (see earlier in this chapter).

Step 4 - Growth Direction

New activities may be undertaken by investing in new products, in new markets, in new technologies or in new geographical regions. Which directions should have the priorities, in the light of available opportunities and capabilities?

By way of example, a perspective may be gained using a simple matrix showing the extent to which totally new business is to be sought, or where existing product lines or markets are to be expanded:

		PRODUCT	
		Present	New
Market	Present	20%	(EXPANSION) 40%
	New	30%	10% (Diversification)

Growth in Region A

Step 5 - New Strategies

- seek alternatives   - select strategies
- criteria for selection   - determine actions needed

Step 6 - Implementation Planning

- planning of time, resources, and people affected
- organisation forms needed
- management potential
- co-operation required
- follow-up.

The above steps are given only as a guide to one formal method for a review of the business scope. According to the business in question, the steps would need more or less depth, time and resources for a full treatment. However, a first rapid orientation is to be recommended.

5. REFERENCES

[1] *Strategic Planning Approach with Philips,* Corporate Strategic Planning, Eindhoven, June 1975.

[2] H.I. Ansoff, R.P. Declerck and R.L. Hayes, *From Strategic Planning to Strategic Management.* Paper presented to the first International Conference on Strategic Management, Vanderbilt University, 1973.

[3] P. Davous and J. Deas, *Design of a Consulting Intervention for Strategic Management.* Paper presented to the first International Conference on Strategic Management, Vanderbilt University, 1973.

[4] Information on the approach developed to make an inventory of the present strategies of a large number of business units within the company, may be obtained from the Corporate Strategic Planning group, Eindhoven.

[5] G. Tavernier (asst. ed.), *The Shortcomings of Strategic Planning,* International Management, 1976, 9, p.45-47.

Chapter 12

CORPORATE PLANNING AT ROLLS-ROYCE MOTORS LIMITED*

Robert Young[1] and David Hussey[2]

[1]Rolls-Royce Motors Ltd
[2]Harbridge House, London

THE COMPANY SITUATION

For the sake of brevity, we shall begin by reporting that Rolls-Royce Motors decided to embark upon a formal corporate planning process in the late summer of 1975 - although that single statement does, of course, encapsulate many contributory events which it is not proposed to dwell upon here. Faced, not with an impending crisis, but with a gamut of opportunities for making the business grow, the Main Board took the view that its traditional planning approach would not be adequate to take the company into the 1980s. By any criteria Rolls-Royce Motors had done well since it was spun off from Rolls-Royce Limited by the Receiver shortly after the collapse of that company in February, 1971. Broadly speaking, the aerospace activities of the old company were nationalized in order to secure their survival, and became Rolls-Royce (1971) Limited. Rolls-Royce Motors Limited - largely the automotive wing of the previous organization - was incorporated as a separate entity and remains in the private sector. Although the company was formed in 1971 and floated publicly in 1973, its manufacturing traditions stretch back over 70 years to the early association of Rolls and Royce. Its record in finance, production and employment (Figure 12.1) is not unremarkable in the aftermath of the parent company's bankruptcy and through the trade recession which soon followed.

Rolls-Royce Motors has two main product lines. Best known to the public is the Roll-Royce car, which holds a unique position in the world's markets, and which is the universal symbol of excellence in automotive engineering. The Car Division production facility is at Crewe, Cheshire, and is supported by a coachbuilding works in London. Better known to the makers of heavy trucks, generator sets and air compressors than to the public at large are the company's diesel engines which are produced at Shrewsbury. Derived activities from the Diesel Division include a 27 per cent share of Moto Equipos SA in Mexico, which makes and sells Rolls-Royce Motors diesels under licence, and a majority shareholding in Thomas Hill (Rotherham) Limited which is a leading manufacturer of shunting locomotives. Within the last few months Rolls-Royce Motors has acquired 16 per cent of the equity of L. Gardner & Sons Ltd., the only other independent British diesel engine manufacturer. The significance of its diesel business to the Rolls-Royce Motors Group thus exceeds by some way public awareness of the activity.

* Originally published in *Long Range Planning,* volume 10, April 1977

	1971	1972	1973	1974	1975
_____	38,354	43,245	48,050	58,391	79,669
Direct Exports:					
£000 ____	10,852	12,631	16,810	22,014	33,083
%	28	29	35	38	42
Profits					
(£000 before tax) __	3825	4023	4599	5424	6241
Cars Sold (units) __	2237	2473	2760	2902	3134
Diesel Engines					
Sold (units) _____	2261	2768	3781	3829	4299
No. of Employees ____	8292	8166	8503	8874	9324

Fig. 12.1 Rolls-Royce Motors Limited - performance

Cars and diesel engines together currently account for 80 per cent of group
turnover and profit. The remaining 20 per cent is derived from precision casting,
machining and fabrication, from light aircraft piston engines (manufactured and
sold under licence), and from heavy duty petrol engines and transmissions which
power, *inter alia*, wheeled military vehicles and specialist emergency vehicles
such as aircraft crash tenders and fire engines.

THE EXISTING PLANNING SYSTEM

The planning system which existed at the time of the Board's corporate planning
decision (and still exists, pending the implementation of the new process) can
fairly be described as extended budgeting. It consists principally of a Five
Year Forecast - a financial extrapolation of current operations and committed
projects, together with a minutely detailed capital budget covering the same
period. In addition, there are engineering project plans covering approximately
7 years. Such a system can work very well for relatively short periods of time
when the company's strategies are unchanging; when the internal and external
factors which affect the business are more or less constant; or when all critical
decisions are made outside the planning process and the extrapolations are used
as background data only. Perhaps the most serious defect of the existing planning
mechanism has been that it works at odds with the management style which the
Group Managing Director adopts and which is encouraged in every corner of the
business. David Plastow and his Board colleagues believe very strongly in the
intelligent delegation of responsibility to Divisional managements, and in
motivating them and their employees to make a real contribution to the running of
the business. Two examples of this philosophy in practice are the organization of

the company and its employee involvement project, both of which are described in
more detail later in this chapter.

The way in which the Five Year Forecasts are constructed is not the same in each
business area, and allows little opportunity for real management involvement. To
quote extremes, in one area it is largely an accountants' exercise, with some
input at Divisional Director level. In another, it is a form completion exercise,
aimed at widespread participation but not achieving it because the people involved
are forced into a compartmental approach which narrows their contribution to a
point where real involvement becomes non-existent. External factors are not
studied in a way that is integrated with the planning system, assumptions are
rarely stated, and different parts of the company frequently work on different
interpretations of the same events. Because of the nature of the extrapolations
and the way in which they are obtained, the strategic elements of planning are
under-emphasized. Strategies are not explicitly stated in support of the plans,
which then makes their interpretation difficult.

Having been ticked off at Divisional level, the Five Year Forecasts reach the
Company Executive Committee (the four Main Board Executive Directors) as a series
of summary financial numbers. No judgement is possible on the risks and sensitivity
of these figures to external changes, or on the strategic paths being followed.
Serious discussions of the validity and meaning of the plans is thus made difficult.
The credibility of the system is stretched, the more so when timetables are over-
run and formal approvals are given too late. It is this state of affairs that
Rolls-Royce Motors decided to change. Much of the research evidence available
suggests that many UK companies who introduce corporate planning do so as a
response to a crisis or a particular problem. Irving[1] found that more than a
third of the companies in his survey began planning as a direct result of major
changes at Board level, and in practically all cases planning was initiated as the
result of a perceived need to meet a factor of change which the company faced or
anticipated. Denning and Lehr[2] among their findings observed a strong positive
correlation between a high rate of technological change and the introduction of
planning. Perhaps the Rolls-Royce Motors situation is evidence of the beginning
of a new trend in British industry: a rational decision based on a desire to do
better, taken by a company already doing well, without any crisis, having had no
traumatic management changes, and facing no environmental challenge which is not
shared by industry as a whole. It is perhaps the rational basis of the decision,
and the healthy state of the company, which makes the Rolls-Royce Motors case
study particularly interesting. Rolls-Royce Motors had both the intention and the
time to make a good job of introducing a Corporate Planning Process: it wanted
some early results for motivational reasons, but appreciated that the full process
would take some time to develop.

                    COMPANY ORGANIZATION

The organization of a company has a direct bearing on how planning is made
effective. The Rolls-Royce Motors organization reflects its management style, and
is based on decentralization of decision making to logical business units. The
Head Office function is deliberately small, consisting of the Group Managing
Director, Group Financial Director, two further Executive Directors (these four
collectively make up the Executive Committee), and supports Planning, Public
Relations, Financial, Legal and Pensions staff. Excluding secretaries the total
Head Office staff of a group employing upwards of 9000 is only 14. Business
activities are organized into divisions and sub-divisions (see Figure 12.2).
These terms do not reflect legal status: some of the divisions consist of one or
more legally incorporated subsidiaries. The three main divisions are Car, Diesel,
and International, each of which has a small number of subsidiaries reporting to it.

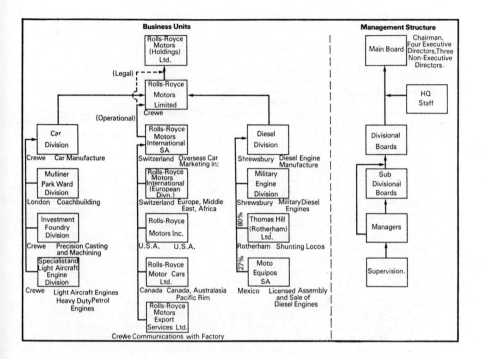

Fig. 12.2   Rolls-Royce Motors Limited - organization

The Managing Director of a subsidiary division normally reports to a non-executive Chairman who sits on the next higher level Board and has an executive role thereon. Thus, the Chairman of the Investment Foundry Division is also the Car Division's Director of Production Resources.

THE EMPLOYEE INVOLVEMENT PROJECT

It is easier to move to a participatory approach to planning in a group which already considers that its employees have a right to be involved in company affairs. Independently of the corporate planning initiative, Rolls-Royce Motors introduced an Employee Involvement Project in 1975, to enhance its already impressive style of communication with employees. A cornerstone of this project is the regular dissemination of information about the company, including explanations of financial results, problems and prospects facing the Company. Although it is not the intention to create a planning process which requires contributions below a fairly senior level in the management structure, the climate created by the employee involvement project was complementary to the new style of planning required.

USE OF CONSULTANTS

A company which wishes to introduce from scratch a new process of planning has
three basic methods open to it:

    (1)   Use outside consultants who can provide the necessary
           expertise;
    (2)   Hire an experienced planner from outside the company;
    (3)   Appoint a man from inside the company, making his first
           task the gaining of the necessary expertise.

The limited research data available suggests that the third option has been the
most popular course in the UK (although not explicitly stated in the research, it
is reasonable to assume that this is sometimes in conjunction with the first).

Knowlson[3] found that 65 per cent of Corporate Planners who were members of the
Society for Long Range Planning had been appointed to their present posts from
within the Company. His report also pointed to the difficulties of either (1) or
(2). Fifty-four per cent of all planners have less than 5 years' experience of
corporate planning and only 11 per cent have more than 10 years' experience. In
addition, roughly one third of all planners are over the age of 45, including the
majority of the most experienced group, which again suggests a relative degree of
immobility. Thus, good experienced planners are hard to find. Brown and
O'Connor[4] found that in the USA some 27 per cent of companies used consultants in
planning either for start up or on a continuing basis, and a further 51 per cent
employed consultants for *ad hoc* studies connected with planning. Whether this
pattern also applies in the UK is not known.

Rolls-Royce Motors elected to use a combination of (1) and (3). Option (2), hiring
from the start an experienced planner from outside, was not thought appropriate
for a variety of reasons. Chief among them were (i) How does a company with no
experience of formal corporate planning actually pick the right man? (ii) Does
not the new planning process present career opportunities for people already in
the company? Even discounting the latter point, options (1) and (3) in combination
offered a better spread of risk. Historically, the company has had no qualms about
engaging consultancy assistance when it has needed to undertake a task for which it
lacks in-house experience. Furthermore, it aims not to use consultancy as a 'hit
and run' approach to problem solving, but rather to ensure that its own staff learn
from the consultant and thereby add to its stock of management skills.

Three consultancy firms were invited to tender. The brief to which they worked may
be summarized as:

    * Examine the effectiveness of existing planning processes
       and recommend how they might be improved.

    * Highlight issues which, in the view of the consultancy
       firm, are currently of strategic significance to the
       company.

    * Show how this work could be used to develop management
       planning skills.

The response of one firm - the London office of Harbridge House Europe - was
especially strong in the third requirement. Indeed, the firm's posture was that,
if the third requirement were strongly pursued, Rolls-Royce Motors would be well
placed to refine continuously any new planning process established during
consultancy work, and to define continuously strategic issues raised by the

planning process. Primarily because of this response, Harbridge House were
selected, and joint Harbridge House/Rolls-Royce Motors work began in October,
1975.

PROGRAMMING THE INTRODUCTION

The Harbridge House proposal for introducing a new planning process was divided
into three distinct stages:

(1) Pre-planning Appraisal: October, 1975 - December,
     1975.

(2) Planning Phase I (Design): February, 1976 - July, 1976.

(3) Planning Phase II (Implementation): July, 1976 -
     June, 1977.

To begin with, Rolls-Royce Motors committed itself only to the Pre-Planning
Appraisal.

PRE-PLANNING APPRAISAL

During the 3 months October to December, 1975, the consultants interviewed and
read papers on the company's planning methodology and on key issues confronting
the car and diesel sectors of the business (it was agreed that the subsidiary
divisions could not be treated in detail at this stage). Throughout this phase
of the assignment, the company emphasized to its senior management that it was not
looking to the consultants to determine corporate or divisional plans, but wanted
to make management aware of independent findings which would sharpen their own
perception of planning. The consultants were assisted, in no more than an
administrative sense, by a senior manager seconded part time from Car Division.
Assuming success of this first stage of the project, he would subsequently be
appointed full time Corporate Planning Executive.

The findings of the consultants were presented to the company's Main and
Divisional Boards, not in the form of the customary brochure, but at a two-day
conference remote from the company's sites, in the Lake District. The effectiveness of presenting material in that way deserves more than a passing mention. A
style of presentation was adopted which sought audience response (and got it,
especially on more contentious topics!), and the effect was not only more
memorable for those who took part than a two-inch report, but it reinforced
unmistakably the company's determination to secure senior management involvement
in any new planning style. At this stage, no new planning process had been
designed. The shortcomings of the old approach had been aired, principally
through debate of the strategic issues which, in the main, it had failed to raise.
The need for a better approach was confirmed.

PLANNING PHASE I

A direct result of the conference was a decision to proceed with the design of a
new Corporate Planning Process; to appoint full time the Corporate Planning
Executive from Rolls-Royce Motors to spearhead this work; to continue with
consultancy assistance from Harbridge House, and to set up a Corporate Planning
Steering Committee which would monitor progress and act as a pool of senior Rolls-
Royce experience to help in the introduction of the process. Phase I was designed

1 Review existing planning and control tools (Five year forecast, profit plan, engineering plan, capital authorization procedure, management appraisal, personal objectives). Build on what is useful; modify and innovate where required.

2 Decide appropriate time horizons for different planning activities.

3 Assist executive committee to define corporate objectives.

4 Design the new process. Document it in the form of a planning guide which aims to assist implementation.

5 Determine and evaluate external issues which should be considered in short, medium and long term planning; evaluate and determine methods of obtaining and processing relevant information.

1 Presentations and papers to divisional and sub-divisional boards on the need for and nature of strategic review.

2 Preparation by divisions and sub-divisions of papers which aim at a common HQ/divisional understanding of problems and opportunities confronting each business unit and the company as a whole.

3 Formal meeting with each unit to review, discuss and agree strategy.

Fig. 12.3 Main tasks in Phase I planning.

to produce two results: the design of a complete process of corporate planning, and a detailed examination/review of corporate and divisional strategies (see Figure 12.3). The Harbridge House role was defined as the provision of expertise and advice which would help the company develop its own solutions to its problems, and involved a teaching style so that knowledge and expertise would continue to be transferred to Rolls-Royce Motors personnel.

CHARACTERISTICS OF THE PROCESS

The aim of those engaged in the project was to design a process which:

* Recognizes the responsibility of the Managing Director and Board of each operating unit to plan and implement change.

* Enables the appropriate degree of management involvement to take place.

* Builds, where appropriate, on the planning and control mechanisms which the company already used.

* Gives additional emphasis to strategic planning.

* Takes due notice of external change factors and integrates the best available forecasts into the planning process.

* Provides monitoring and control functions.

* Assists in the development of management skills and potential.

The definition of planning used for the project appears in Figure 12.4.

> "Corporate planning is a comprehensive, future-orientated,
> continuous process of management which is implemented
> within a formal framework. It is responsive to relevant
> change in the external environment. It is concerned with
> both strategic and operational planning, and, through the
> participation of relevant members of management, develops
> plans and actions at the appropriate levels in the organiza-
> tion. It incorporates monitoring and control mechanisms and
> is concerned with both the short and the long term."

Fig. 12.4   Definition of corporate planning for Rolls-Royce
            Motors Limited.

THE CORPORATE PLANNING STEERING COMMITTEE

The Committee consists of the Group Managing Director, the Group Commercial
Director, and a Director from each of the Car and Diesel Divisions, assisted by
the newly appointed Corporate Planning Executive and the outside consultant. Its
main purpose was to assist the Group Managing Director in guiding the work which
would lead to the new corporate planning process, and to ensure that both corporate
and divisional needs were effectively covered. The Committee's terms of reference
covered only planning processes and methods. As a Committee it had no responsibility for agreeing specific matters of strategy or setting corporate or divisional
objectives. During Phase I the Committee met at intervals of 4-6 weeks, heard
reports on progress to date, reviewed the proposals developed, and gave general
guidance. Each meeting lasted between 1 and 2 hours, with documentation issued in
advance. In addition, members of the Committee were consulted individually between
meetings as required.

The corporate planning executive

The corporate planner was appointed from within the organization in January, 1976,
reporting to the Group Managing Director. A brief synopsis of his job description
appears in Figure 12.5.

Design of the new process

The intention was to involve a wide spread of managers in the design of the new
process and in the identification of good and bad points from the old system. To
this end:

  * Some forty senior managers were interviewed as part of
    the programme to establish the strengths and weaknesses
    of the old system, and to discuss ideas for improvement.

  * Written briefs on the project and its objectives were
    given a wide circulation.

  * Discussions were held with managers who operated in
    departments critical to the planning design, and parts of
    the new process were agreed with them as they developed.

  * Formal presentations on the project were made to each
    divisional and sub-divisional Board.

1 The prime function of the corporate planning executive is
  to establish and maintain planning procedures which effectively meet the needs of Rolls-Royce Motors as a whole and
  of its operating units.

2 It is not the function of the corporate planning executive
  to determine strategy for or impose objectives on the operating units. He will advise and assist in the formulation of
  strategy and objectives, but responsibility for their adoption lies wholly with the chief executive of the unit(s)
  concerned.

3 He must secure the widest practicable involvement of
  management in the planning process, and encourage the view
  that involvement in the process makes a cardinal contribution to the development of management skills.

4 He will assist the group managing director and executive
  committee in *(inter alia)* defining corporate objectives;
  assessing the corporate implications of divisional plans;
  analysing the gap which may arise between group requirements and divisional plans; exploring the planning implications of capital investment projects and new ventures;
  monitoring achievements against plans.

5 He will report to the group managing director.

Fig. 12.5 Summary job description - Corporate Planning
           Executive.

* Special seminars and discussions were held in the United
  States and Switzerland, where distance made normal casual
  communication difficult.

* Ideas were exchanged on planning matters with other
  managers whenever opportunities arose.

Gradually, the specific planning needs and problems of the different areas became
apparent, solutions were found, and the broad conceptual model which Harbridge
House[5] had brought with them changed to something that was uniquely Rolls-Royce
Motors.

The broad outlines of the system and a description of its components appear in
Figure 12.6. Particular elements of the system have been expanded into more
detailed schematics: for example the method of approaching environmental
assumptions, which appears in Figure 12.7.

THE STRATEGIC REVIEW

The strategic review, which conceptually is the first stage of the new planning
process, was carried out (unusually) in parallel with the design of the new
process. There were a number of reasons for this:

        * It was desirable that as many people as possible should be
          involved in some concrete aspect of planning at an early
          stage in order to secure continued interest.

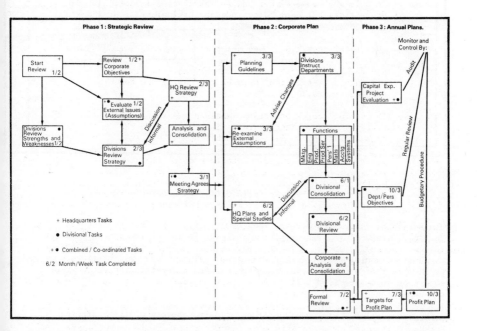

Fig. 12.6   Rolls-Royce Motors Limited - outline planning
            process.

* Strategy is an important part of planning, and Rolls-Royce
  Motors had to ensure that their plans had a firm base.

* The review was likely to bring (and did in fact bring)
  some immediate and obvious results, thus helping to add to
  the credibility of the new style of planning.

* The second phase of planning work would be to obtain a
  wider involvement of managers in planning. This was likely
  to be more successful when Directors had a common understanding of current strategies, and could respond more
  positively to ideas and challenges from below.

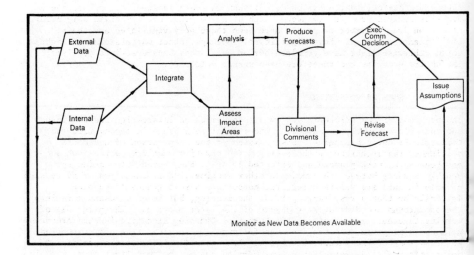

Fig. 12.7 Process of setting external assumptions.

The strategic review started in mid-February with a memorandum from the Group Managing Director, and was completed when the formal review meetings were held towards the end of June. A short paper on how to do it was prepared by the Corporate Planning Executive and consultant jointly, and presentations were made by them to the various Boards. Active help was offered in the preparation of papers on an as required basis: some divisions made greater use of the planner and consultant than did others.

Each paper included statements on the following aspects of the business:

        * Key assumptions used in preparing forecasts.
        * Strengths and weaknesses.
        * Opportunities and threats.
        * Current objectives of the business.
        * Estimated current and future financial resources required.
        * The major issues which the divisions wish to raise with
          corporate management.

In addition, the Executive Committee gave every division a number of specific questions on matters which were causing concern at corporate level. These had to be answered, but the rest of the paper was developed at the discretion of the division. All divisions received a note of the questions put to other divisions, as well as a copy of each divisional paper and minutes of the review meetings. This facilitated cross-divisional understanding, and tended to stimulate a corporate approach.

Some of those who attended the review meetings, which were consciously structured by the Executive Committee in such a way as to encourage and support strategic analytical thinking, stated that these were the most constructive senior level meetings they had attended. One divisional Managing Director in his written submission stated, 'While the burden of work was very substantial, so are the benefits derived from it. Matters which hitherto might have received only brief attention from a number of people have been thoroughly ventilated and their significance assessed. More significantly perhaps, other matters came to light which otherwise might have remained buried until they became serious problems. The entire exercise has therefore been warmly welcomed'.

ROLE OF CONSULTANT

The progress of the strategic review also provides an interesting insight into the role played by the consultant. The initial work began in tandem with the Corporate Planning Executive, and consisted of the preparation of documents setting up the structure of the review. The briefing meetings, which took about one hour each, were planned and executed jointly, the presentation being split roughly equally between the two. In other meetings, where animation of discussion or help in analysis was required, the consultant's role gradually changed. Initially he took a very large part at the meeting, but moved more and more into the background and did not attend some of the later meetings. The principle of working together, and of having the Corporate Planning Executive in the foreground as much as possible, was one that was followed rigorously. (The only exception was that some of the interviewing work, which normally followed the pattern of joint effort already established, was carried out by the consultant alone.) This principle of working with the client's representative(s) is an essential feature of process consultancy, and enables a client to be helped to find the solution to his problems rather than to have solutions thrust upon him. It is also indispensible to the transfer of expertise between consultant and client.

THE RESULTS OF PHASE I

The completion of Phase I has left Rolls-Royce Motors with a fully designed but only partly implemented planning process, accepted by each Board and by those individual managers who have played a key role in the old process. At the same time, benefits have been derived in the form of better communication between the Divisions and the centre and in improved understanding of strategy which came out of the formal reviews. This, of course, is not enough. The philosophy behind the new process is that planning should involve at least the two levels of management below Divisional Directors (see Figure 12.8). Involvement of directors and managers is construed as more than filling in a form relating to their own

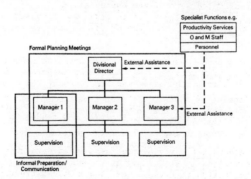

Fig. 12.8 Planning by director functions

---

1 A series of meetings with divisional and sub-divisional
   boards to ensure that the new process is fully understood, and that directors are aware of the practical
   implications and the part they have to play in securing
   wider management involvement (August 1976).

2 A series of meetings with groups of 5-10 managers across
   the organization, to explain the new process and ensure
   an understanding of the principle. Roughly 20 meetings
   are envisaged, each of 1-2 hours duration (September-
   October 1976).

2(a) A seminar, along similar lines, to be held in the U.S.A.
   (December 1976).

3 Working with planning groups during the planning cycle
   (Fig.12.6) to secure adequate depth of involvement and
   to improve the cross-functional approach (January-May
   1977).

4 Modifying the process to meet any problems which arise
   during its implementation.

Fig. 12.9 Main tasks in Phase II planning.

activities. Involvement should contribute firstly to solving the problems which
face all the activities under a particular director. Secondly, it should achieve
a measure of improved decision making by ensuring that representatives from other
departments who have something to contribute are able to do so. Thirdly, it
should create an opportunity for each management function to contribute to the
wider strategic thinking of the Division: more specifically, it aims to stimulate
new ideas and analytical thinking, and to ensure that the inputs obtained are
properly handled. It does not attempt in any way to remove the decision making
duty from Divisional Boards.

Figure 12.9 shows the way in which these tasks will be approached during Phase II
of the planning introduction. These are very important to bring about the new
attitude which corporate planning requires. It cannot be achieved by edict; only
by example from the top, supported by practical help in adopting the new approach.
This help can best be provided in a real working situation. The group work shown
in Figure 12.9, which is designed to bring about the depth of involvement required,
will therefore take place during those periods of the planning cycle when managers
are called upon to make a contribution. As Phase II has still to take place, it
is not yet possible to evaluate it. We hope to make it the subject of a second
article in due course.

PLANNING, A TOOL NOT A STRAITJACKET

We see corporate planning as a tool. It is not being applied in a way which will
make it into a straitjacket, nor does any one expect it to be a universal panacea.
We are well aware that the process of managerial decision making is very complex:
much too complex for anyone to expect that every strategic decision can be neatly
tagged and pasted like a photograph into an album which is labelled X YEAR PLAN.
Research (for example, Mintzberg[6] and Grinyer and Norburn[7]) clearly demonstrates
the way in which managerial decisions normally do take place as distinct from the
way in which they are often thought to take place. The Rolls-Royce Motors plan
is seen as a background document, showing a strategic path which the company
chooses consciously to follow at a given moment of time. The involvement philosoph

coupled with the day-to-day role of the Corporate Planning Executive in strategic decisions, will ensure that the planning philosophy is continuous, even though a particular plan may become outdated by events.

REFERENCES

1 P. Irving (1970) Corporate Planning in Practice: a study of the development of organized planning in Major UK companies. University of Bradford, M.Sc. Dissertation.

2 B.W. Denning and M.E. Lehr (1971-2). The extent and nature of corporate long range planning in the United Kingdom, Parts 1 and 2. *Journal of Managerial Studies* Vol.8, May 1971, Vol.9, Feb. 1972.

3 P. Knowlson (1974) Organization and Membership Survey, Society for Long Range Planning, March 1974.

4 J.K. Brown and R. O'Connor (1974) Planning and the Corporate Planning Director, *The Conference Report,* No.627.

5 B.W. Denning. Unpublished Harbridge House manuscript.

6 H. Mintzberg (1975) The Manager's job: folklore and fact, *Harvard Business Review,* July-Aug. 1975.

7 P.H. Grinyer and D. Norburn (1974) Strategic Planning in 21 UK Companies, *Long Range Planning,* Vol.7 No.4, August, 1974.

FURTHER READING

1 D.E. Hussey, *Corporate Planning: Theory and Practice,* Pergamon Press, Oxford (1973).

2 E.K. Warren, *Long Range Planning: The Executive Viewpoint,* Prentice-Hall, New Jersey (1966).

3 P. Baynes (Ed), *Case Studies in Corporate Planning,* Pitman, London (1973).

4 B.W. Denning (Ed), *Corporate Planning: Selected Concepts,* McGraw-Hill, New York (1971).

Part 5

CHOOSING A FUTURE

Extrapolative forecasts as a base for planning have been found to be unsuitable in the present era of discontinuity. What is more useful for the avoidance of "corporate surprise" is to work on alternative scenarios of the future as a basis for the preparation of strategic policy options, better decisions, risk avoidance and contingency planning. In Chapter 13 Bernard Taylor surveys the methods available for the preparation of scenarios, and discusses their use in corporate planning.

An example is given of the importance of the environment in Barrie James' chapter on the social environment of the pharmaceutical industry, which demonstrates the need for social forecasting techniques in this industry.

In Chapter 15 David Hussey discusses the importance of another environmental factor, inflation, and stresses the danger of thinking too simplistically of the impact high inflation rates have on corporate strategy.

Chapter 13

THE USE OF SCENARIOS IN PLANNING*

Bernard Taylor

Managers in business and administrators in government are now using scenarios and
other futures research techniques to try to cope with what they perceive as
'discontinuities'.   1974, the year of the oil crisis, is seen as a watershed,
marking the end of an era of relative stability and affluence and the beginning of
a period of turbulence and economic stagnation.   In this new environment a number
of trends - political, social, economic and technological - seem to be gathering
momentum and interacting to create a business environment which is highly volatile.

Nationalism in developing countries has increased the political risks to western
business, and expropriation - outright or 'creeping' - has meant handing over
control of companies in Angola, Uganda, Iran, India and Nigeria.   In the industrialised world itself social and political movements, ranging from women's liberation
to anarchist violence, have applied increasing pressures, while local and international economic crises, with collapsing markets and shop floor demands for greater
participation and benefits, created 'discontinuities' which had dramatic effects
on corporate profits, particularly in large corporations.   Environmentalists have
blocked the development of oil, mineral and chemical companies, and new technologies
have put one industry after another into difficulties.   Industrial disputes and
growing resort to the strike weapon in Italy, Britain, Canada and Australia, have
also taken a mounting toll.

As managements witnessed successive plans being rendered obsolete by unforeseen
changes, they began to doubt the value of traditional forecasting and planning
systems based on extrapolation and budgeting, and looked for other approaches
better suited to a complex and turbulent environment.   They were convinced of the
need to expand their planning and forecasting procedures to cover not only
economic and market trends but also social and political changes which might be
reflected in legislation and in the activities of trade unions and social pressure
groups.

The result was a spate of experiments in the use of modern forecasting techniques:
delphi studies, cross impact analyses, trend impact analyses etc.   And there was
an increase in the use of simple financial models aimed at examining the sensitivity
of company plans to changes in the assumptions, about prices, levels of sales,
costs of raw materials, wages and salaries, interest rates etc.   Companies began

---

* Originally published in *Chelwood Review*

to make tentative contingency plans confidentially and informally, to provide
for such major risks as strikes, changes of government, new legislation, shortage
or non-availability of a key raw material or component, or a substantial delay
in the construction of a new facility.

However, the most impressive of these changes in planning techniques has been the
increasing use of scenarios. In the late 1960s, Herman Kahn and Anthony Wiener
defined scenarios as:

> 'Hypothetical sequences of events constructed for the purpose
> of focusing attention on causal processes and decision points'.[1]

In business, scenarios usually take the form of 'qualitative descriptions of the
situation of a company, an industry, a nation or a region at some specified time
in the future'.

Recent scenarios developed in the UK cover, for example: the British economy,
unemployment, supply and demand for energy, finance, the chemical industry,
television, the world pharmaceutical industry and Japan in 1980.[2] In the USA well
known centres of futures research include the Institute for the Future, and the
Hudson Institute. A recent study by the Conference Board noted 30 large businesses
using scenarios. Other centres for futures research in Europe include the Berlin
Centre for Futures Research, Bertrand de Jouvenal's organisation, Futuribles, and
Aurelio Peccei's Club of Rome.

ACCEPTING UNCERTAINTY

Scenario planning has been criticised as being 'a practice without a discipline':
as lacking the exactness of traditional economic forecasting techniques and
affording no proof of its effectiveness. On the other hand, it is the very
precision and the bogus authority of conventional approaches to forecasting which
have led to the search for other methods which reflect the real uncertainty in
the environment. The supporters of scenarios assert that 'it is better to be
approximately right than precisely wrong'. To quote Alvin Toffler: 'Linear
extrapolation, otherwise known as straight-line thinking is extremely useful and
it can tell us many important things. But it works best between revolutionary
periods, not in them'.[3]

In response to suggestions that scenarios are not sufficiently rigorous, futures
researchers reply that forecasting and planning are essentially a matter of
judgement. To quote Professor Lynn White: 'Quantity is only one of the qualities:
thus all decisions, including the quantitative, are inherently qualitative'.

Scenarios are not intended to predict the future, but to help executives to deal
with a highly uncertain environment: to assist the executive who is used to
extrapolative forecasting and budgeting, in coping with the unexpected.

Scenarios are not supposed to provide an accurate picture of the future, but to
challenge the imagination: to encourage managers to plan, not just for the most
likely future but also for other alternative futures which are less likely.

Scenario planning should help managers to be more flexible in various ways:

Environmental scanning should stimulate managers to search the business environment
for 'weak signals', especially social and political changes, which might fore-
shadow a crisis.

Sensitivity analysis should encourage executives to produce plans which are 'robust', that is, which may not be optimal but would keep the business profitable under a wide range of conditions.

Contingency planning should prompt managers to be prepared for crises, for example, strikes, revolutions or a slump in demand.

Risk analysis should make decision-makers more realistic about the threats to their business - social, political, technological and competitive - and persuade them to minimise the risk of over-dependence on any one source: a customer group, a technology, a range of products, a national or regional market.

Investment in flexibility. Scenario planning also invites businessmen to consider the advantages of building flexibility into their operations, that is:

> Designing facilities which can be used in different ways.

> Training staff for a broad range of tasks.

> Consciously carrying 'slack resources' (skilled staff, extra stocks, back-up generators etc.) in case of a crisis or a new opportunity.

> Diversifying one's business so as to have enterprises, suppliers, production facilities, stockholding or computer operations in more than one country or region.

Scenario planning is unique in that it offers a framework for thinking about the socio-political environment. Scenarios provide a language and a methodology for talking about social futures and their likely consequences for the firm. If we believe that social and political changes are likely to have a critical impact on the future of business then scenario planning must have an important role to play in corporate planning. To quote a senior executive of Shell:

> 'I believe that an oil company's continued success could depend as much on its ability to respond to this wave of pressures as on its commercial skills in the nuts and bolts of the business .... Solving these complex problems requires a special dimension of management. What does this entail? For many people it means a new way of life. A company must now ensure that while its managers get on with the job, they are also sensitive to changing social attitudes, they can anticipate the resultant pressures, and that they will be able to cope imaginatively with the unavoidable problems.'

SUBJECTS FOR SCENARIOS ARE:

1 *Economic Growth*

The most popular topic for scenarios appears to be the rate of economic growth. Indeed scenarios are most commonly written in terms of 'high growth', 'low growth' and 'most likely'.

Between 1960 and 1974, the Organisation for Economic Co-operation and Development area grew at an average rate of around 5% per annum, that is, gross domestic product in real terms. In 1973 the growth rate rose to about 7%, and in 1974 it fell below 2%. A vital question for forecasters is 'what will be the trend in economic growth during the 1980s?' Will growth return to the levels of the 1960s, that is, 5-6%? Or will growth in the OECD economies stabilise at a lower level of 3-4% or even less?

2 *The Trade Cycle*

An important subject for scenarios in the short term is the forecasting of the
next trade cycle. In recession we need to know: will there be a quick up-turn,
a slow up-turn or no up-turn?

Alternatively, in a boom phase we want to predict whether there will be too
rapid growth, limited growth, or if the recovery will turn back into a recession
before trade picks up.

The world trade cycle has been a fairly regular phenomenon in the post-war period
with recessions and recoveries occurring every three to four years on a slightly
different time-scale in each country. However, 1973 was an exceptional boom year
when all the industrialised economies peaked together. Unprecedented shortages
and high prices in world commodity markets resulted and, with the oil price
increase of 1973-74, led to high inflation, balance of payments problems and
government action to limit growth. The timing of the trade cycle in the eighties
is a matter for conjecture and hence for the use of scenarios.

3 *Protectionism*

The oil crisis caused chronic balance of payments problems for oil importing
countries. The USA has had large trade deficits and a depreciating currency, and
the Germans and Japanese have mounted powerful export campaigns to maintain their
trade surpluses and their constantly rising exchange rates. Western governments
generally have seen their home markets invaded by manufactured goods from Japan,
the developing world and Comecon countries.

The natural response in the USA and the European Economic Community has been to
restrain imports - by imposing quotas, minimum prices, import duties, and non-
fiscal barriers to trade. These restraints have grown markedly during the 1970s
in food, textiles, steel and ships. A crucial question for business is how fast
this trend towards protectionism will continue because it could restrict the
growth of world trade.

4 *Nationalism*

Third World countries in the 1970s have reacted against what they see as 'economic
colonialism', that is continued economic dependence on western countries. They
particularly resent many of their major businesses being owned and managed by
foreign companies, and they have sought to assert their independence by:

> - imposing restrictions on foreign ownership.
> - insisting on the development of local management.
> - putting limits on the payment of dividends, royalties and
>   fees for management service.
> - requiring foreign companies to invest locally in manu-
>   facturing facilities.
> - diverting their investment into businesses which bring
>   in new technologies and expand exports, etc.

As a result the pattern of international businesses is changing. They are
becoming more truly multinational in culture, in ownership and in management.
Also, from the western viewpoint they are becoming more difficult to control and
possibly more risky.

Crucial issues for business are:

> What pattern of business is likely to emerge?
> Will economic nationalism deter western companies from
> investing in certain economies?
> Will there be more joint ventures between local governments
> and western multinationals?
> Will we see more trade in knowhow, more turnkey projects,
> more management contracts?

5 *Energy*

It is important to understand the factors determining the price of oil. On the
one hand the Middle East producers wish to keep the oil in the ground because it
is a wasting asset and the dollars and the manufactured goods which they get
depreciate in value.

On the other hand, their investments, their oil markets and some of their political
allies are in North America and Western Europe so it would not be in their long-
term best interests to undermine the western economies by insisting on too high
a price for their oil.

It may be that low economic growth and the action of consumer governments, for
example, in conservation, the development of nuclear energy and various alternative
energy sources, will avoid further energy crises. Or, a series of crises may
occur as demand rises above supply. This would precipitate a price rise and a
fall in demand, and probably a fall in production and higher fuel costs in western
industries. More political crises in the Middle East are possible, and such
political problems could interrupt supply and increase oil prices overnight. In
any case, many experts predict that demand for oil will outstrip supplies in the
1980s. It seems it is only the nature and the timing of the crisis which we need
to forecast.

6 *Employment*

The growth in unemployment, especially among young people, is an anxiety for all
western governments, particularly as the trend appears likely to persist throughout the 1980s. Predictions depend on assumptions about: the growth in the labour
force owing to the baby boom of the 1960s and more women working; the reduction
in demand for labour, particularly from manufacturing industry; and technological
changes such as the introduction of microprocessors which seem likely to eliminate
certain jobs and create others. Other scenarios are being produced in an attempt
to anticipate training needs, for example, shortages of instrument technicians
and chemical engineers. One of the ironies is that employers are unable to open
up new facilities because they are short of skilled staff: engineers, tool-
makers, computer programmers, systems analysts, nurses, etc. In developing
countries the problem is much worse: among such oil producers as Algeria, Libya
and Venezuela, the absence of management and craftsmen seriously impedes the
development of local industries.

7 *Industrial Policy*

The pattern of international trade has changed radically in the past five years -
and to the disadvantage of Western Europe - with the rapid growth of Japan, the
entry of Russia, the rise of emerging countries such as Brazil, India and South

Korea. It is therefore important to forecast how international trade is likely to change in the 1980s. Already we have seen a remarkable transfer of basic manufacturing industries to Eastern Europe, and to the emerging countries. Government leaders and businessmen in Western Europe should work together to rationalise traditional industries and to build up new businesses where they will be internationally competitive. This involves governments and large companies in producing long term forecasts for their national markets, for example, over a ten-year period in terms of total supply and demand, investments in new facilities and improved technology, production levels, productivity improvements, inflation in costs of labour and raw materials and price levels for major competitors.

8 Social Changes and Social Values

Some significant changes affecting business over the past decade have emanated from changing social values - consumer protection, conservation, equal opportunity, civil rights, health and safety at work, employee participation. Thus, large businesses are now trying to determine what will be the social movements of the 1980s. In western societies some of the basic social trends are well established:

Employment and training. High levels of unemployment, shortages of key skills, the re-entry of women into the labour force, early retirement, re-training for new careers, and the development of 'life-long education', not just for work but also for leisure.

Public participation. Citizens and work forces with high expectations and a desire to be informed and involved in decisions which affect their lives.

Resistance to large systems. Alienation and resistance to large-scale bureaucracy in business and government; worries about large scale technology which is vulnerable to strikes and terrorism.

Crime. Growth in crime and less respect for law and order, particularly among young people; an expansion of private security firms.

Freedom for women. More social freedom and career opportunities for women leading to lower birth-rates, two-career families etc.

Regionalism. Separatism and regionalism in Northern Ireland, Scotland and Wales, the Basque Country, Brittany, Quebec, etc.

Quality of life. An insistence on a minimum 'quality' in life in terms of clean air, unpolluted water, freedom from noise.

Product liability. A belief that business should be responsible for any damage to property or personal injury which results from the use of its products.

Redistribution of income. A continuing erosion of the rewards which society is willing to pay for skill, responsibility and risk-taking.

Predictions based on such trends are leading some companies to anticipate even greater challenges to business and further legislation to limit management autonomy. Other forecasters expect western governments to see the need for greater rewards for risk-taking and more incentives for innovation and entrepreneurship to create more jobs and growth. For business the crucial issue is: whether governments will provide an environment which will support or be hostile to business. This will inevitably affect management's allocation of resources.

ROP - J

9 *Political Changes*

War and peace, revolutions, the rise and fall of political leaders - these are
most difficult events to predict and yet can affect business significantly. The
consequences of the appearance of China as a world power, the long term future
for the Middle East after Iran, and the future of Rhodesia and South Africa must
concern both governments and business leaders. Will we see more communist
takeovers in central Africa - following those in Angola and Mozambique?
In Europe can we expect a continued swing to the left and the development of
Euro-Communism as part of the establishment?

10 *Technological Trends*

A most important use of scenarios is to try to anticipate the likely effects on
business and society of future changes in technology. These can be most
disruptive, particularly when a breakthrough occurs and an entirely new technique
means that a production or distribution process is cheaper, faster or requires
less skill or less labour.

Hence the current concern over micro-processors which promise to hasten the
automation of various operations - *via* industrial robots in the factory, word
processors in the office, and mini-computers in supermarkets. The use of lasers
and fibre optics in telecommunications, the application of bio-engineering in
medicine, new power sources for automobiles, oceanic exploration and engineering,
also offer fruitful areas for scenario-writing.

In each case the approach might be to work with 'informed opinion' to forecast
technology changes, then to examine the likely social impact and the response of
governments, and finally, to establish the important issues to be decided now or
in the near future and how one might influence these decisions.

The penalty for not anticipating technological change is to be caught flat-footed
like the Swiss watch-making industry, when new technology arrives and makes
present systems obsolete. The penalty for not predicting social and political
resistance to a new technology is to find yourself over-investing in new production
facilities and new products just as many construction companies over-committed
themselves to industrialised building in the 1960s.

The word 'scenario' is used to describe an attempt to write a history which
extends from the present into the longer term future. It should be credible and
internally consistent and it should include a number of 'alternative futures'.

The writing of scenarios typically involves using a number of futures research
techniques. For example, the approach recommended by the General Electric Company
(shown in Figure 13.1) includes the use of a delphi study, trend analysis, trend
extrapolation, trend impact analysis and cross impact analysis. A number of
techniques most commonly used in the development of scenarios are listed below:

Trend analysis involves regularly scanning and analysing a number of publications
inside and outside the enterprise to plot long term trends. The approach is used
by a wide range of enterprises and a number of these analyses are published, for
example, by the American Council of Life Insurance and the Canadian Department of
Environment.

Computer simulation entails building a computer model of an enterprise or an
industry and making projections on different assumptions. For example, the UK
Department of Energy and various fuel industries use computer models to forecast

---

1 Prepare background

Assess environmental factors - social, regulatory,
technological, economic and competitive.
Develop crude 'systems' model of the industry.

---

2 Select critical indicators

Key indicators (trends).
Future events affecting key indicators (literature
search).
Delphi panel to evaluate industry's future.

---

3 Establish past behaviour for each indicator

Historical performance.
Reasons for past behaviour of each trend.
Delphi questionnaire.

---

4 Verify potential future events

Delphi panel.
Past trends, future events, impact/probability, future
trends.
Assumptions for forecasts, rationale for future trends.

---

5 Forecast each indicator

Range of future values for each indicator.
Results from literature search and Delphi study.
Trend Impact Analysis and Cross Impact Analysis.

---

6 Write scenarios

Guidelines for Strategic Business Units.
Annual revision.

Fig. 13.1 Constructing scenarios for an industrial sector
(General Electric USA)
See Rochelle O'Connor, *Planning Under Uncertainty,* Conference
Board, New York, 1978, p.8.

the total market for energy, the growth rate, the energy mix and the breakdown by
type of usage. Volkswagen use similar models to forecast the future competitive
situation in the world automobile industry.

In *decision analysis* the analyst creates a 'road map' of decisions relating to a
particular issue or project. At each step he plots the alternatives available to
the 'decision-maker', the estimated pay off or loss for each course of action and
the probability of success or failure. The technique is useful to determine the
broad dimensions of a decision and as a means of keeping various options open.
In analysing real decisions, however, the range of alternatives available is
often far too wide for a planner to carry out a comprehensive quantitative
analysis.

Sensitivity analysis. One of the commonest ways to explore alternative futures
is by analysing the sensitivity of a plan to variations in the assumptions. For
this purpose access to a simple computer model is helpful. Thus the planner can
produce an operating statement, a cash flow analysis or a balance sheet based on

different assumptions about investments, sales, costs, prices, interest rates etc.
Many companies require their subsidiaries or divisions to explore the effects of
a 10% or 15% increase or decrease in the major assumptions underpinning any
major new project.

A Delphi study is a systematic way of carrying out a poll among experts, who are
asked questions, usually concerning the likelihood of events occurring at certain
dates. Then the results are fed back to the panel and they are asked further
questions. Experience to date suggests that the technique is valuable in
eliciting the opinion of specialists on a narrow subject such as the probability
of a breakthrough in a particular technology which they know well. It seems to
be less useful in exploring social and political issues which are much less
structured and where there are fewer experts. However, General Electric (USA)
have used this technique to explore likely trends in population, employment,
education etc.

Impact analysis implies setting up a matrix of events likely to affect other
events (cross impact analysis) or exploring the various impacts a particular
trend may have (trend impact analysis). These techniques involve weighing the
likely effects and then estimating which are the most important. Monsanto and
Bell Telephones are well known for their use of this approach in assessing the
likely social impacts of technology.

'Without vision the people perish,' said the prophet. And certainly it is around
visions that we build the future of our society. Our towns are shaped around
visions of modern architecture which includes concepts such as tower blocks,
shopping centres, arts centres and pedestrian precincts. Our education system is
based on social inventions such as nursery schools, comprehensive schools,
polytechnics and the Open University. Our transportation systems consist of
modern inventions such as container ships and super-tankers, jumbo jets and
package holidays, motorways and juggernauts, parking meters and multi-storey car
parks.

Now, our leaders are debating what kind of society we should have in the 1990s,
using concepts such as:

Self-service banking with fewer bank branches, more cash dispensers and point of
sale terminals in supermarkets.

The electronic office with secretaries using word processors instead of typewriters,
data transmitted by telephone and computers 'talking' to computers.

The workless society. Made possible by micro-processors and industrial robots,
with shorter working hours, more holidays, early retirement and life-long
education to equip people for new careers and for leisure.

The communications revolution which may enable the individual to work from his
home, communicating via a video-phone and a home computer with a visual display
unit, and will reduce the time businessmen spend travelling by using 'confraphone',
video-cassettes and closed circuit television.

Bio-feedback. The use of electronic devices to monitor the functions of the body.
This could make it possible for doctors in a central location to diagnose the
illnesses of patients in small cottage hospitals, or even in ambulances on the
way to hospital.

But how are these visions of the future to be created? Should we leave our future
in the hands of our political masters? Can we rely on the inspiration of the

scientists and planners in our big businesses - ably supported by small businessmen and the entrepreneurs who are supposed to be a major source of innovation? Or will the public servants devise our grand design, with the aid of think tanks and consultants like the Hudson Institute? Futures researchers are pressing for an open debate: the wider the discussion the better, and for the public to have a say in decisions which affect them. Alvin Toffler calls it Anticipatory Democracy - telling the public what the issues are and having them settled publicly rather than behind closed doors.

But public participation is not easy to arrange. The issues are complicated. The public who participate are often vocal minorities. All too often the result of public consultation is a decision for the *status quo* - or a decision not to build it here. So we seem to be working towards an uneasy compromise which involves public consultation and debate followed by political decision-making. And all too often this is seen by the cynics as manipulation: first consult, then take the decision you would have taken anyway.

THE PHILOSOPHY

The futurology or futures research movement is one of the most significant developments to affect planning in the last decade. Futures research offers a perspective complementary to that of the 'control systems' school. The controller starts from where the system is now and he tries to develop a guidance system which will take it in a certain direction. He uses techniques such as budgetary control and forecasting approaches based on extrapolation.

Futures research or scenario planning starts with a vision of the future and asks 'What different futures are feasible?'. 'What will happen to our enterprise in these new conditions?'. The futures researcher envisages not one future but a number of alternative futures. And he aims to produce strategies and plans which will be robust enough to enable the organisation to survive and prosper under a wide range of conditions. He uses qualitative techniques which explore the future, taking the opinions of specialists, examining the possible impacts of certain events and constructing scenarios describing futures which could happen given certain assumptions.

REFERENCES

[1] Herman Kahn and Anthony Wiener, *The Year 2000,*Macmillan, New York, 1967, p.6.

[2] Sources

Associated Business Programmes, *The Hudson Report,* 1976; Henley Centre for Forecasting, *The Year 2010,* 1977; Colin Leicester, *Unemployment 2001, A.D.,* Institute for Manpower Studies, 1977; James Robertson, *The Structure of British Financial Institutions in the 1980's,* in B. Taylor and G. de Mowbray's *Strategic Planning for Financial Institutions,* Bodley Head, 1974; Energy Policy: A Consultative Document, HMSO, 1978; Working at the Future Strategy for 1977/82, CAPTIB, 1976; Raymond Williams, *Television Technology and Cultural Form,* Fontana, 1974; Barrie James, *The Future of the Multinational Pharmaceutical Industry to 1990,* Associated Business Programmes, 1977; Boston Consulting Group, *Japan in 1980,* Financial Times, 1974.

[3] Senate Committee Report, *Choosing Our Environment: Can We Anticipate the Future,* Washington, 1976.

[4] Rochelle O'Connor, op.cit., pp.7-8.

Chapter 14

SOCIAL IMPACT: THE PHARMACEUTICAL INDUSTRY*

Barrie G. James

Management Information and Research,
Merck Sharp and Döhme, New York

The impact of the Social Environment is today of such magnitude on corporate activities that to ignore social trends in both short-term tactical and long-term strategic planning significantly reduces the level of operating efficiency and seriously questions the very survival of all companies.

AN ERA OF SOCIAL DISCONTINUITY

The current social profile in the industrialized countries is one of great unrest and can be realistically termed an era of social discontinuity.

The transition towards a post-industrialized community in a service economy with pragmatic social democracy in a participative society has radically changed many of the traditional norms of society. Changes in contemporary cultural preferences, values and perceptions of need and of abuse have greatly influenced social behaviour. Constant quantitative increases in wealth have given increasing access to education, communication, mobility and travel and have contributed to the rise of social phenomena such as environmentalism, consumerism, feminism and liberalism. These changes in social attitudes have also led to intense social scrutiny and public dissatisfaction with the way in which business operates, the tripartite interface between business, technology and government and the effects of industrialization on the social and economic systems. The greater participation in, and the growth of, wealth in the industrialized countries has re-oriented societal goals away from the basic economic necessities and the material pursuit of quantitative increases in the standard of living towards increases in the quality of life. This reorder of social priorities and public morality has strengthened the trend of the transfer of power away from the institutions towards the state and organized pressure groups.

These societal trends are forcing a fundamental change in business ideology and strategy as business seeks to adjust to the demands of a participative society.

---

* This chapter is adapted from the author's book *The Future of the Multinational Pharmaceutical Industry to 1990* (Associated Business Programmes, London, 1977). It was originally published in Long Range Planning, Vol.11, February 1978.

SOCIAL CHANGE AND THE PHARMACEUTICAL INDUSTRY

The effects on a company and an industry due to the changes in the social
environment can be dramatic and current business is littered with examples of
companies who have failed to identify and adapt to social change.

One of the best examples of the impact of social change is in the contemporary
pharmaceutical industry.

Prior to the early 1960s management in the pharmaceutical industry was faced
solely with tasks centered around discovering, financing, producing and marketing
ethical drugs[1] under relatively *laissez-faire* conditions. From the early 1960s
these operating characteristics progressively changed as a set of societal
conditions were superimposed by government acting at the behest of, and as the
guardian of, society. Since these societal demands largely originated in countries
which can be realistically termed post-industrial and which account for the bulk
of world drug innovation, production, consumption and trade, the impact on the
pharmaceutical industry has been severe.

In the post-industrialized countries two key conditions triggered a major
transformation in the operating characteristics of pharmaceutical companies:

1. *Health Care Systems*

The formation of public and private health care systems in the industrialized
countries from the late 1940s and increased public funding of these systems
spurred by consumer demand for higher quality and greater quantity of health care
services. This situation was intensified by the ideological commitment by growing
liberal and socialist political strength to the fundamental right to health care
on a need basis and equality of access to all services. At first the Health Care
systems offered a major commercial opportunity for the pharmaceutical industry
since with free or nominal cost drug supply consumers were released from previous
economic constraint.

It became apparent by the early 1970s that the philosophy of unlimited health care
on a need basis was open to high levels of abuse and unnecessary over-utilization
of scarce resources and almost infinite interpretation. After basic needs have
been met there appears to be a law of diminishing returns where despite increased
funding there does not appear to be a commensurate increase in the overall health
of society.

The initial services of individual physician treatment and hospitalization rapidly
spread to secondary services such as dental treatment and later into diverse
tertiary services, more sociological in nature, such as birth control counselling.

Successive expansion of health care service quality and quantity greatly increased
operating costs and outpaced the ability of public and private systems to finance
demand. During the 1950s most countries increased health care expenditure by
about 1 per cent of GNP. By the 1960s this had increased by a further 1½ per cent
of GNP. In other words a country which had spent 3½ per cent of GNP in 1950 on
health care was spending 6 per cent of a very much larger GNP by 1969.[2] This
problem will be compounded in the industrialized countries in the future both by
increased economic constraints on GNP growth and by continuing low birth rates
and increasing longevity. The indications are that this will produce an inverted
population pyramid with a progressively smaller number of tax payers supporting a
growing number of non-tax contributing senior citizens.

The majority of health care systems are now in the traumatic process of trying to
freeze or lower services to more financially acceptable levels. Heavily increased
taxation to gain funds and reductions in existing services are frequently
incompatible with contemporary political policies given liberal and socialist
political strength in the industrialized countries. Health care systems have
therefore turned their attention to stringent control of prices, profits and
promotion of ethical drugs as the pharmaceutical industry has largely become the
only private sector in health care delivery in the industrialized countries.
These moves have been made despite the facts that ethical drugs rarely exceed 15
per cent of the total health care costs, have not risen in cost at anywhere near
the indexed cost increases of medical personnel or hospitals and are highly cost
effective and thus of greater economic benefit than higher cost, labour intensive
surgery and capital intensive hospitalization where such substitutes exist.

The complex interactions of these economic pressures on the operating environment
of the pharmaceutical industry are illustrated in Figure 14.1.

2. *The Quality of Life*

Public demand for quantitative increases in the quality of life, fears that a
technology dependent society could produce unacceptable conditions and
consumerism have had a great impact on the pharmaceutical industry.

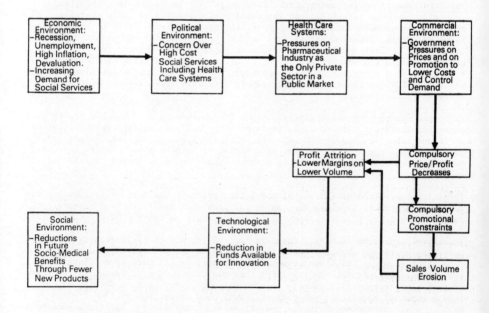

Fig. 14.1 Interactions of economic pressures on the operating
environment of the pharmaceutical industry.

The public has shown great interest in the pharmaceutical industry since its
early origins because drugs are perceived to offer the perpetuation of life
through the eradication of disease and the alleviation of suffering.

Although many outstanding advances have been made in drug therapy, drugs still
cannot control some illnesses at all and they control other illnesses only
partially. Drugs still cure relatively few illnesses and frequently treat only
the symptoms leaving the causes untouched. For example, arthritis cannot yet be
cured and chronic degenerative conditions such as asthma, bronchitis and
emphysema cannot be effectively treated let alone cured. Vaccines prevent a
number of infectious diseases and antibiotics cure many others and some forms of
cancer are curable with drug therapy. Aside from these drugs and vitamins which
can eliminate nutritional deficiency, drug therapy tends to be palliative rather
than curative. Both insulin and tranquillizers revolutionized the treatment of
diabetics and the mentally ill. However, neither therapy is curative. To a
society conditioned by the lay media to expect miracle drug cures, this apparent
lack of success at a time of critical personal need raises serious doubts as to
the credibility of the drug industry despite the fact that drug therapy in general
provides remedies where no others exist and significantly contributes to personal
well-being.

Consumerism has also been active in the pharmaceutical industry. Ethical drugs
are not purchased out of choice but out of necessity. The patient, who is the
ultimate consumer, does not select a specific drug since he cannot evaluate the
medical criteria underlying a physician's choice of a particular drug. This
degree of direct consumer choice isolation by scientific based decision making
which is upheld by law, and the necessity to obtain a prescription from a
licensed physician and supplies from a licensed pharmacist appears to produce a
high level of suspicion due to the lack of consumer sovereignty.

Possibly the most critical aspect is that of safety. It is generally accepted
that therapeutic progress can cause harm since no drug is completely non-toxic
nor does any drug not produce unwanted side effects in certain circumstances.
The more potent and efficacious a drug the more likely that unwanted effects can
be produced if the drug is not used within its therapeutic dosage range. In line
with this is the demonstrated fact that no amount of testing before general use
can ensure absolute safety of a new medicine.

The current trend of society in demanding quantitative increases in the quality
of life has programmed itself, in terms of ethical drugs, to accepting a lower
level of risk for drugs. The case of oral contraceptives illustrates the impact
of society's perceptions of drug safety. With large population growths in the
underdeveloped countries accompanied by mass starvation as a result of maldistri-
bution of food and poverty there is an overwhelming immediate need for contra-
ceptive agents. Oral contraceptives, however, are not curative agents and offer
marginal benefits to the user and the risks are assumed to be great. The long
duration of usage and cumulative effects on basic human physiological mechanisms
and side effects, although rare, can occur. Whilst mortality rates in normal
childbirth outweigh the risks of oral contraceptives, public concern has resulted
in unprecedented controls in standards and the duration of, and number of patients
involved in, clinical trials.

These social pressures for increased safety and consumer protection have been
translated into progressively more stringent government control over pharmaceuticals
and more recently compulsory product liability insurance. This change in social
values and attitudes can be traced back to the early 1960s. The U.S. Senate's
investigation into the industry in 1961 coupled with the multi-country Thalidomide
tragedy resulted in the 1962 Kefauver-Harris amendment to the 1938 Food, Drug and

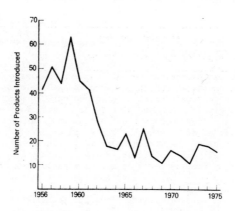

Fig. 14.2   Marketing of newly synthesized drugs (U.S.A. 1956-1975).
Source: Paul de Haen Inc.

Cosmetic Act. These events triggered a chain reaction worldwide as other governments applied more stringent controls.

These social pressures for increased safety, translated into government action, had a significant impact on all sectors of the pharmaceutical industry's operating environment.

New product innovation fell dramatically due primarily to more stringent control criteria. In the USA new product introductions fell from a peak of 63 in 1959 to a current level of around 17 newly synthesized drugs per annum[3] (see Figure 14.2). Whilst it has been argued that this was due to a technological plateau,[4] a comparison with other post-industrial countries indicates that as late as 1969 the USA was suffering from over-control rather than a lack of innovation in terms of new product introduction (see Figure 14.3). From the early 1970s a real technological plateau was reached in many therapeutic areas which intensified economic pressures on the pharmaceutical industry worldwide. The U.S.A. has managed to maintain its lead in overall innovation, however, this has been due to the high levels of basic product research in the U.S.A. combined with an increasing trend towards applied and development research overseas - particularly in countries with a more pragmatic approach to safety. Figure 14.4 details new product innovation in key innovative countries between 1961 and 1973.

Overall the time lag of getting new products into the market and the added bureaucracy have increased economic and social costs to the community by denying society access to important therapeutic advances in the shortest possible time.

Figure 14.5 illustrates the interactions of social pressures for increased safety on the operating environment of the pharmaceutical industry.

The evidence points squarely to the Social Environment being the key factor in the future of the pharmaceutical industry due to the pervasiveness and the power of social constraint. However, a recent attitude study[5] of the future of the multi-

| Country | \|\| Year of First Introduction ||||||||||||| | Totals ||
	1961	1962	1963	1964	1965	1966	1967	1968	1969	1970	1971	1972	1973	No.	%
France	10	24	19	16	16	24	19	19	23	20	15	14	21	240	23.6
BRD	12	17	23	14	14	12	12	15	13	6	5	4	6	153	15.1
Japan	6	3	12	6	13	8	11	7	7	8	11	8	2	102	10.0
U.K.	9	5	17	6	4	8	10	10	7	4	8	6	6	100	9.8
U.S.A.	26	12	7	7	4	6	5	1	3	6	6	4	5	92	9.0
Italy	4	10	2	1	6	2	7	4	7	5	6	9	4	67	6.6
Switzerland	8	5	6	3	4	1	5	4	2	4	6	2	4	54	5.3
East Bloc	3	-	1	5	2	7	7	4	2	1	4	6	3	45	4.4
Benelux	3	6	4	2	3	3	-	4	2	1	7	-	6	41	4.0
Scandinavia	2	3	1	2	-	3	2	2	1	2	3	1	1	23	2.3
Austria	3	-	1	2	2	1	3	1	-	2	-	-	-	15	1.5
Others	5	4	3	5	5	7	4	9	9	8	11	8	7	85	8.4
Total Yearly	91	89	96	69	73	82	85	80	76	67	82	62	65	1017	100

Fig. 14.3   New drug entities by countries of introduction
1961-1973.
Source: Ries-Ardt, E.: Pharmazeutische Industrie,
4/75.

national pharmaceutical industry through to 1990 amongst an international sample
of involved industry and non-industry experts produced some surprising results.

Environmental Ranking

In comparison with other environmental factors the Social Environment was given an
overall third place ranking, and, whilst all respondents in Europe and Asia gave
a high relevance to the Social Environment, industry respondents in North America
viewed the future of the Social Environment with considerably less concern (see
Figure 14.6).

These responses tend to indicate that there is a low value placed on the Social
Environment, and possibly, an absence of knowledge of the effects which the
attitudes of society could have on the future of the pharmaceutical industry.
The changing values[6] and expectations[7] of post-industrial society in the
developed countries which account for the bulk of drug innovation, consumption,
trade and production will require a high degree of management sensitivity[8] to
ensure that the pharmaceutical industry matches values and attitudes to those
demanded by society. All major laws regulating the pharmaceutical industry have
been forced by public concern and this trend is expected to continue due to the
industry's involvement in a highly emotive area, personal well-being, and
society's growing role in political decision making.

By concentrating, as the study indicates, on the Political Environment, companies

Country	Year of Invention													Totals	
	1961	1962	1963	1964	1965	1966	1967	1968	1969	1970	1971	1972	1973	No.	%
U.S.A.	31/1	20	22/1	14	13	22	20/1	18/2	18/1	21/1	25	13	10	247/7	23.9
France	11	21	20	8	14	19	19	17/1	22	17	15	13	17	213/1	20.9
BRD	11	14	16/1	14	10	7	8	12/1	11	7/1	5	4	14/1	133/4	12.9
Japan	7	3	12	9	13	8	7	7	5	7	11	8	1	98	9.6
Switzerland	12/1	8	7	5	7	3	8	5/1	3	6	5	3	8/1	80/3	7.8
Italy	4	6	2	4	6	2	5	7/1	8	1	6	9	6	66/1	6.5
U.K.	6/1	3	9	4	4	4	5/1	4	3/1	2	2	3	3	52/3	4.9
East Bloc	3	-	1	5	2	7	7	4	3	1	4	6	3	46	4.5
Scandinavia	3/1	5	4	2	1	3	3	3	2	2	3	1	2	34/1	3.3
Benelux	2	7	2	1	1	4	-	3	2	1	4	1	2	30	2.9
Austria	3	-	1	2	2	1	3	1	-	2	-	-	-	15	1.5
Other	-	2	1	1	-	2	1	2	-	1	2	1	-	13	1.3
TotalYearly	91	89	96	69	73	82	85	80	76	67	82	62	65	1017	100

N.B. Numbers After the Main Number Indicate that More than one Company or Group of Companies Occasionally Synthesized the Same Substance at the Same Time.

Fig. 14.4   New drug entities by countries of invention
1961-1973.
Source: Ries-Arndt, E.: Pharmazeutische Industrie,
4/75.

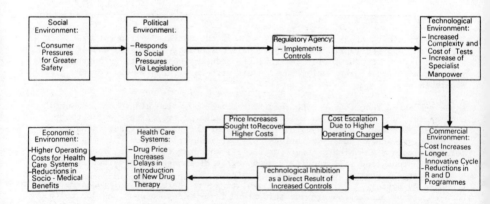

Fig. 14.5   Interactions of social pressures for increased drug
safety on the operating environment of the pharmaceutical industry.

Environmental Factors: Which of the Following Factors do you Feel will have the Most Impact on the Future
Development of the Pharmaceutical Industry in and International Context

Issues	Europe		North America		Asia		International		Total Score
	Industry	Non-Industry	Industry	Non-Industry	Industry	Non-Industry	Industry	Non-Industry	
Economic	141	43	92	42	21	13	254	98	352
Social	139	41	116	70	20	9	275	120	395
Political	81	23	63	41	22	10	166	74	240
Commercial	192	47	132	78	26	15	350	140	490
Technological	169	51	115	71	14	10	298	132	430

N.B. Raw Scores Only, Lowest Scores Indicate Highest Ranking

Fig. 14.6

Social Environment: Do You Feel that Any of the Following Factors Will have a Continuing Effect Through the
1975 - 1990 Period and How Severe do You Rate These Conditions

Issues	Europe		North America		Asia		International		Total Score
	Industry	Non-Industry	Industry	Non-Industry	Industry	Non-Industry	Industry	Non-Industry	
Consumerism	165	58	92	48	20	11	277	117	394
Drug Safety	90	27	73	38	15	5	178	70	248
Social Responsibility	144	38	132	79	18	14	294	131	425
Adverse Public Opinion	165	39	101	65	27	14	293	118	411
Compulsory Product Liability	186	66	132	82	25	15	343	163	506
Influence of Female Employees	264	53	217	125	42	24	523	202	725

N.B. Raw Scores Only, Lowest Scores Indicate Highest Ranking

Fig. 14.7

are focusing attention on the end results, political action, rather than the causative agents, social attitudes, needs and demands.

Specific Social Issues

The study also probed several social issues specific to the pharmaceutical industry (see Figure 14.7).

The unanimous concern of respondents to the issues of Drug Safety whilst having the important economic implications of more stringent requirements and attendant cost increases, have possibly a more significant long-term strategic implication for management in the industry as well as for society as a whole. More stringent safety requirements will tend to accelerate the industry's trade-off in new product efficacy to meet higher safety standards thus reducing the market potential for new products. The attendant risk for society in inhibiting innovation is the loss of future qualitative increases in both socio-medical and socio-economic benefits from new drugs which could significantly upgrade health care delivery.

The issue of drug safety appears to be the political result rather than the cause which is linked to the attitudes, perceptions and demands of society in the developed countries, which are pursuing increases in the quality of life with the acceptance of a lower level of risk for drug therapy. Similarly, the issues of Consumerism, Social Responsibility, Product Liability and Adverse Public Opinion appear to be the results of social attitudes towards the contemporary environments.

Notably the issue of Compulsory Product Liability was ranked fairly low despite the fact that many countries are pursuing legislation for product liability which not only implies future cost increases but also legal conflicts arising from the assignment of individual company or collective industry culpability. Similarly, despite widespread legislation granting equal opportunities for female employees there appears to be little interest by all respondents in this social aspect.[9]

The strategic implications for pharmaceutical company managements is the need to acquire a profound understanding of the social context of all facets of health care and the role which drug therapy plays if they are to survive and grow in a future which is largely controlled by society. Possibly a type of environmental assessment group such as that operated by General Electric in the U.S.A.[10] to appraise major issues of social importance and their interlinkage with the economic, political, technological and commercial environments will be necessary to accomplish constant monitoring of social change affecting the pharmaceutical industry. The pharmaceutical industry must be able to successfully identify, track and diffuse social issues before they become politicized, since once social issues become part of a political programme or are enmeshed in the legislative machinery it can become virtually impossible to rationalize the issue or reach a working compromise.[11] The more personal an industry's products and services are to society the more emotive the appeal to politicians and legislators.

The social environment has become the central strategy issue in the pharmaceutical industry since the attitudes of society can critically influence the Economic, Commercial, Political and Technological environments. The provision of health care is being changed fundamentally by society's attitudes towards the pharmaceutical industry's activities in the area of development, safety, usage, promotion, pricing and profitability of ethical drugs in post-industrialized countries. Through perceptions of need society can influence resource allocation and exercise public control over most facets of innovation, production, distribution and marketing of drugs and in the funds available by controlling both prices and profits.

Company	Country	Issue
Abbott	U.S.A.	Safety: Cyclamate
Akzo	France	Protectionism: Acquisition of RETI
Beecham, Boots	U.K.	Antitrust: Acquisition of GLAXO
Ciba - Geigy	U.S.A.	Antitrust: Divestiture of Geigy Line
	Japan	Safety: Smon - Clioquinol
Commercial Solvents	EEC	Antitrust: Restrictive Practices, Dextroethambutol
Distillers	U.K.	Safety: Thalidomide
Dow-Lepetit	Italy	Business Practices: Currency Evasion
Givaudan	France	Safety: Hexachlorophen
	Italy	Ecology: TCDD - DIOXIN
ICI	U.K.	Safety: Practolol
Leo	Sweden	Safety : X-Ray Contrast Media
Nicholas	France	Labour: Redundancies
Richardson - Merrell	Italy	Labour: Plant Closures
Robins	U.S.A.	Safety: IUD
Roche	U.K. + 16	Antitrust: Pricing, Tranquilizers
	EEC	Antitrust: Restrictive Practices, Vitamins
Schering A. G.	U.K.	Safety : Primodes
Searle	U.S.A.	Safety: Aldactone and Aldactazide
Sherwin - Williams	U.S.A., Canada	Safety: Saccharin
Thomae, Wyeth, Mack	Germany	Antitrust: Abuse of Market Position, Tranquilizers
U.S. Government	U.S.A.	Safety: Swine - Flu Vaccine
Warner - Lambert	U.S.A.	Antitrust: Divestiture of Parke, Davis Lines
Various Companies	Worldwide	Safety: Oestrogen Content in Oral Contraceptives

Fig. 14.8 Trigger issues in the pharmaceutical industry.

Figure 14.8, a brief review of social trigger issues, gives some idea of the magnitude of social censure which companies have been recently or are at present facing in the pharmaceutical industry.

CONCLUSIONS

There is sufficient evidence to conclude that changes in the social environment can have important consequences on pharmaceutical companies and there is reason to believe that many of the social trends and trigger issues could have been forecast, albeit with a degree of open-mindedness and imagination. However, little has been, or is being, done to ensure that pharmaceutical companies respond effectively to social change by considering the social environment as the central strategy issue and adopting effective social forecasting techniques.

Most companies in any industry will have difficulty in matching corporate goals with those of the social environment. However, the gap in values between the pharmaceutical industry and society due to the industry's involvement in a highly emotive area will require a greater level of management sensitivity to social issues to minimize conflict in the future than has been the rule in the past.

The speed, complexity and utter pervasiveness of social change and the potential impact of social trends on the operating environment of the pharmaceutical

industry have contributed to the rise of the social environment as the key
planning issue. Until pharmaceutical company managements accept that the social
environment is the key planning issue and are committed to effective social
forecasting the pharmaceutical industry will continue to suffer increasing
pressures of public control where both the industry and society as a whole will
forfeit better drug therapy and its social and industrial rewards.

REFERENCES

[1] Ethical drugs are those pharmaceutical preparations which can be obtained
only on prescription from physicians and are dispensed either by physicians
and private or hospital pharmacies.

[2] R. Maxwell, *Health Care: The Growing Dilemma,* McKinsey, New York (1974).

[3] P. DeHaen, *New Products Parade,* New York (various issues).

[4] Statement by FDA Commissioner Schmidt, 16.4.1974, at the Kennedy-Nelson
Health Sub-Committee Investigations, Washington, D.C.

[5] B.G. James, *The Multinational Pharmaceutical Industry to 1990,* Associated
Business Programmes, London (1977).

[6] M. Abrams, *Changing Values in our Society,* in Business Strategies for Survival,
W.K. Purdie and B. Taylor, Heinemann, London (1976).

[7] B. Taylor, *Strategic Planning for Social and Political Change,* paper at the
Third International Conference on Corporate Planning, Brussels (1973).

[8] V.B. Day, Business Priorities in a Changing Environment, *Journal of General
Management,* 1, (1973).

[9] Lady B.N. Seear, *The Impact of Social Change: Women,* in Business Strategies
for Survival, W.K. Purdie and B. Taylor, Heinemann, London (1976).

[10] E.B. Dunckel, W.K. Reed and I.H. Wilson, *The Business Environment of the
Seventies,* McGraw-Hill, London (1970).

[11] B. Taylor, ibid.

Chapter 15

STRATEGIC PLANNING AND INFLATION*

David Hussey

Few experienced planners claim that corporate planning is easy, and recent
experience with what for most of us are abnormally high rates of inflation has
left many of us feeling that it is very difficult indeed. A large number of
corporate plans prepared in 1972-1973 will inevitably have been based on assumptions about inflation and economic growth that could hardly have been more incorrect.
Many of the world's businesses moved into situations in late 1973 that had not been
forecast, were outside any previous company experience, and for which no worthwhile
plans had been prepared.

In theory all planners will have carefully forecast and assessed the economic
assumptions, examined their impact on the company, carried out sensitivity analysis,
prepared alternative strategies, and come out with plans that are easily monitored
and infinitely flexible.   In practice life is never quite like this and most
planners will have skipped or skimped certain of the theoretical planning steps.
One reason for this is that most of us find it difficult to do what planning should
do: 'plan for the unforeseeable', and despite all our brave words we are severely
limited by our own experience. Another reason is that many of us have been too
busy, too lazy, or too uncommitted to follow the theory, and have given scant
attention to many of the environmental factors affecting the plans.

Inflation is a particularly good example of a neglected area. Many companies have
refused to give any real consideration to the subject, and have assumed that the
rate of inflation is nothing more than an accountant's numerator which increases
all costs and all prices equally, has no effect on corporate or consumer
behaviour, and strikes all companies and all industries with equal effect leaving
competitive positions unchanged.

Many companies will have been shocked out of this position by the events of 1974.
Nevertheless, I know of at least one multinational company which still requires
its subsidiaries to ignore inflation in the preparation of their long range plans,
and to provide a notation at the bottom of the forms which gives the magic one-
number inflation rate which can be used to put inflation back into the plans.
Not all of us can learn from experience!

---

*This chapter was originally published in *Long Range Planning*, April 1976.

Of course accountants and economists have given thought to inflation. Unfortunately many of the efforts of the former have been directed towards accounting for
inflation rather than solving the strategic issues resulting from inflation and
(until the Sandilands report[1] at least) elected the constant purchasing power
approach which fails because it depends for success on using one magic numerator
to adjust for the impact of inflation. On project analysis the argument has
centred around the d.c.f. rate of return required under inflationary conditions,
instead of the more critical matter of how inflation will alter the basic project
itself, and the forecasts used in its appraisal. Economists who interpret the
meaning of 'inflation' according to their basic school of thought, seem to have
spent their energies at the macro-level instead of the micro-level of the
individual company.

The planning problem which companies face because of inflation is easy to define
and difficult to solve. It consists of a number of analytical steps:

> (1) Define what is meant by inflation and find a method of
>   measuring it.
>
> (2) Forecast the future of this measured inflation.
>
> (3) Identify the impact on the company's business and
>   develop means of combating it.
>
> (4) Review strategy and develop a new one where necessary
>   in the light of the foregoing.
>
> (5) Carry out risk and sensitivity analysis.
>
> (6) Select a strategy.
>
> (7) Implement.

My experience is that steps 1 - 3 lead to immediate changes in tactical decision-
making, for the impact of inflation is often urgent.

If there is one lesson that planners can learn from the recent experience of
inflation, it is that it cannot be ignored. If there is another, it is that it
has a direct impact on every major area of business from marketing to production:
industrial relations to finance. Previous decisions may now be wrong, inappropriate, or impossible to implement.

DEFINITION AND MEASUREMENT

The planner must decide what he means when he talks about inflation. At times he
will be considering national and international rates of inflation, without too
much concern for the economist's problems of definition or cause of inflation.
Even at national level there is no one measure of the inflation rate. Most
quoted measures are based on indices (retail prices, wage rates, raw material
prices, and wholesale prices). Each is only typical of the items the index
measures, and even then subject to problems of interpretation, and the limitations
of averages. The planner should ensure that he has a clear understanding of the
national indices which he may need to use in his consideration of inflation.

Some national series, such as industry raw material purchases or wage rates, can
be used as a guide to calculating a company's own internal rates of inflation.
A much better way is for the company to produce its own internal inflation indices.

With a little statistical knowledge, and some care in selection, sampling and
weightings it is possible to produce company indices which give a prompt
indication of actual inflationary trends, can give accurate short term forecasts
and provide a reasonable base for the longer term, and which themselves can
provide 'triggers' for management action over, for example, prices.

Using pareto principles, it is possible to construct indices for raw materials,
labour costs, and combinations of these which I call a 'cost direction' index.
These can be directly compared with a series of indices based on selling prices.
All series can be compiled on a product, group of products or company basis,
depending on requirements. Indices can be compared directly with government
figures (see Figure 15.1). Their main advantages are that they measure the
company situation, are available up to 2 months quicker than national series, and
carry a built in early warning system. Depending on how they are constructed,
they can give reliable forecasts of up to 3 months ahead, and beat the usual cost
accountant's variance report by 1 to 2 months. Although they cannot replace
accounting data, they can be used to stimulate decisions in advance of the
conventional management information.

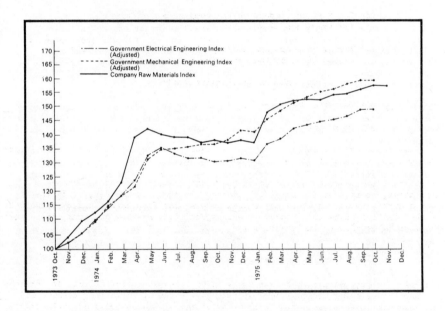

Fig. 15.1 Comparison of government statistics with company
raw materials index.

Tactical uses and the detailed construction of the indices are beyond the scope
of this chapter. Their use in a planning sense for measuring and monitoring the
progress of internal inflation is immediately obvious.

FORECASTING INFLATION

The indices provide an excellent base from which to forecast the main elements of
inflation as they affect the company's cost structure. They offer a mechanism
through which forecasts of the cost trends of different raw materials or types
of labour can be integrated. My experience is that expressing planning assumptions
about inflation through the extension of the indices at once makes them
intelligible and unambiguous. The more common statement like 'raw materials will
increase by 20 per cent next year' is capable of numerous interpretations, for
example:

> (a) The average cost next year will be 20 per cent higher
>   than the average cost for this year.
>
> (b) The cost will be 20 per cent higher than today's cost.
>
> (c) It will be 20 per cent higher at the end of the year
>   than it will be at the beginning.
>
> (d) The cost will be 20 per cent higher than today's standard
>   cost.

Indices of this type help the company to study the impact of the inflation
forecast on the company itself. Cost direction indices for different products
will highlight potential problems, such as the products which are the most
susceptible to inflation, the degree to which prices must change to maintain or
improve margins, or the amount of cost reduction effort needed to hold the price
increases to what is considered an acceptable level.

Statistical forecasting techniques can be used if the indices have been running
for a sufficient length of time. This is an aspect I have not personally explored
as I prefer to build up the forecast by a study of the individual external factors
which influence it.

In addition to the indices it is necessary to forecast other relevant measures of
inflation which will affect the environment in which the company operates, and
the social and political trends which will result from this inflation. This form
of forecast is more than a numbers game, and will include such things as the
industrial relations climate and government inflation control measures.

Most modern companies should also have an interest in international comparisons,
for changes in inflation rates can affect international competitiveness and
therefore strategic decisions.

IDENTIFY THE IMPACT

The most accurate of forecasts is of no more than passing academic interest unless
it causes appropriate decisions to be made: these can only result when the impact
of inflation on the individual business is understood. Inflation can bring
opportunities as well as problems, although they are usually harder to identify.

Internal indices, as described, lead logically to an appraisal of at least part
of the impact. What must also be fully appreciated is that inflation is a change
factor, which can alter social patterns, market reactions, the availability of
finance and the behaviour of the company's own work force. Special studies may
have to be mounted in order to answer many of the questions which arise as
inflation is studied.

Part of the impact analysis can be undertaken centrally by planning departments. It is also important for line managers to understand and give thought to what inflation means to their areas, and the achievement of this need may require special efforts from the planners. My experience has been that without this effort, operating plans will continue to be exactly the same whatever rate of inflation is taken as the base assumption. The deep and conceptual thinking, necessary to identify change areas, is very difficult to bring about.

Part of the development of strategic thinking will be defensive and will arise directly from these studies. One major way to combat inflation is to reduce costs through greater efficiency, and a new approach might be indicated. Planned profit improvement schemes, working to pre-set targets, have been successfully tried in a number of companies[2] and should certainly be considered.

Administrative systems may require overhaul to improve cash flow: for example the methods used for handling debtors and creditors, and the mechanisms for implementing price increases.

REVIEW AND DEVELOP STRATEGIES

The heart of the inflation problem is its impact on corporate strategy, and all the steps described so far lead up to a reassessment of current strategies, and the development of new ones. It must not be forgotten that the reasoning behind the selection of a strategy may be invalid in the light of new conditions and a review is essential. Inflation may change the marketing prospects, costs structures, or cash flow situation.

A number of strategic issues can be identified in general terms: this concentration does not suggest that inflation is the only factor affecting these issues for the real-life situation is concerned with a multiplicity of influences of which inflation may not always be the most significant. The fact that inflation must always be treated as a serious factor justifies the exclusion of other issues in this analysis.

A changed expectation of inflation may well make it necessary for the company to review its objectives, particularly its profit objectives. The challenge is to meet growth objectives which allow for real growth: the difficulty is that when inflation is rife it is often impossible to do more than stand still in real terms. Consideration should be given to linking profit objectives to cash flow objectives, as cash flow is likely to be the most critical factor for corporate development.

Strategies can be divided into two closely related headings: What? and How? These are taken in reverse order, because the consideration of the alternative means available to implement a strategy can condition the choice of what strategy to follow. It seems to me that the expected continuation of heavy inflation must, if only for cash flow reasons, lead to a serious re-consideration of how strategies might be implemented, and a number of previously rejected options may become more desirable. For example:

> (1) Preference for capital expenditure projects that can be speedily implemented, and when thus have an investment requirement which can be known reasonably accurately. Long, drawn-out projects are subject to greater uncertainty from inflation, and true capital requirements are more difficult to forecast. The extent of this problem is demonstrated in the Concorde saga (see

Date of Estimate	Previous Estimate	£ Million Design Changes	Inflation	Other	New Estimate
November 1962	—	—	—	—	150–170
July 1964	150–170	45	65	—	275
March 1965	275	—	—	50c	325
1966	325	⌞——95——⌟		80d	500
May 1969	450a	90	150b	40e	730
October 1970	730	55	40	—	825
May 1971	825	30	15	15c	885
May 1972	885	25	60	—	970
June 1973	970	—	75b	20c	1065

Fig. 15.2　Revision to the estimated cost of developing Concorde

Figure 15.2), although it may be relevant to question whether inflation was the cause of all the increases ascribed to it.

(2) Preference for projects that can be divided into several viable stages. This provides for greater flexibility, and the opportunity to withhold further involvement should this become desirable.

(3) Projects with a fast positive cash flow are likely to be preferred to higher return projects with a longer period of negative cash flow. This condition may be related to (1) above, but is not necessarily the same. It can be brought about in a variety of ways, including (4) below.

(4) A new look at methods of expansion which avoid or reduce capital investment. These may include development by selling knowledge and skills rather than goods (granting licences); the acquisition of licenses; through partnerships or joint ventures; or by giving preference to projects which make maximum use of existing assets over those which do not.

Many of these criteria would ensure that the project rated fairly high in any case in any ranking of projects by d.c.f. methods. There will still be many good projects in d.c.f. terms which do not match the criteria: it is these which I suggest require a re-examination for as long as conditions of high inflation prevail.

The principles which surround the choice of what strategy to follow are even more general in nature than those which can be derived from the 'how'. The suggestions given are meant as thought generators rather than hard and fast rules which apply to every company. What is stated is offered as an area for investigation and cannot be more than this.

Markets

Perhaps the most important principle is an acceptance of the possibility that inflation can change market behaviour and brand share, either by bringing about a structural change in the market itself, or a preference for competitive products benefiting from a lower rate of inflation, or a transfer of market allegiance to a cheaper substitute. These factors are not easy to forecast, but an acceptance of their possibility (in many cases their probability) may lead to a completely different appreciation of future prospects for particular products, which can have far reaching prospects on marketing strategy, production and R & D. At the very least a product profitability strategy should be defined, with a plan for maintaining margins at a time when government control or market forces act to restrict price increases.

There should be a new assessment of the validity of each product to the company's future prospects (for example see Drucker's[3] classifications). Inflation may turn the previously planned 'future breadwinner' into a doubtful prospect, with a shattering impact on all aspects of corporate strategy. A measure of ruthlessness is required to eliminate all poor performing products for when inflation is rampant they are more likely to get worse than better. Strategic views of the product mix often will change.

One aspect of inflation which is never apparent from the economic measures is the loss of consumer choice which is caused by the death of products or a reduction of their quality. No marketing strategist likes to consider a reduction of quality: nevertheless inflation may make the reduction of cost an essential for product survival. Quality reduction need not necessarily be the physical attributes of a product: it can be the intangibles like guarantees, after-sales service, delivery, or personal service. Certainly these policies should be reviewed.

Such re-assessments of marketing emphasis should be made against a multi-national background. Rates of inflation are not identical in all countries, and the competitive position may change so that export prospects are reduced, and imports have an edge in the domestic market. The world view will have implications on other areas of strategy besides marketing. Under modern business conditions it becomes increasingly less profitable for businesses to take a narrow, insular view of their strategic options.

The problem of price has already been raised. Assessments of future prospects must be based on some form of price plan. The possibility that price changes will affect market behaviour has been mentioned, and there is obviously a price/volume relationship which can be changed by inflation. Higher prices may mean a lower volume of sales, with all that this entails. Static prices will inevitably lead to loss of profits and what are probably unacceptable margins. Every company has to walk this tightrope between the market and its costs. Attention needs to be given to the frequency with which prices can be changed, as well as the company's ability to change. A new attitude to price may be required, including consideration of price escalation (or price variance) policies, long a feature of construction related businesses and recently extended to other areas: for example the rental of fork lift trucks.

Promotion and advertising strategies may also require consideration, for it is
unlikely that products, prices and anticipated volumes can change without their
being some need to look at the aims and costs of promotional activity.

Major changes to sales volumes, the product mix, the quality and constitution of
the product. The way it is promoted and the future expectations of products must
lead the company to fundamentally different strategies. The need for diversification may appear greater (or lesser), the change of emphasis to a new 'breadwinner'
and the need to reduce costs to stay in business will all have far reaching
implications which cannot be ignored.

Production

If marketing prospects change there is likely to be some effect on production.
Even without this, production can come under the influence of inflationary changes,
because of alterations in the comparative costs of different options. What was
good business logic at a 5 per cent inflation rate may be bad at 15 per cent, or
above.

The production aspects of strategy, like marketing, should be decided against a
multi-national backcloth. This immediately raises the possibility that production
should be transferred from one country to another, because costs in a lower
inflation country are more competitive, or because a combining of production
requirements in a market where volume will decline is the only way to maintain
reasonable economies of scale, or because new investment requirements to remain
competitive require a larger throughput to give a reasonable return.

Any change in expected production volumes will have an effect on the company's
factories. At best a fall in output will lead to a redeployment of resources:
at worst it may involve redundancies. These problems may be difficult enough in
a domestic situation, and the considerations of strategy on an international front
is likely to make them even more complex. It may, however, be critical for the
company's future.

Planned investment in production must be re-studied. On the one hand it may be
unwise to sink more capital into a product whose future is now doubtful, or whose
source is likely to change. On the other hand inflation may bring a need for
additional investment to assist the product's survival. This may happen when a
new process of manufacture is essential for the reduction of costs, or if
substitute raw materials have to be considered. What was right last year may not
be right in the future: changing expectations of raw material inflation compared
with labour inflation may make a previously rejected project not only viable but
absolutely essential.

Make or buy decisions should be re-examined, not only for components but for the
product itself. A company may assure its future more effectively by giving up
production of an item and importing from a lower cost country, instead of hanging
on in an unprofitable situation.

Inflation can be the change factor which alters emphasis. A study of this
emphasis moves a long way from the blind assumption that all inflation will do is
move costs and prices upwards in the same proportion, leaving all else unchanged.

Research and Development

The line of thought resulting from a consideration of R & D strategy follows similar lines. Changed marketing prospects may alter priorities, leading to the discontinuation of some and the expansion of others. There is little point in pouring further resources into research when the marketing prospects have been killed by inflation. Similarly new perceptions of marketing needs may lead to research or development in completely new areas.

There may also be a requirement to direct thought to new processes of manufacture, or to the development of substitutes. Research which leads to cost reduction may prove of greater benefit than research into new products.

Overall, changed cash flow expectations may mean that resources allocated to research have to be changed. The uncertainty of success in research coupled with the high failure of new product launches may mean that R & D should be rejected as a strategic growth option in favour of another method, or if not rejected at least curtailed.

Industrial Relations and Personnel

Inflation, because of its effects on output and therefore manpower requirements can bring very big changes to the manpower plan. In addition changes in attitudes may occur and industrial relations strategy is likely to require modification because of this. A new approach to wages and salaries is likely to be required under conditions of high inflation (unless these are controlled by government).

Risk and Sensitivity Analysis

For a long time planners have stressed the desirability of subjecting strategic alternatives to risk and sensitivity analysis. As there can never be any certainty about any forecast this is always a desirable action to take, for it enables the company to assess the magnitude of any effect of incorrect assessments of the results of a particular course of action, and the impact on those results of alternative views of environmental factors. In the inflation context this action can help in the choice of the preferred company strategy. Some strategies are more prone to the ravages of a higher than expected inflation rate than others, and analysis can help to eliminate these.

For practical reasons only the crudest analysis is possible unless the company has a computerized planning model. Even with computer assistance the analysis will require some skill and supporting data. The question is not simply 'what will happen if costs increase by a further 10 per cent' but 'if costs increase by 10 per cent more, how will this affect prices, demand or cost reduction requirements?'

Unfortunately too few companies appear to undertake even the simplest form of sensitivity analysis, and are satisfied with a 'one point' plan. When conditions are as uncertain as they are today, the lack of sensitivity analysis can mean that the company takes the wrong decisions. Lack of attention to this aspect of planning, is, I think, one of the failings of corporate planners in general, although there are many notable exceptions to this criticism.

Select a Strategy

Inflation affects the choice of strategy (or strategies), but not the process of selection. Out of the complexities of the analysis the company will have to make decisions and choose a strategic path.

Implementation

Action should follow, for planning without action is theory, not management. The fact that action must be monitored and controlled is another reason for trying to take account of inflation in plans. Some urge that plans should only be expressed in terms of constant prices, never in terms of current prices. Unless figures take account of inflation it will be impossible to measure whether the action at some future date equates with the planned expectation. Thus plans would become impossible to monitor.

It is easy to be wise after the event, to look back at the recent past, and from this deduce the sort of actions that organizations must take in order to develop under conditions of severe inflation. One can criticize organizations such as the Greater London Council which (unless they have recently changed) ignore the inflation problem in their long range plan: one can query the value of such plans.

Perhaps the real question to consider is not whether planners have learnt to cope with inflation, but whether inflation has taught us anything about planning. If another environmental factor suddenly becomes critical, will we be ahead of the game, or will we once again be caught out? It is only when we bring the practice of planning closer to the theory that we will, as planners, be able to claim that we are doing a good job.

REFERENCES

[1] Inflation Accounting Steering Committee, *Inflation Accounting*, HMSO, London (1975).

[2] (a) D.E. Hussey, *Corporate Planning: Theory and Practice*, Chapter 17, Pergamon, Oxford (1974).
(b) W.J. Bayley, Method Change at BOC, *Long Range Planning*, 5(2) (1972).

[3] P.F. Drucker, *Managing for Results*, p.67, Pan (1967).

FURTHER READING

Inflation General

R.U. Ball and P. Doyle (Editors), *Inflation*, Penguin (1969).
J. Burnett, *A History of the Cost of Living*, Penguin (1969).
I.S. Friedman, *Inflation a World Wide Disaster*, Hamish Hamilton (1973).

Inflation and Business Strategy

D.E. Hussey, *Inflation and Business Policy*, Longmans, (1976).
J. Morrell and R. Ashton, *Inflation and Business Strategy*, Economic Forecasting Publications (1975).
D.E. Hussey, *Corporate Planning in Inflationary Conditions*, I.C.M.A. (1978).

Profit Improvement

R. Dick-Larkham, *Profit Improvement Techniques: An Action Programme for Managers,*
Gower (1973).

J. Winkler, *Company Survival During Inflation: An Approach to Profit Improvement,*
Gower (1975).

INDEX